THE BRANCH LINES OF EAST ANGLIA

Bury, Colne Valley, Saffron Walden and Stour Valley Branches

Andy T. Wallis

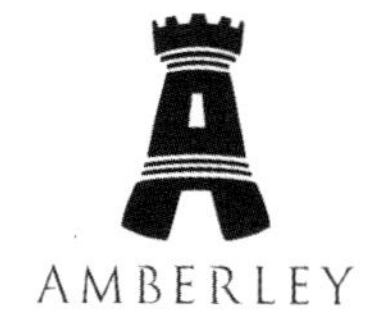

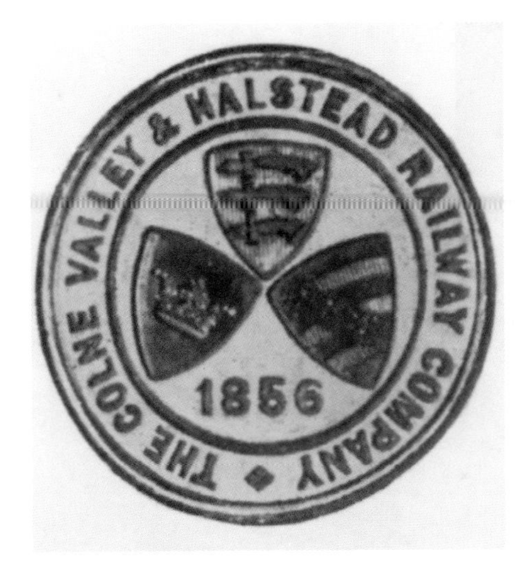

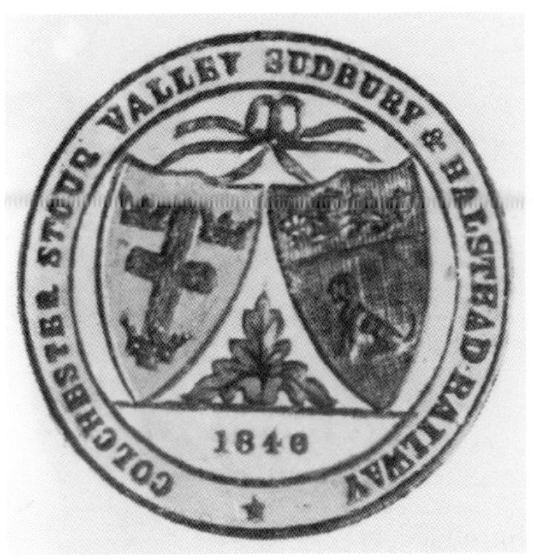

Above left: The original crest of The Colne Valley & Halstead Railway Company, dated 1856.

Above right: The original crest of The Colchester, Stour Valley, Sudbury & Halstead Railway, dated 1848.

First published 2015

Amberley Publishing
The Hill, Stroud
Gloucestershire, GL5 4EP

www.amberley-books.com

British Library Cataloguing in Publication Data.
A catalogue record for this book is available from the British Library.

ISBN 978 1 4456 4827 9 (print)
ISBN 978 1 4456 4828 6 (ebook)

Typeset in 10.5pt on 13pt Sabon.
Typesetting and Origination by Amberley Publishing.
Printed in the UK.

CONTENTS

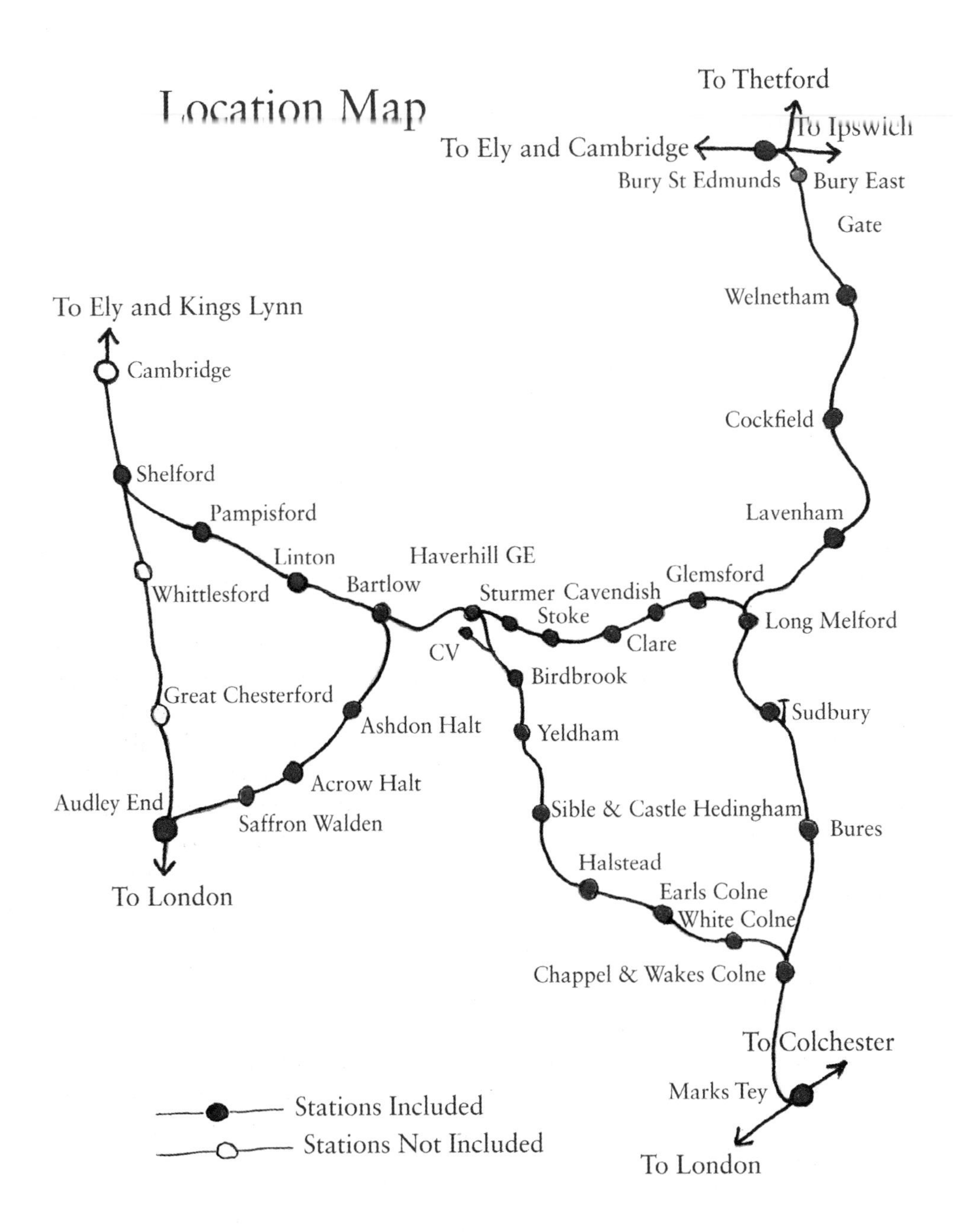
Location Map
To Thetford
To Ely and Cambridge
To Ipswich
Bury St Edmunds
Bury East
Gate
Welnetham
To Ely and Kings Lynn
Cambridge
Cockfield
Shelford
Pampisford
Lavenham
Linton
Haverhill GE
Glemsford
Whittlesford
Bartlow
Sturmer
Cavendish
Stoke
Long Melford
Clare
CV
Birdbrook
Great Chesterford
Sudbury
Ashdon Halt
Yeldham
Acrow Halt
Audley End
Sible & Castle Hedingham
Bures
Saffron Walden
Halstead
To London
Earls Colne
White Colne
Chappel & Wakes Colne
To Colchester
Marks Tey
Stations Included
Stations Not Included
To London

Introduction

At the height of railway building during the nineteenth century most towns and villages had access to a railway, which helped considerably in the movements of goods and people who previously had to rely on horses and carts and the canals to move freight long distances.

East Anglia was predominantly an agricultural area with some heavy industry in the major towns and cities. By the end of the nineteenth century the railway had reached to most parts of East Anglia, with two main lines reaching out from London to Norwich, Cambridge and Kings Lynn, with plenty of small secondary and branch lines filling in the gaps between.

In this volume it is intended to cover four lines in north Essex, Suffolk and Cambridgeshire; these have all now closed apart from one section of the Stour Valley line which is still serving the community as originally planned. We start our journey at Marks Tey and travel along the Stour Valley to its end, calling at all stations on route. We will also include the branches from Long Melford to Bury St Edmunds, the Saffron Walden branch and the former Colne Valley & Halstead Railway from Chappel & Wakes Colne to Haverhill. Every station will feature, with photographs taken before the purges of the 1960s. Each line will also feature a short history.

The first of our lines to open was part of the Colchester, Stour Valley, Sudbury & Halstead, which opened between Marks Tey and Sudbury in 1849; the second was the Colne Valley & Halstead, which built the branch from Chappel to Halstead following failures by the Eastern Union and Eastern Counties railways to complete the authorised lines of the former CSVS&HR. The rest of the lines had to wait until the formation of the Great Eastern Railway in 1862 and the remaining lines opened in 1865. The final piece was the Saffron Walden extension to Bartlow, which opened in 1866.

This book will be well illustrated and will include a selection of photographs from both the steam and diesel era. This book should appeal to those interested in railway history and those interested in history generally. The area covered by this book benefits from two railway preservation sites at Castle Hedingham and Chappel & Wakes Colne.

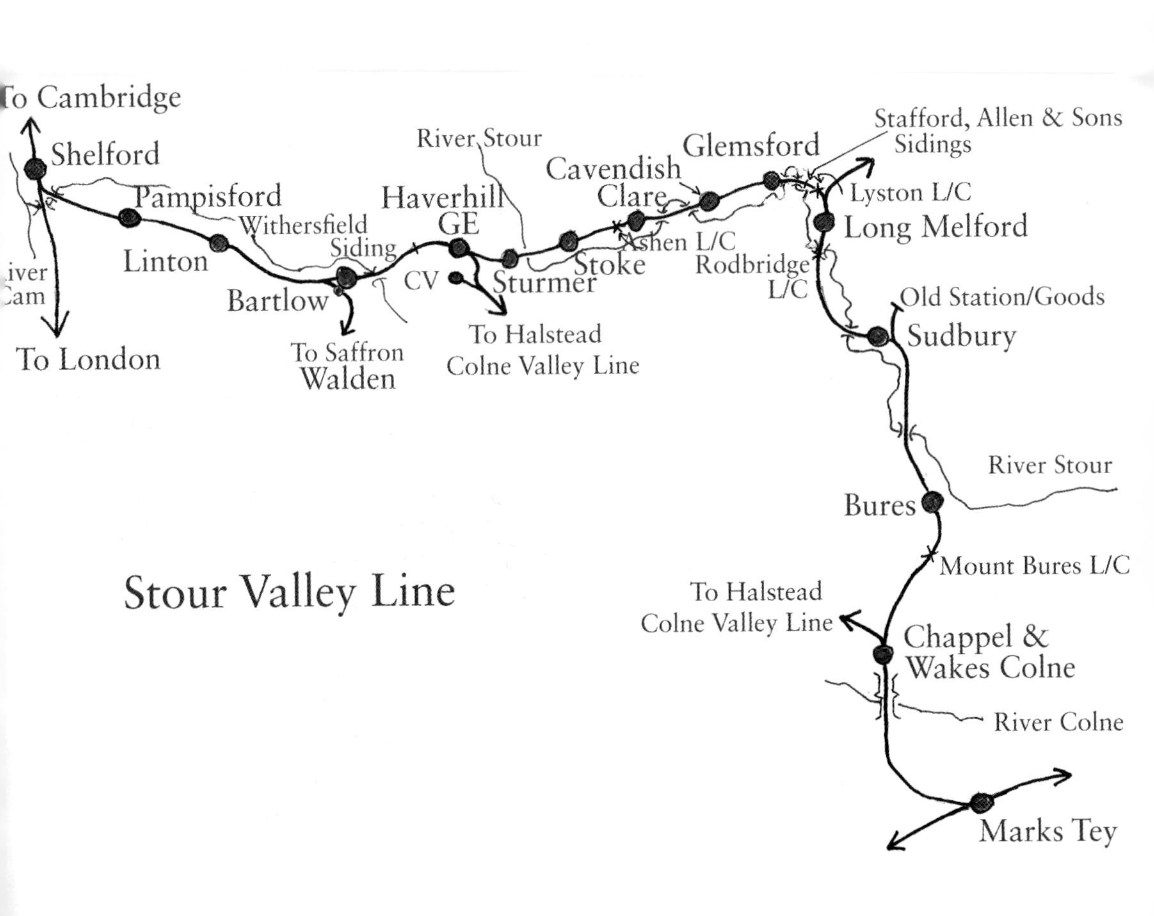

Stour Valley Line

The Stour Valley Branch: Marks Tey to Shelford

Our first line was built by the Colchester, Stour Valley, Sudbury & Halstead Railway, which had been authorised by an Act of Parliament in 1846; there were to be two lines, the first from Colchester to Hythe and the second from Marks Tey to Sudbury with a branch to Halstead. The Sudbury line was duly opened on 2 July 1849; the branch to Halstead was not built due to lack of finance. Extensions were authorised to Melford (later Long Melford), Lavenham and Bury St Edmunds, but they were never built due to there being no money. Meanwhile, the CSVS&H Railway was leased to the Ipswich & Bury Railway, which in turn was leased to the Eastern Union Railway. By 1854 the EUR was leased to the larger Eastern Counties Railway (ECR), which had leased or taken over most of the railways in its area of influence. The lack of interest by the ECR in building the Halstead branch forced the local inhabitants to go it alone and the Colne Valley & Halstead Railway was authorised in 1856 to build the branch; see chapter two.

The ECR and the majority of the other railways of East Anglia were merged into the new Great Eastern Railway authorised by an Act of Parliament in 1862. The new company was empowered to build the long-forgotten extensions from Sudbury to (Long) Melford and onwards to the Cambridge main line at Shelford via Haverhill and Bartlow, there was to be a branch from (Long) Melford to Bury St Edmunds. All these new lines opened in 1865.

By the end of the nineteenth century the fortunes of the line had nearly reached their peak in traffic, with large amounts of freight being carried as well as passenger traffic; like most lines, the zenith was just prior to the First World War in 1914. After the war, the railways were grouped into four large companies and the former Great Eastern Railway became part of the London & North Eastern Railway. The LNER purged costs and closed duplicate signal boxes as well as finishing the installation of Token working over the remaining single sections not already equipped. With the advent of paid holidays, excursion trains on bank holidays and on Sundays were a common site on the line.

After the Second World War all the railways were run down after seeing heavy use throughout the war years. The LNER ceased to exist as from 1 January 1948 when the railways were nationalised; the new company was known as British Railways and this was later shortened to British Rail. The branch benefitted from the modernisation plan of 1955 and diesel railbuses and multiple units took over the passenger workings from 1 January 1959; some limited steam workings on excursion trains carried on for a short while before these were replaced by diesel-hauled trains. Freight was worked from this time by diesels.

Unfortunately the losses continued to be made, and after close examination passenger services on the neighbouring Bury and Colne Valley lines were withdrawn in April 1961 and January 1962 respectively.

Following the publication of the Beeching Report in 1963, the whole of the Stour Valley line was proposed for closure. In April 1965 the closure plan was announced; there was strong opposition to the closure, principally led by the local authorities. A public meeting was held in August 1965 to hear the objections to closure; the outcome of that meeting was published in November 1965 and reprieved the line from Marks Tey to Sudbury, but the rest of the line through Haverhill was doomed.

A subsidy of some £26,000 was paid to British Rail to keep the whole line open in 1966. Meanwhile, freight facilities had slowly been withdrawn from all the branch stations, a process that was completed by 31 October 1966. BR demanded a higher subsidy of £52,000 in January 1967, and when this was not forthcoming the closure proposals went ahead and the last trains duly ran on Saturday 4 March with the line closing formally on Monday 6 April, a sad day for the line and especially for Haverhill as this town had been designated as a London overspill town, which would see the town grow to some 24,000 persons by 2011 and is still growing.

The derelict line remained silent, with weeds growing up through the ballast until the autumn of 1969, when demolition contract was placed. Work commenced from the Sudbury end and this carried on through 1970.

Today, most of the track bed has been sold off. Fortunately some of the stations have found new uses as private houses, with the station and surrounding area at Clare designated as a country park, albeit without any financial support from the local authority. Also, at Chappel & Wakes the former goods yard and surrounding area is now the East Anglian Railway Museum, which keeps part of the old line very much alive; this is well worth a visit.

As for the remaining part of the line still open, the line struggled through the early 1970s with further proposals for closure but the fuel crisis of 1974 aided the retention of the line. Much-needed investment took place in the 1990s and early 2000s and the line's future goes from strength to strength, vindicating the decision not to go with the original proposal for closure. On the other hand, the people of Haverhill can only look on with envy at what good rail communications can do for an area.

Marks Tey

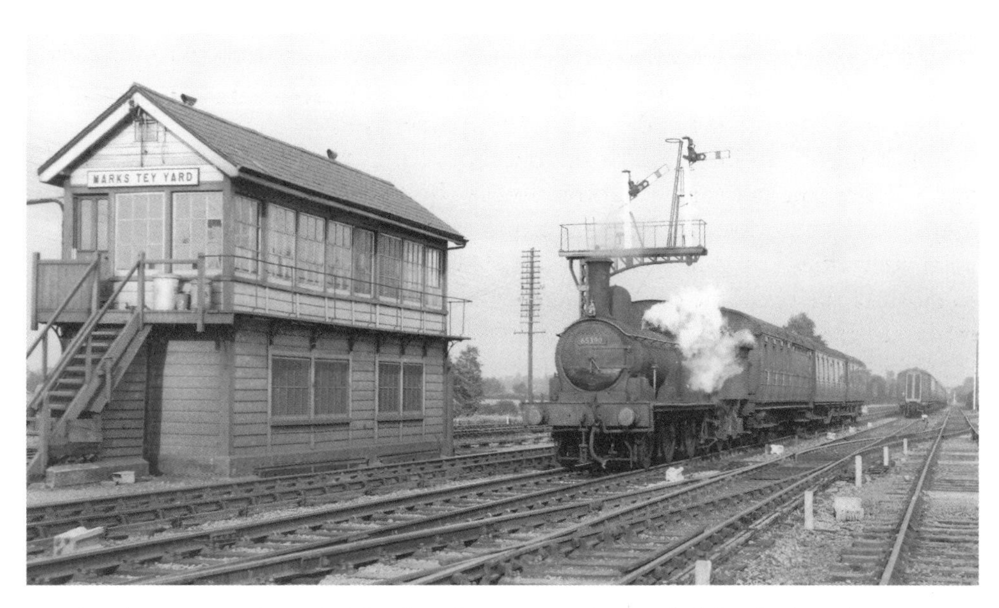

J15 class locomotive No. 65390 hauling three coaches is signalled for the branch as it passes Marks Tey Yard signal box on 6 October 1956. This locomotive was much travelled, being allocated to Cambridge shed on 10 August 1952 then moving onto March on 21 April 1957; two short months later it was allocated to Kings Cross Depot for one week before going onto Neasden Shed, where it was withdrawn from service on 13 December 1958. (R. C. Riley/Transport Treasury)

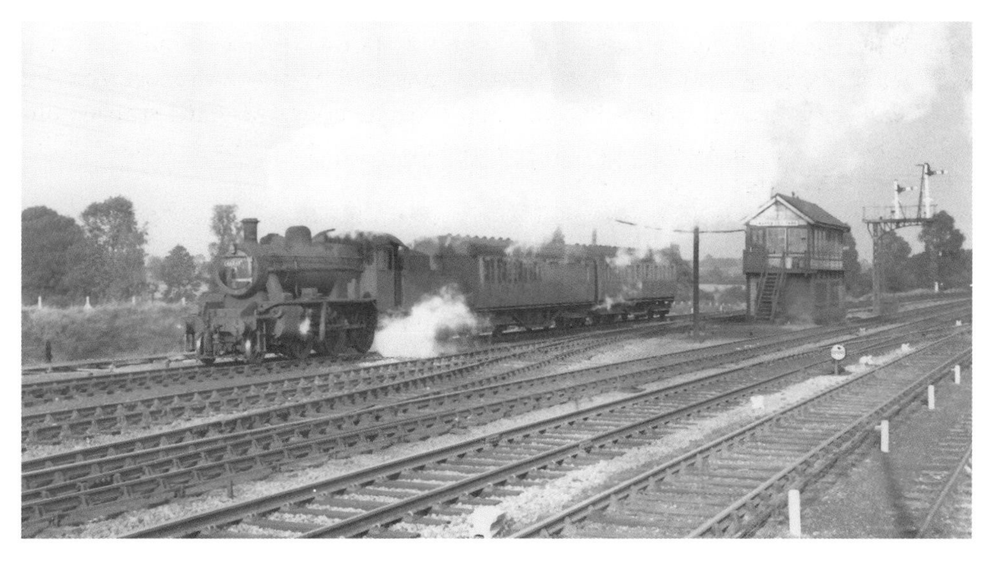

Apparently right behind the previous movement, 2MT class locomotive No. 46469 plus two coaches moves from the down loop lines into the branch platform with a separate Colne Valley working on 6 October 1956. (R. C. Riley/Transport Treasury)

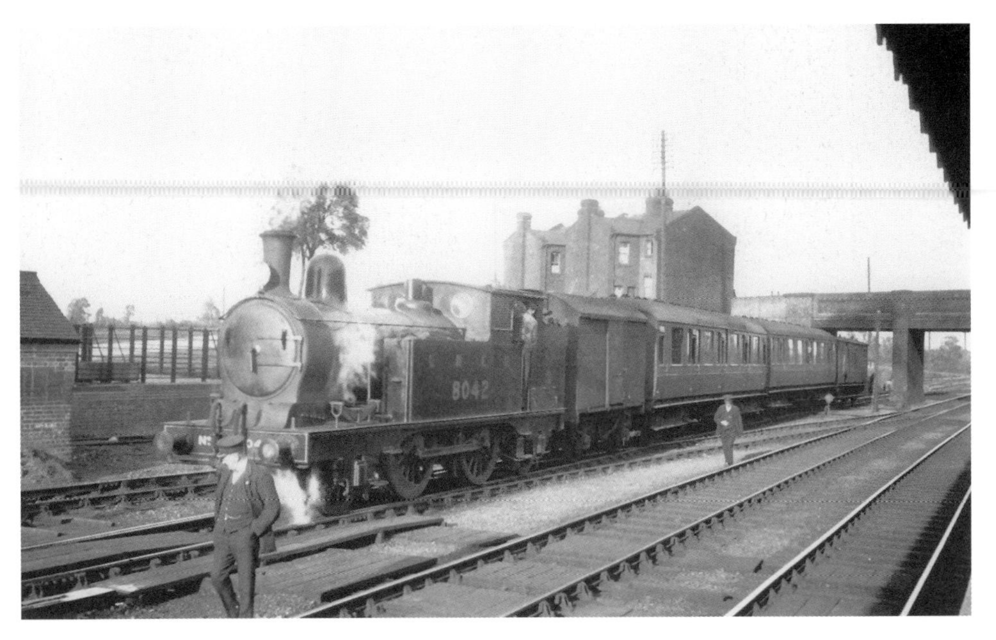

In LNER livery, F3 class locomotive No. 8042 is seen at Marks Tey with a train for Cambridge during October 1931. Prior to the Second World War there was no facing connection from the up main line to the branch, so all trains had to be shunted over to the branch if the train had come from the direction of Colchester. (Dr I. C. Allen/Transport Treasury)

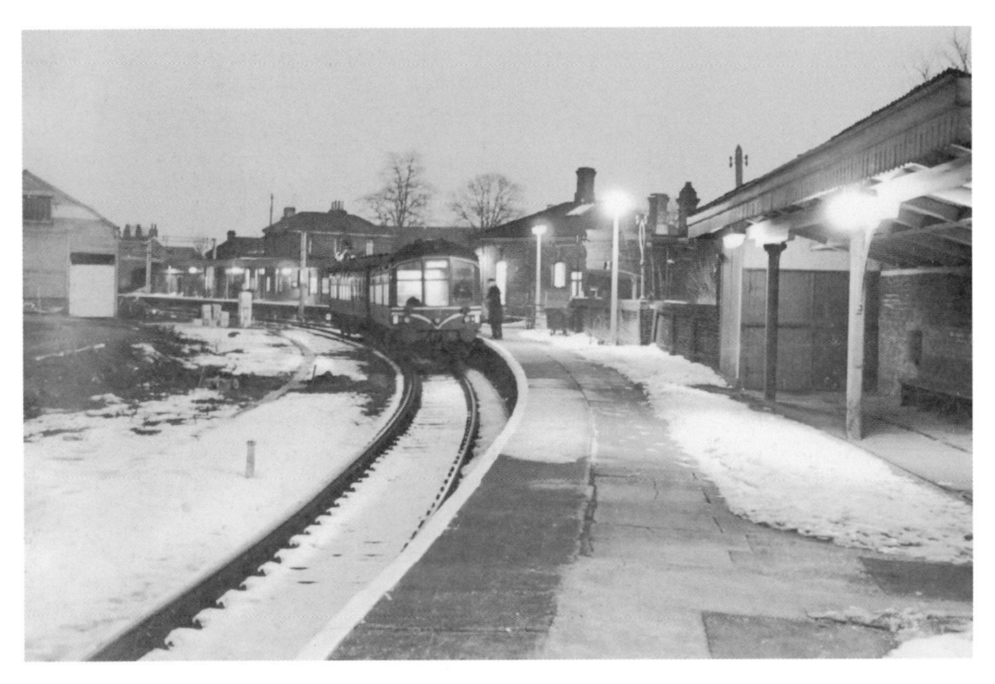

Some thirty-four years later, we see a Derby Lightweight diesel multiple unit standing at a snowy branch platform *c*. 1965; by this time the track in the goods yard had been lifted. The former goods yard is now turned over to car parking. (Malcolm Root)

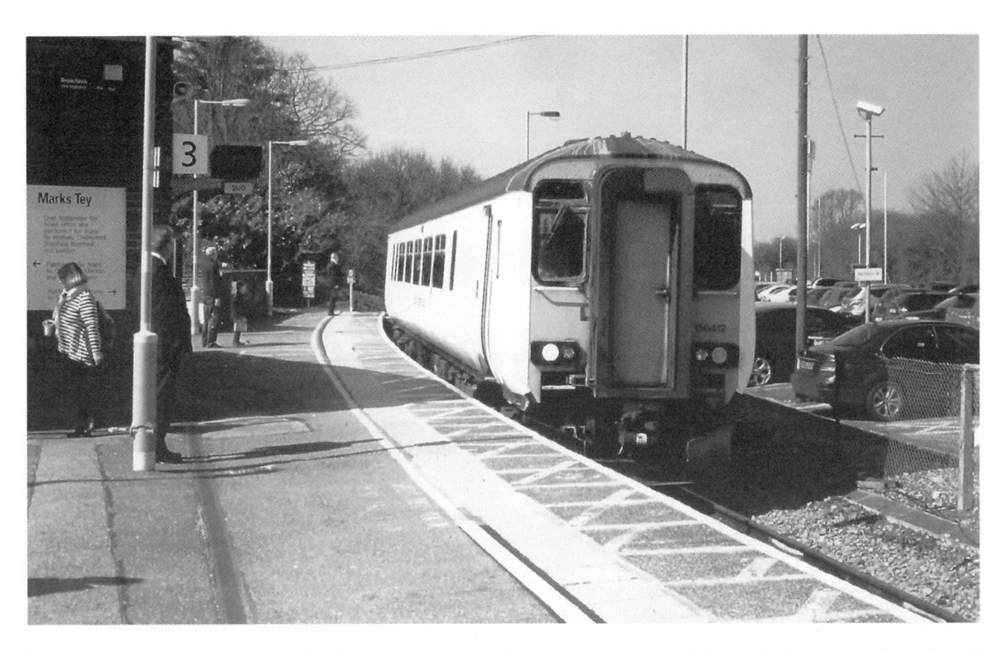

The branch platform today has been reduced to just over two coach lengths long. Modern diesel multiple unit No. 156412 is seen arriving in April 2015 with a train from Sudbury. The former goods yard is now given over to car parking. Most branch trains now just shuttle between Sudbury and Marks Tey, with some workings going to and from Colchester. (Ray Bishop)

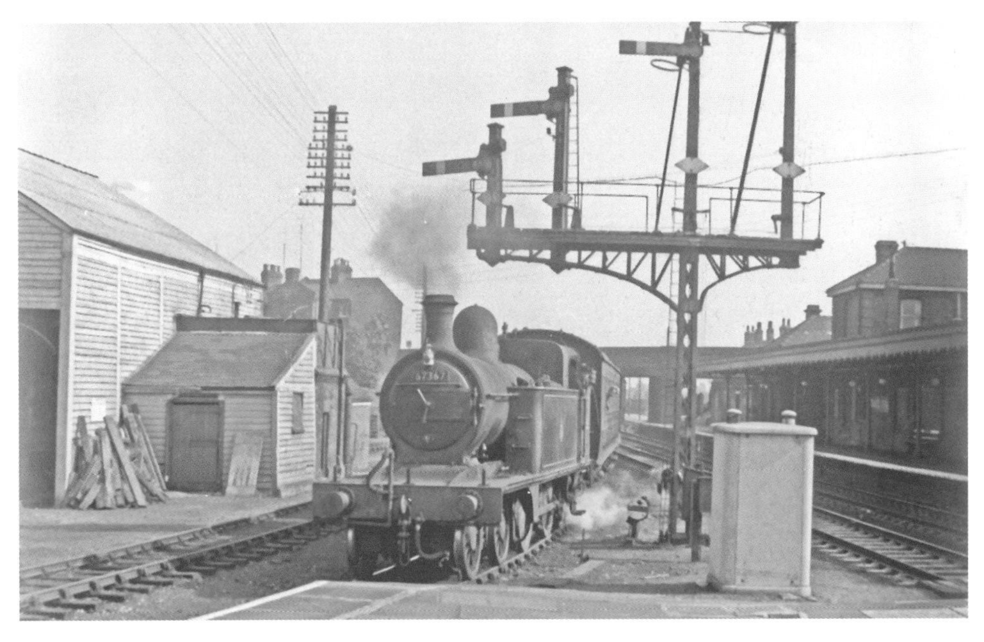

C12 class locomotive No. 67367 plus a passenger train arriving at the branch platform, passing the magnificent semaphore bracket signal, in happier times on 22 September 1956. In their later years the C12s were allocated to Bury St Edmunds shed and could be seen working on the Bury branch and the Stour Valley line between Long Melford and Marks Tey or Colchester. (Brian Pask)

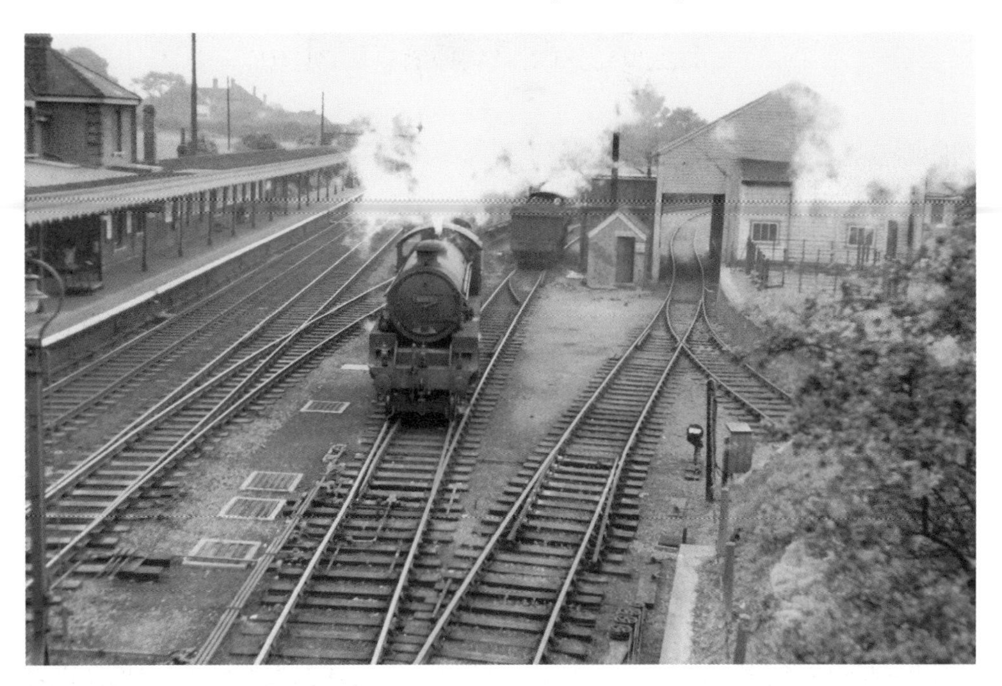

An undated view of B1 class locomotive No. 61323 shunting while another locomotive stands on the branch siding. Note the road through the goods shed to the goods yard beyond. Although not in railway use, this building is still standing today. (Dr I. C. Allen/Transport Treasury)

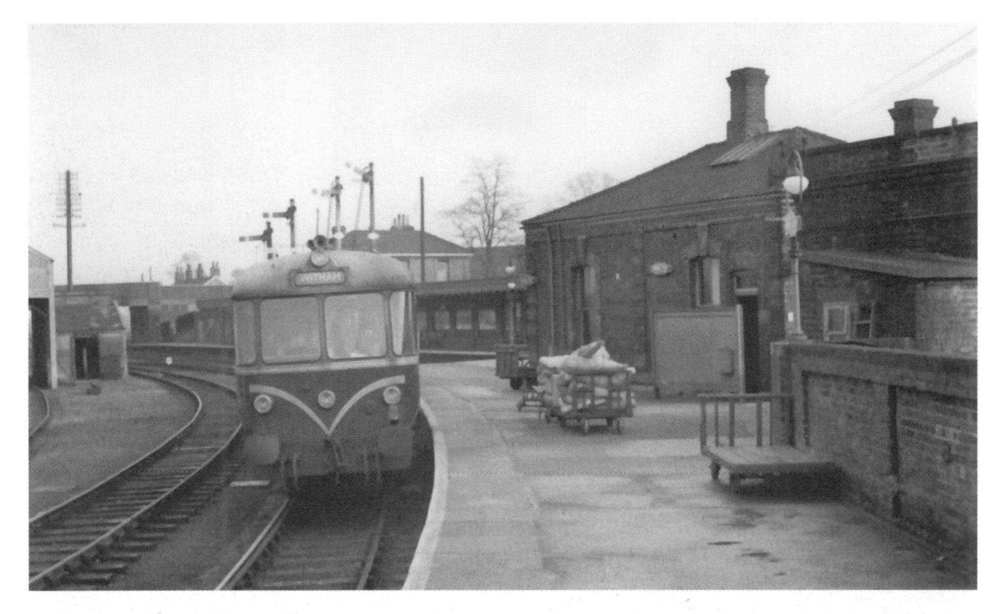

A Waggon und Maschinenbau diesel railbus standing at the branch platform on 21 November 1959; the destination board reads Witham, so whether it was going to that destination is anybody's guess. Five of these small machines were built and used on the Braintree, Saffron Walden, Mildenhall, Colne and Stour Valley lines as well as the Witham to Maldon branch. (A. E. Bennett/Transport Treasury)

Chappel & Wakes Colne

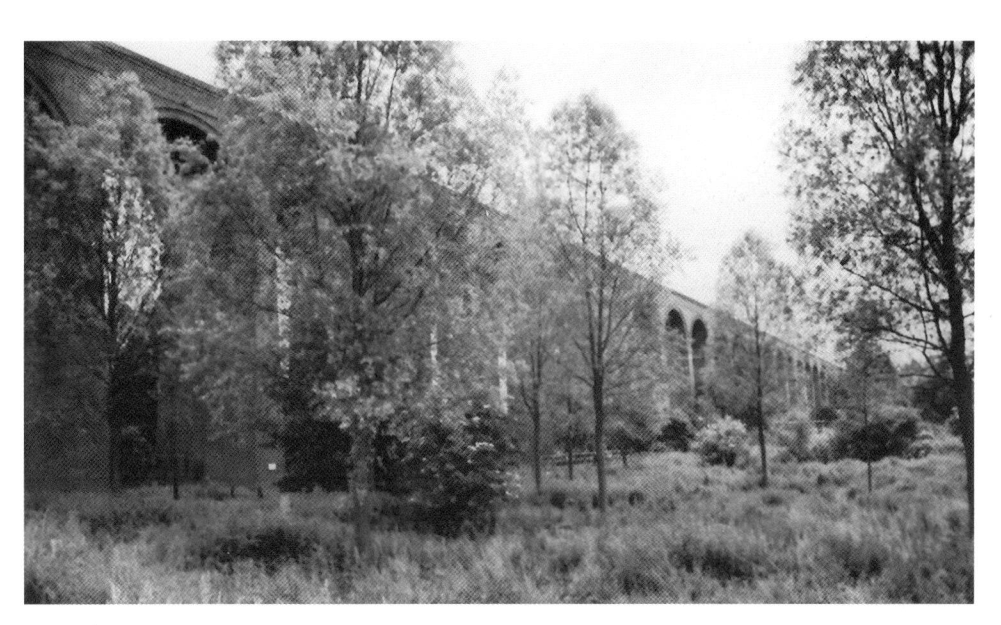

The magnificent Chappel Viaduct, which spans the Colne Valley just to the south of the station, is some 1,066 feet long and has thirty-two brick arches, each one having a span of 30 feet; this used some 7,000,000 bricks to build. The highest point on the viaduct is 75 feet above the valley floor and it cost £32,000 to construct; a refurbishment programme in 1997 cost considerably more than that! (Historical Model Railway Society/AAD585)

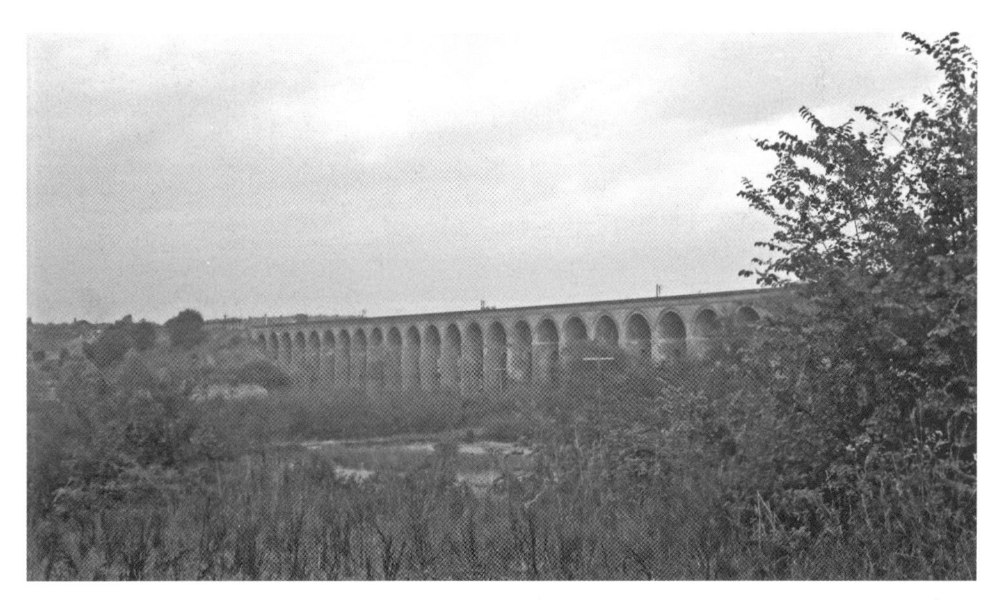

A 1961 view from the other side of the valley showing the viaduct in all its glory; as well as the River Colne, the viaduct also spanned the former A604, the Colchester to Halstead road. (Brian Pask)

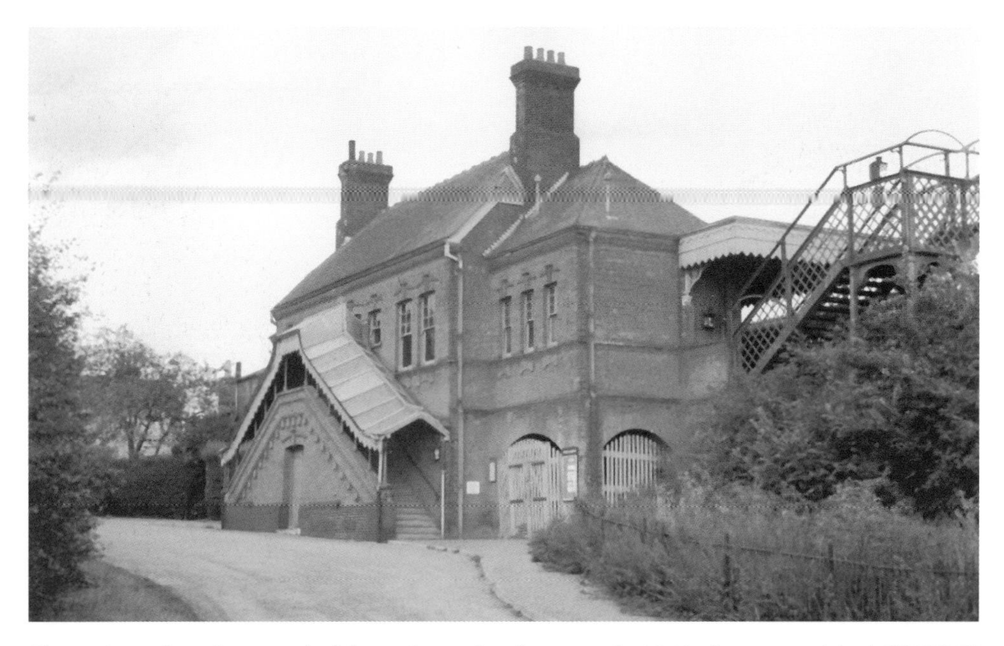

The main station photographed from the station forecourt in 1961; these are original CSVS&H Railway buildings. They are now well looked after by the East Anglia Railway Museum (EARM), who lease the buildings and goods yard from British Rail; later they were purchased outright. (Brian Pask)

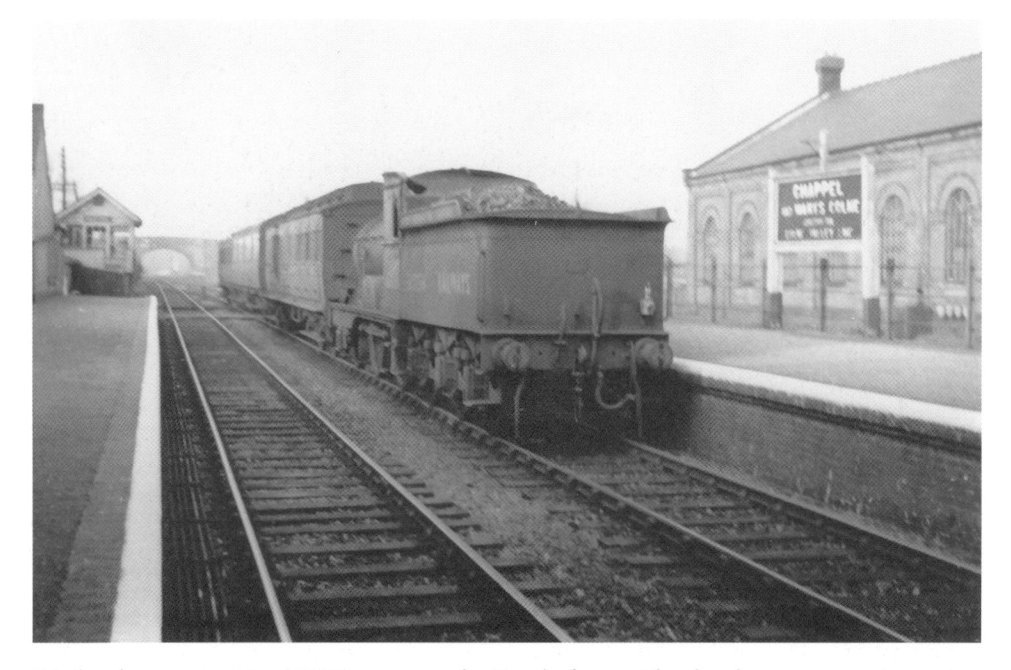

E4 class locomotive No. 6278X runs into the Up platform with a local passenger train service; note the large running in board stating, 'Change here for the Colne Valley line.' This view was taken on 15 April 1949. (Stephenson Locomotive Society – 28919)

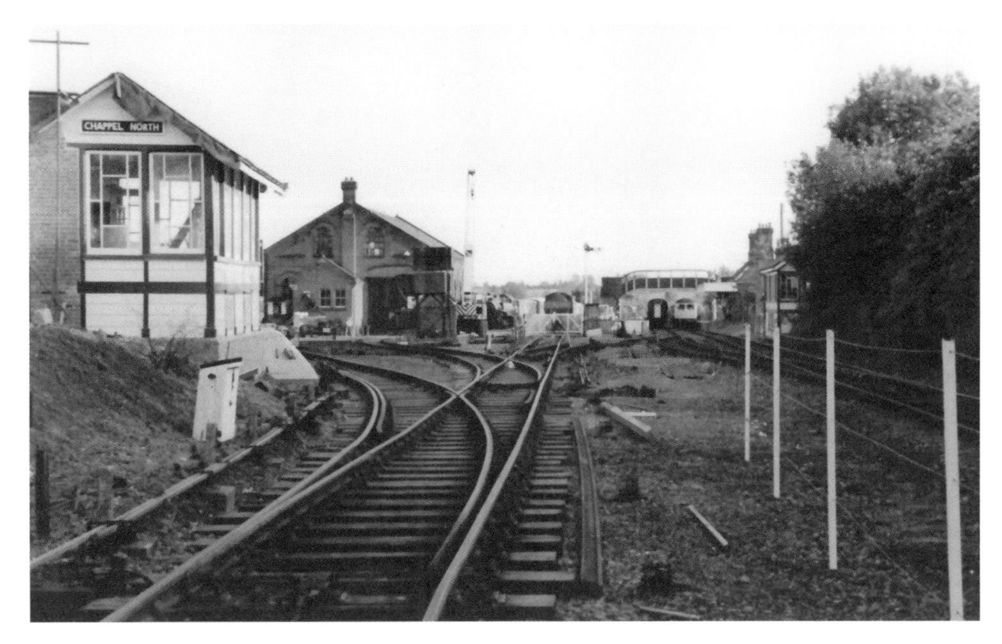

A 1990s view taken at the north end of the museum site looking south, showing the recently installed signal box from Mistley and, in the centre left, the goods shed. The BR line is on the extreme right with a DMU in the platform; a permanent connection now joins the BR line to the museum and is controlled by the museum ground frame. (Andy T. Wallis)

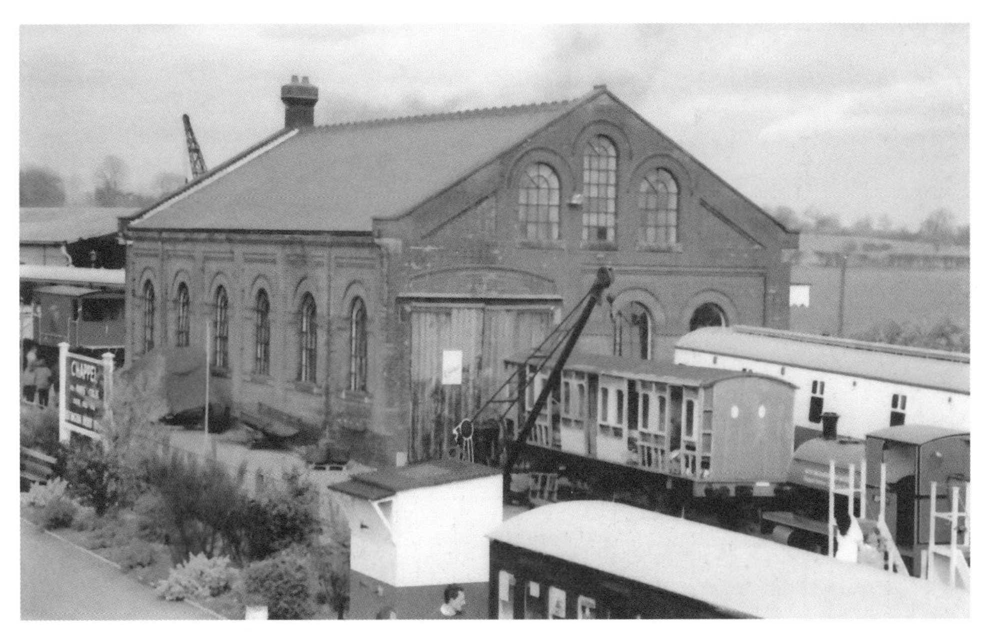

A view taken in 1991 of the goods shed with various restoration projects ongoing in the goods yard. At the top left of the picture, the new museum restoration building, which had been built in the 1980s, can just be seen. The museum has since been further expanded behind the goods shed. (Historical Model Railway Society/AAD357)

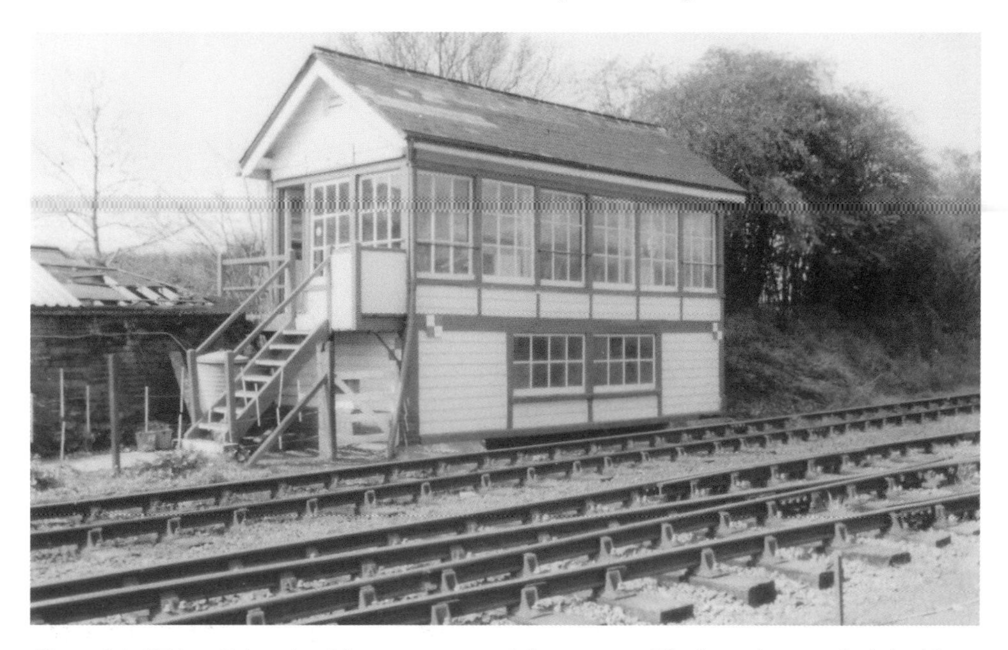

Chappel & Wakes Colne signal box, now part of the museum. The lever frame, which had been removed by BR, was found in pieces in the yard and was rebuilt with parts from other frames to its original thirty-eight levers by museum members. (Historical Model Railway Society/AAD758)

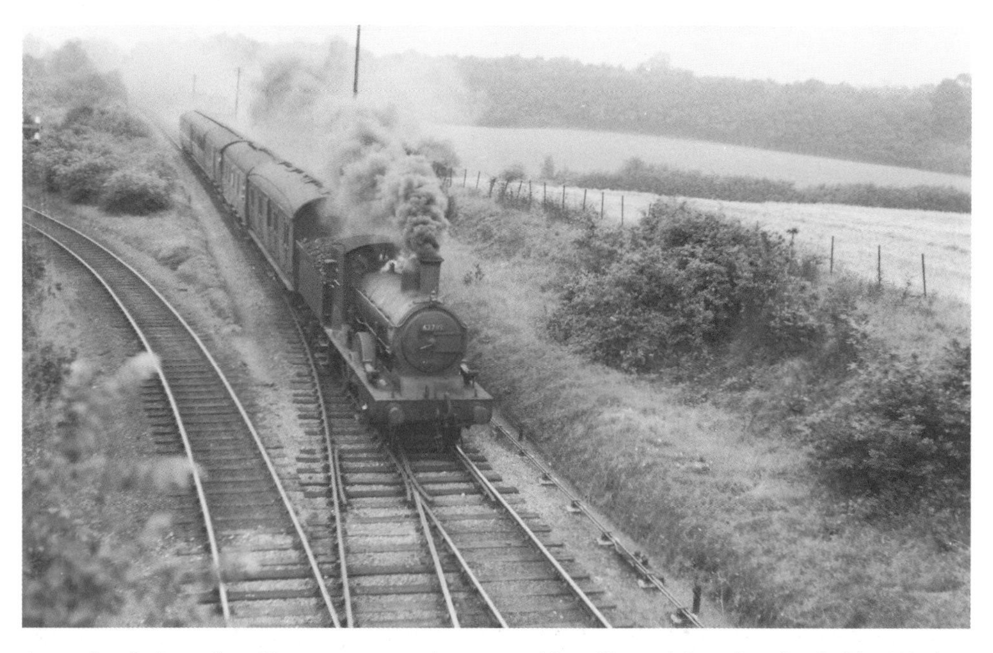

An undated view of an Up passenger train approaching Chappel Junction, hauled by E4 class No. 62789. As this locomotive was withdrawn from traffic in December 1957, this gives a clue to the date of the photograph. The Colne Valley branch can be seen curving away on the left; the gradient at this point is downhill towards Chappel & Wakes Colne station. (Dr I. C. Allen/ Transport Treasury)

Bures

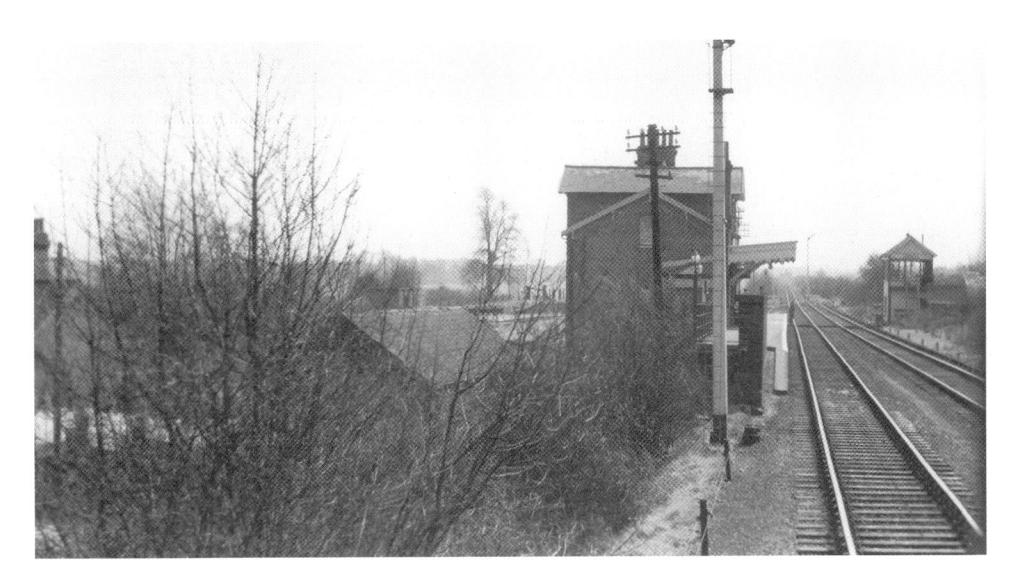

A view taken from a train running from Marks Tey to Bury St Edmunds looking back at the station, which at this time was complete and still fully signalled. The station only ever had one platform and could pass goods trains using the loop line, which could be entered from each end. Today, there is just a bare platform with a small waiting shelter. (R. E. Vincent/Transport Treasury)

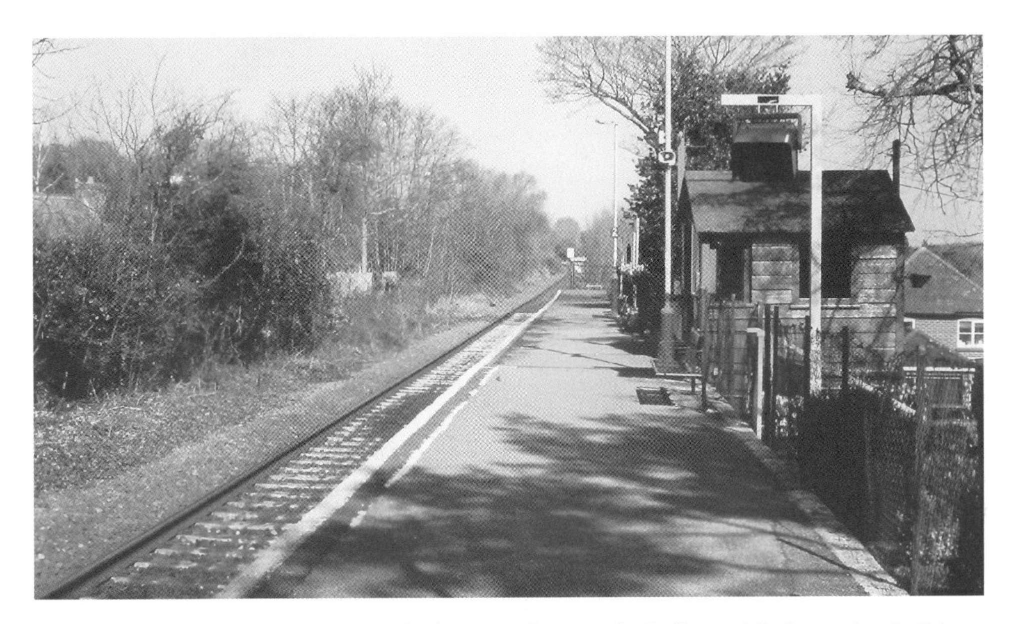

An April 2015 view of the station, looking north towards Sudbury. All the station buildings were demolished by British Rail many years ago and waiting passengers have a wooden waiting shed for shelter from the elements; the station now has modern lighting and a long line announcing system to keep passengers informed of any disruption. (Ray Bishop)

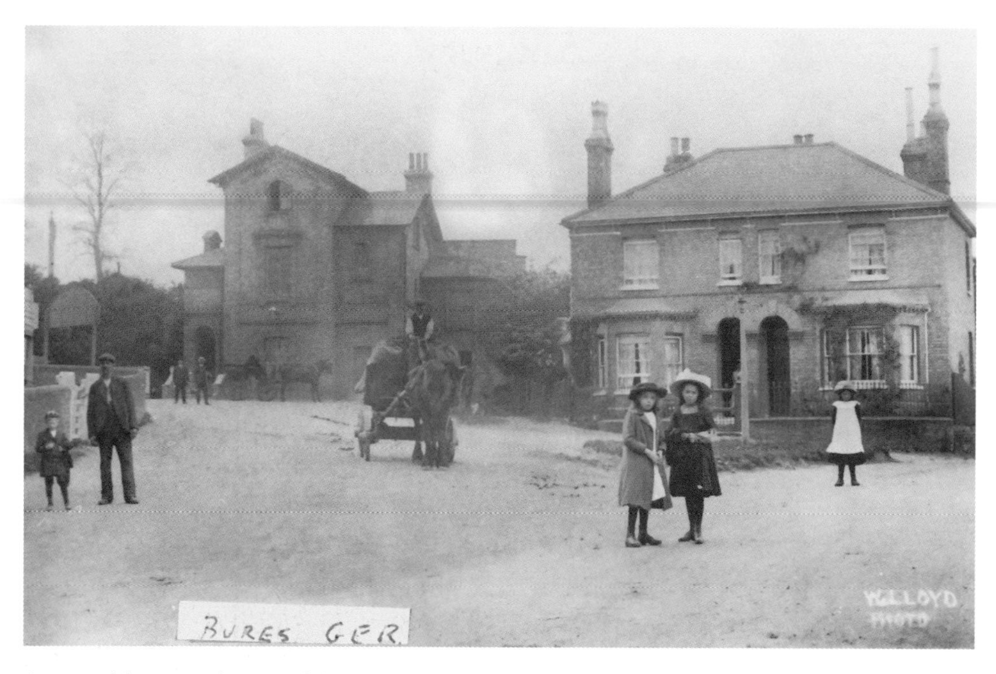

A very old postcard view of the station taken from the forecourt; the fine CSVS&H Railway buildings are shown, together with a couple of station cottages. The horse-drawn vehicles probably date this view to the early twentieth century. (Lens of Sutton Association)

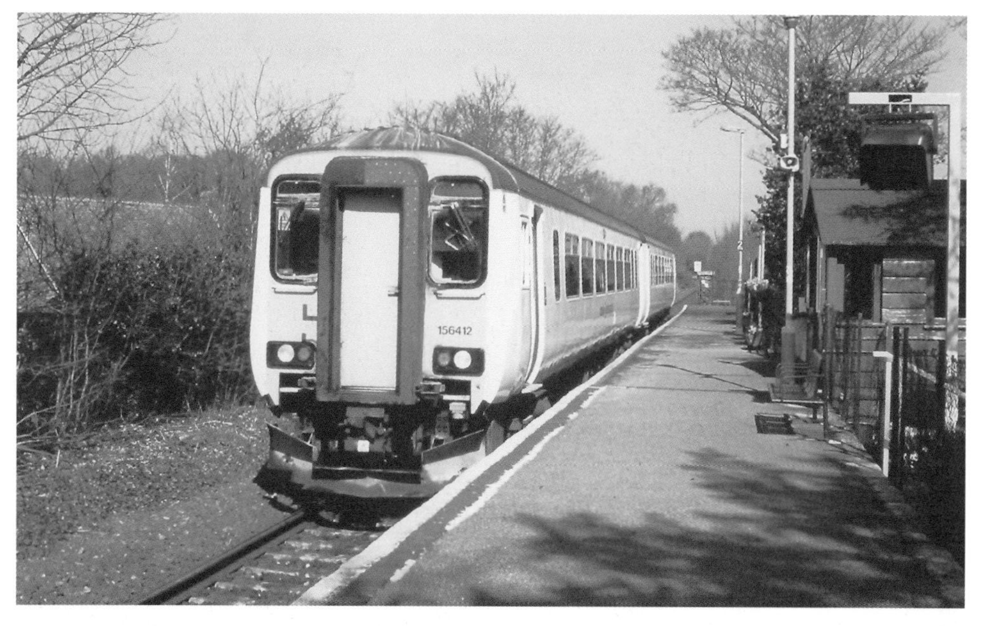

A two-coach Class 156 calls at the station on a lovely spring day with plenty of sunshine and blue sky. The branch line has benefitted from major investment in both the track and signalling infrastructure; the line is now controlled by Liverpool Street Integrated Electronic Control Centre (IECC). (Ray Bishop)

Sudbury

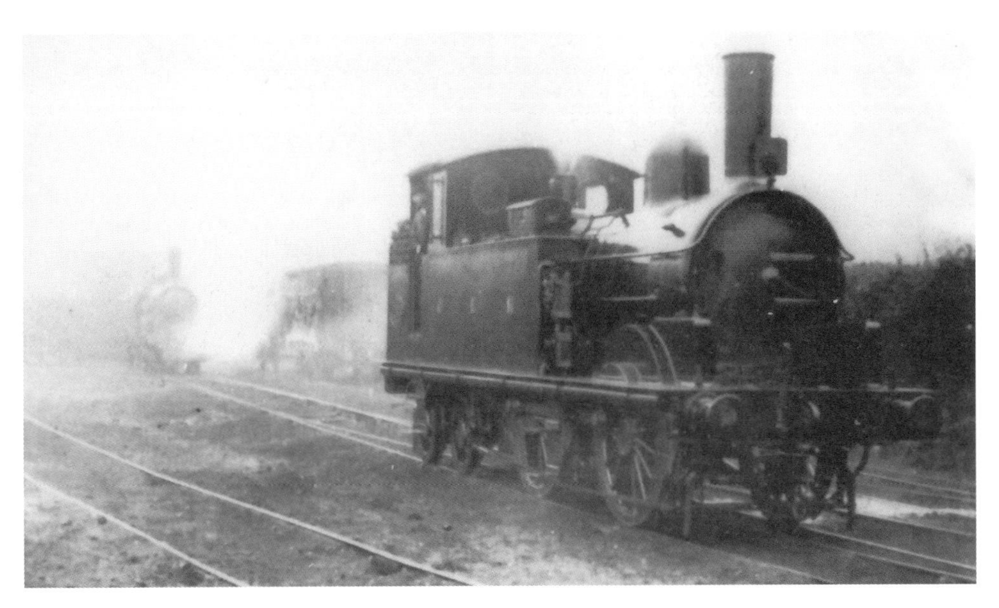

A *c.* 1900 view of a Massey Bromley GER Class E10; this 0-4-4 tank locomotive is seen at the station. Although this print is not completely clear, this view is included due to this photograph being over 110 years old. (Historical Model Railway Society/ACE 103)

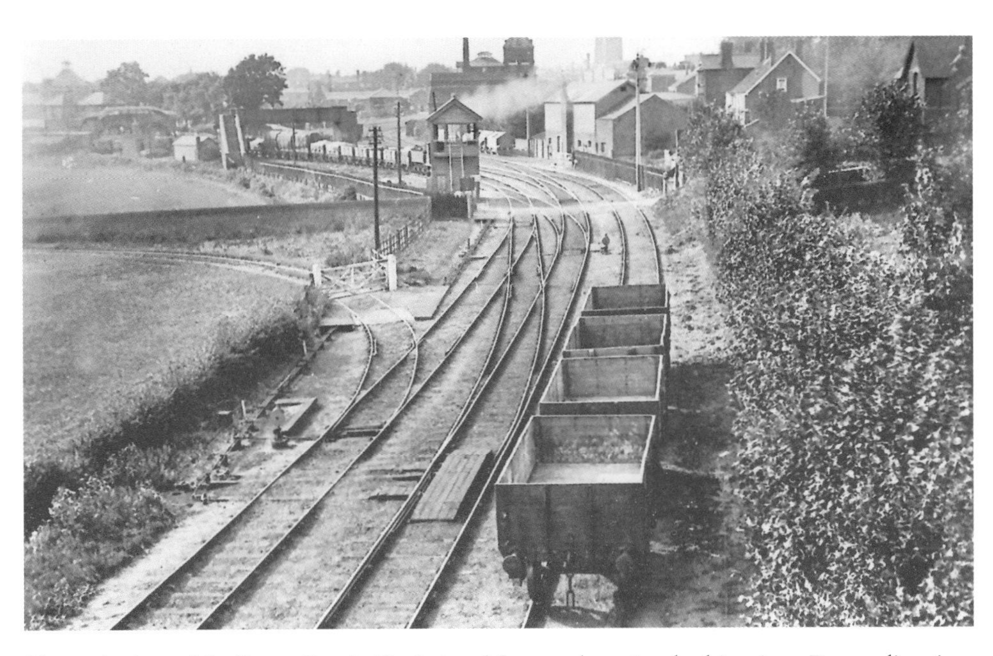

Elevated view of Sudbury Goods Yard signal box and station looking in a Down direction; the siding beyond the gate led down to the river. This view is dated *c.* 1911. (Historical Model Railway Society/ABB315)

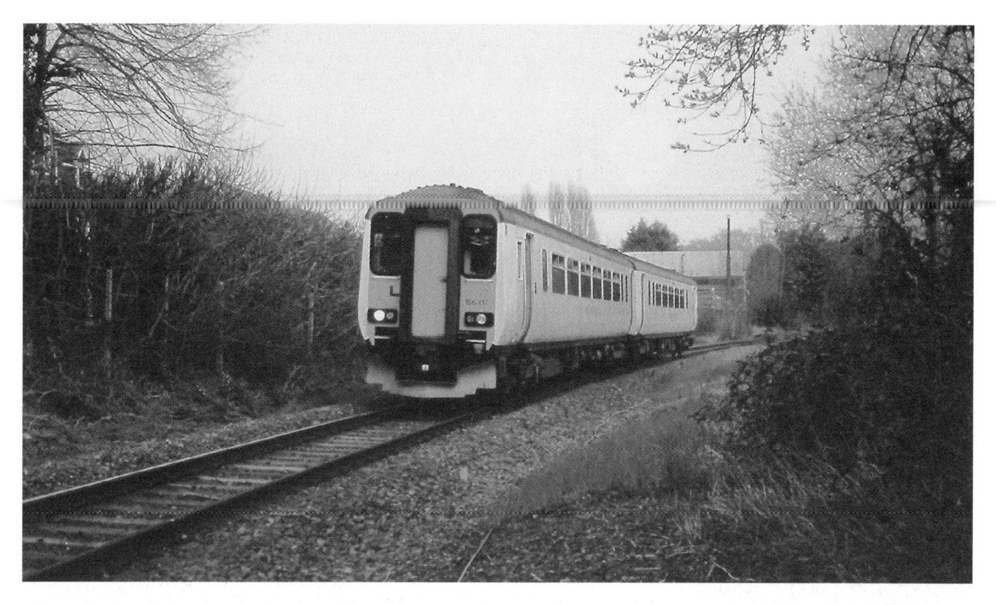

A modern view taken in 2015 of a Class 156 approaching Sudbury near to Ladysbridge level crossing, which was once adjacent to the former goods junction signal box. This view is looking south towards Marks Tey. (Ray Bishop)

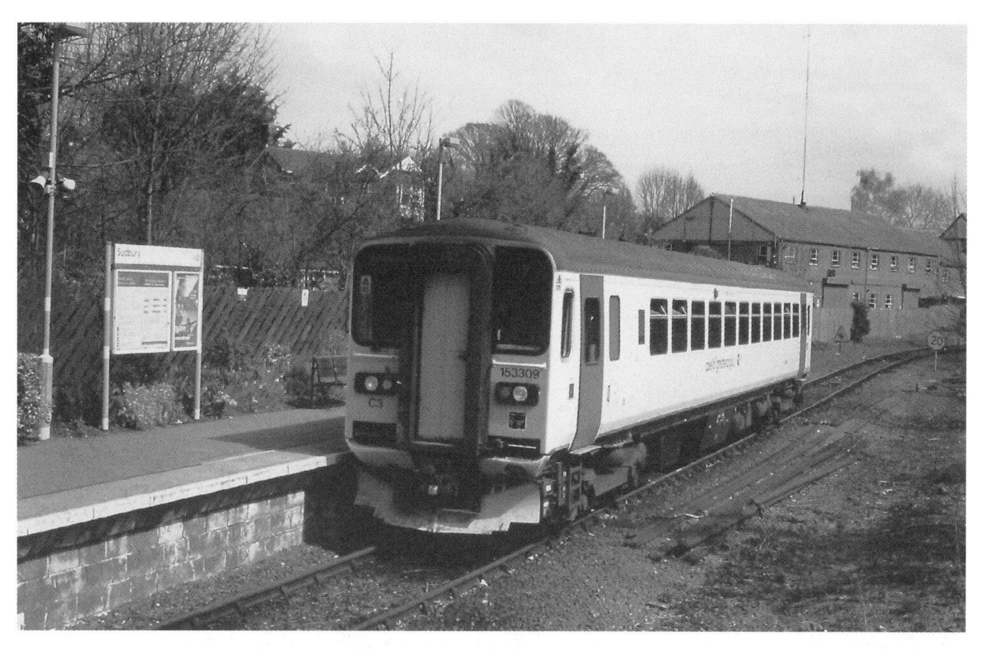

On Saturdays and Sundays the one-coach Class 153 diesel units make an appearance on the branch; this unit, No. 153309, is seen entering the new Sudbury station. This short platform replaced the original GER station, which had been boarded up for many years; the whole site was levelled and cleared away to make way for a new car park. The old footbridge, a favourite with photographers, was demolished at the same time as the footpath was diverted through the new car park, now clear of all railway lines. (Ray Bishop)

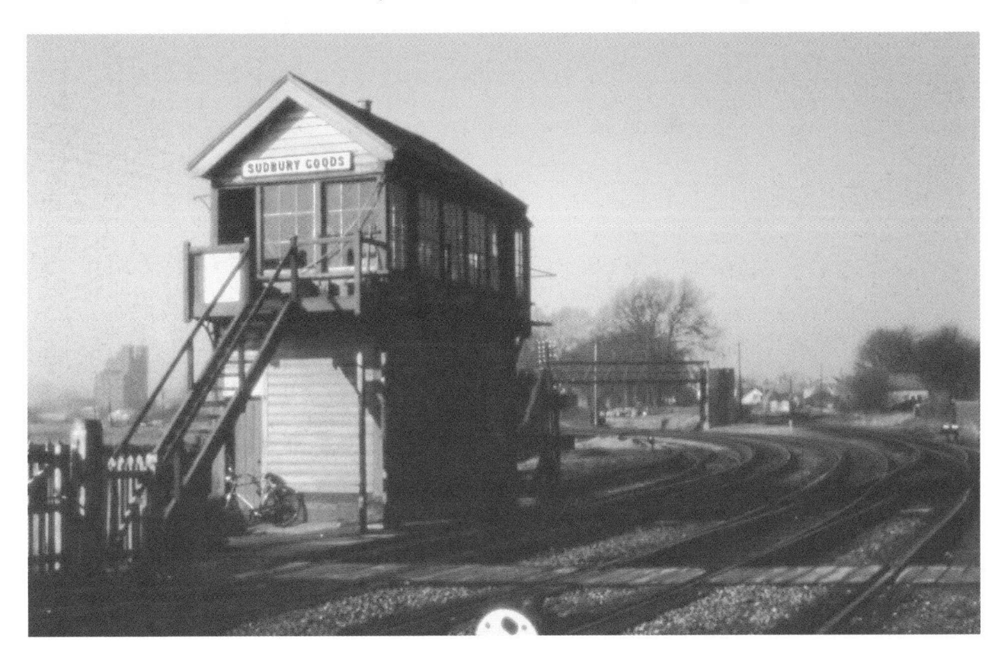

A view of Sudbury Goods Junction signal box as seen on 18 February 1967, just a few weeks before through trains were withdrawn. After the line closed towards Cambridge the signal box remained to control the remaining signals until closure. (D. J. Plyer)

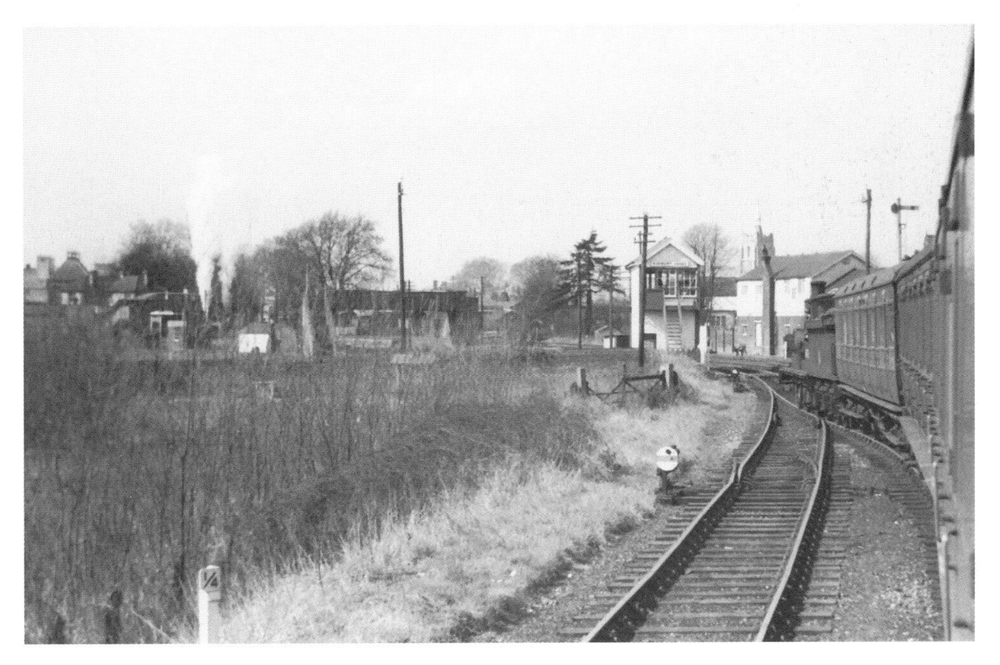

A view from the train of Sudbury Goods Junction signal box; as the train crosses from the single line to the Down loop, another train can just be seen blowing off in the platform. Note the old gate adjacent to the single line siding that used to be a siding leading down to the river (see picture on page 19). (R. E. Vincent/Transport Treasury)

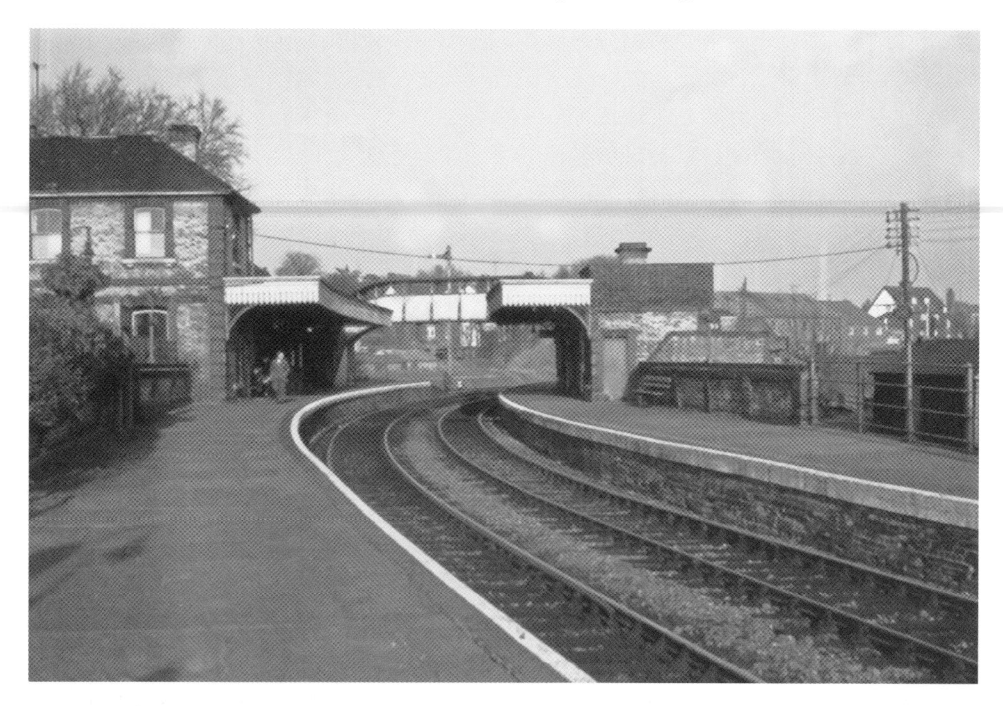

A view of the station, fully intact, not long after the services to Cambridge had been discontinued; the track in the station area was lifted when demolition commenced in 1969. The date is May 1967. (Brian Pask)

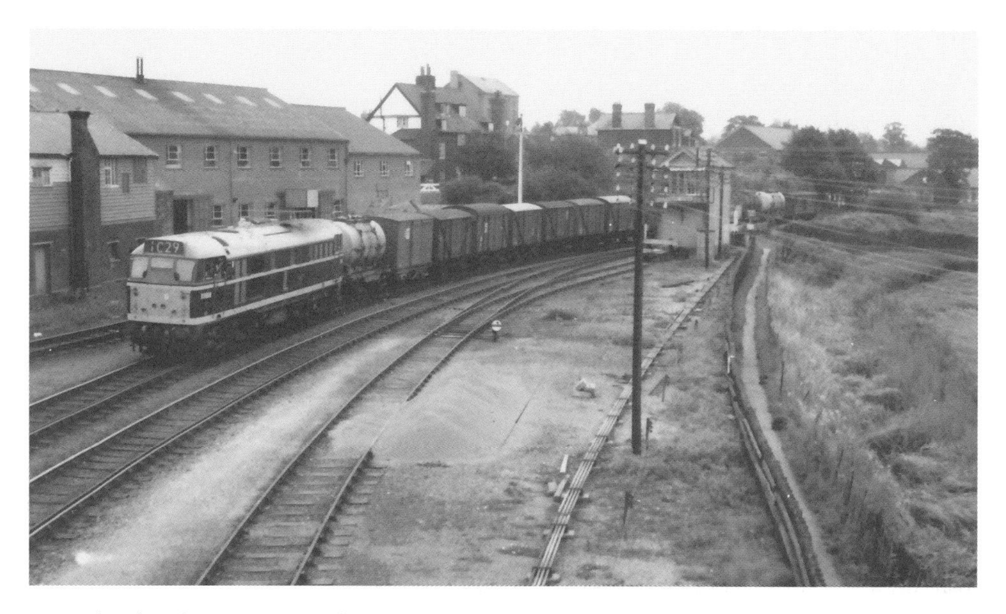

An undated early 1960s view of a Class 31 diesel, D5659, propelling a goods train along the Up loop line; the 1C29 head code on the locomotive is a bit of wishful thinking for a goods train! A few years later Sudbury was the limit of the goods working from Cambridge once Cornard Siding and Bures goods yard had closed. (Dr I. C. Allen/Transport Treasury)

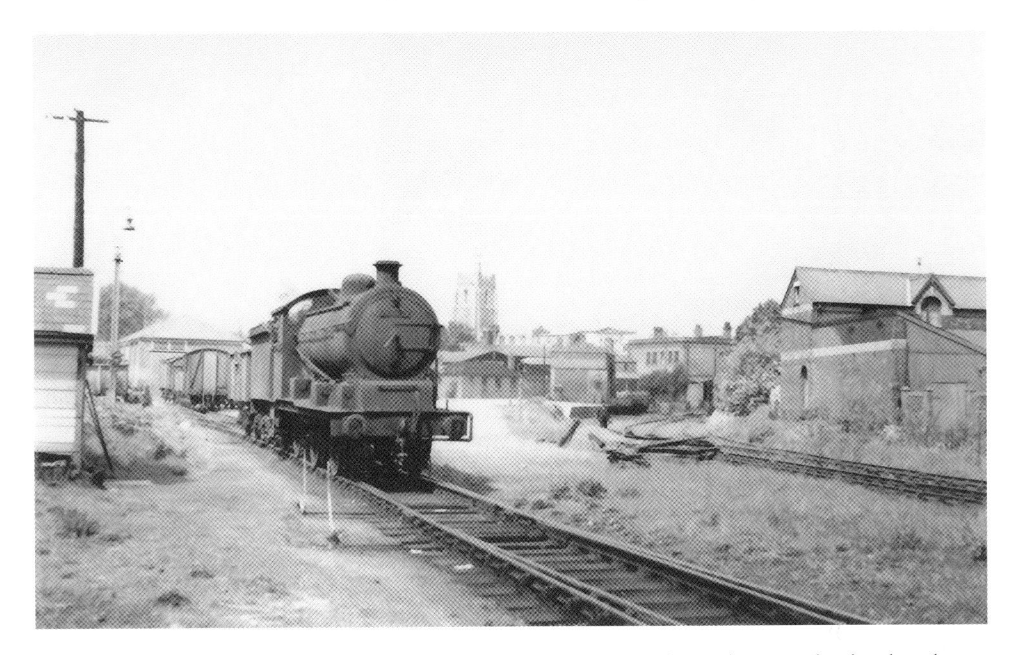

An undated view of a J19 class locomotive shunting the goods yard. St Michael's church can be seen in the background; the old passenger station is seen on the right. Sudbury finally lost its freight facilities on 31 October 1966 as part of the rundown of the line. (Dr I. C. Allen/ Transport Treasury)

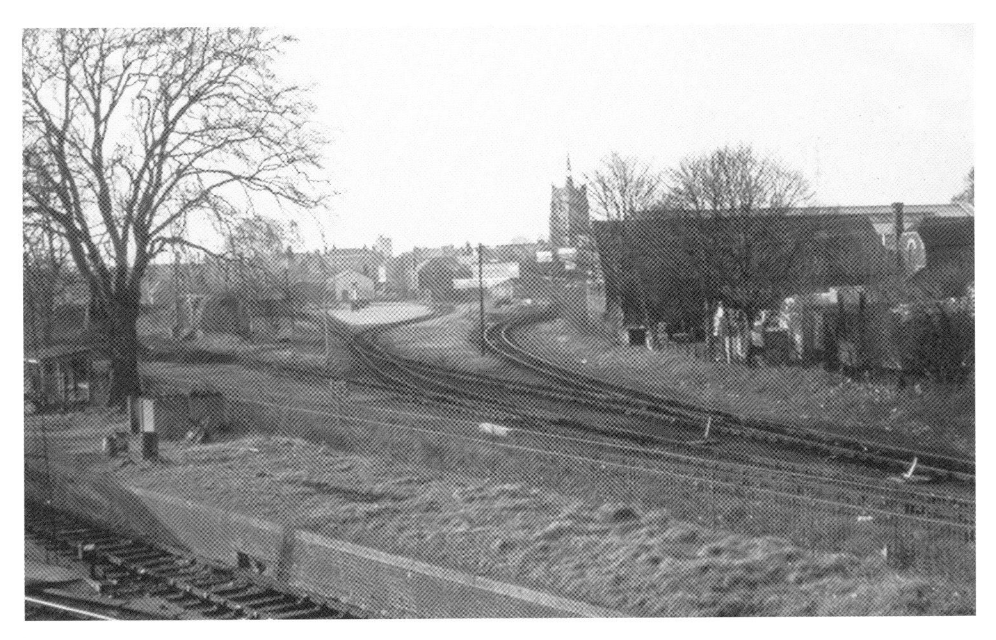

A view of the disused goods yard in May 1967. The goods service from Cambridge to Sudbury had been withdrawn on 31 October 1966, which some would say left the way open for complete closure when the passenger service was withdrawn; it had only taken four years to run down the goods service over the whole line. (Brian Pask)

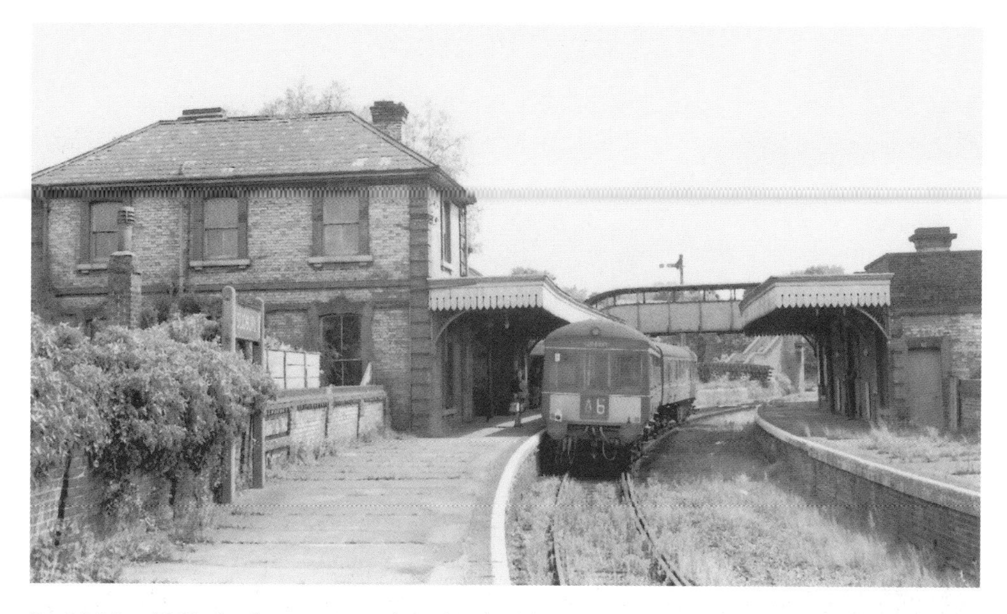

By 26 May 1969, the former Down loop line had been lifted and weeds were beginning to take control as a Class 100 Gloucester-type diesel multiple unit waits in the former up platform to work the next service to Marks Tey and Colchester. (Railway Correspondence & Travel Society Archive)

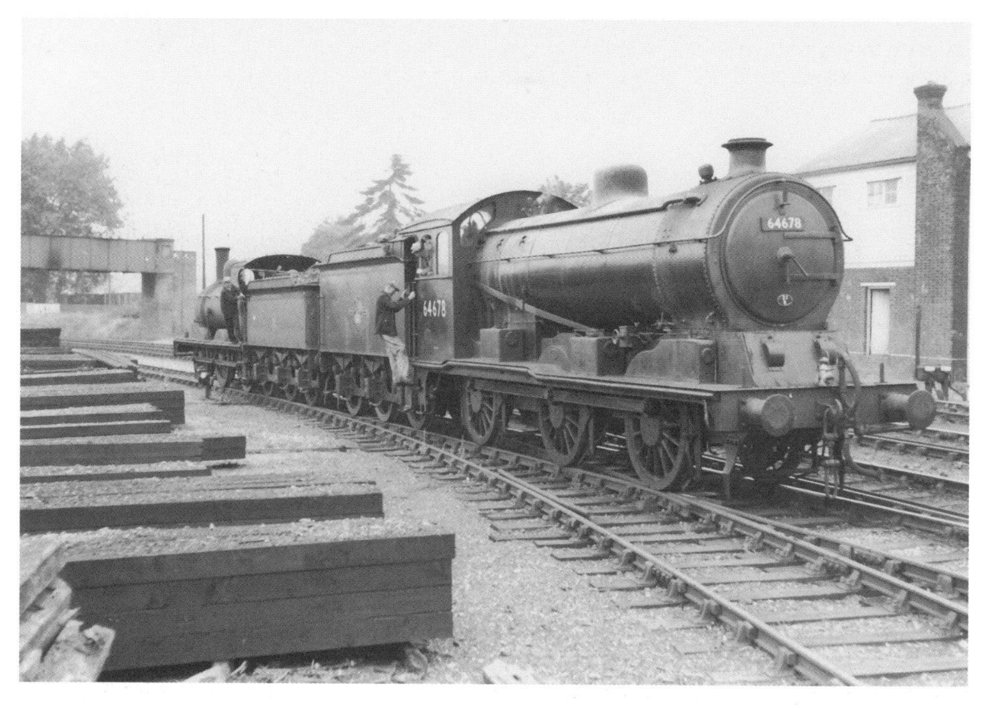

J20 class locomotive No. 64673 is seen shunting a J15 class loco near to the goods junction signal box; the size difference between the two classes of engine is very apparent. Note the piles of new timbers and sleepers all neatly stacked on the left ready for some relaying work in the vicinity. (Dr I. C. Allen/Transport Treasury)

Long Melford

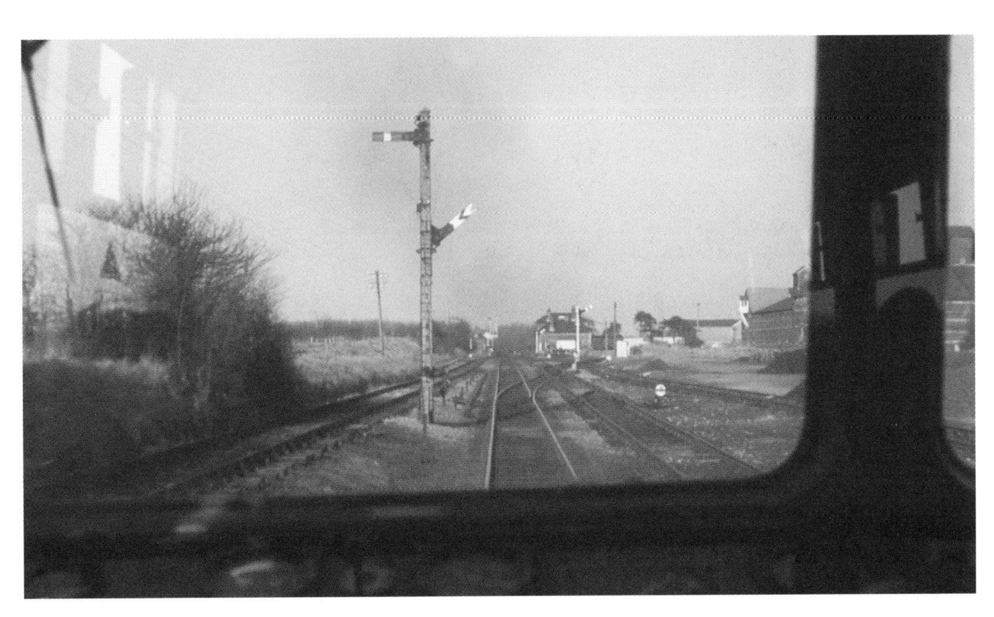

A rear view taken from a departing diesel multiple unit looking back at the station, dated Saturday 4 March 1967. By this time the former goods shed had been demolished following the withdrawal of freight facilities on 12 September the previous year. The distant signal is the gate distant signal for Rodbridge level crossing. (D. J. Plyer)

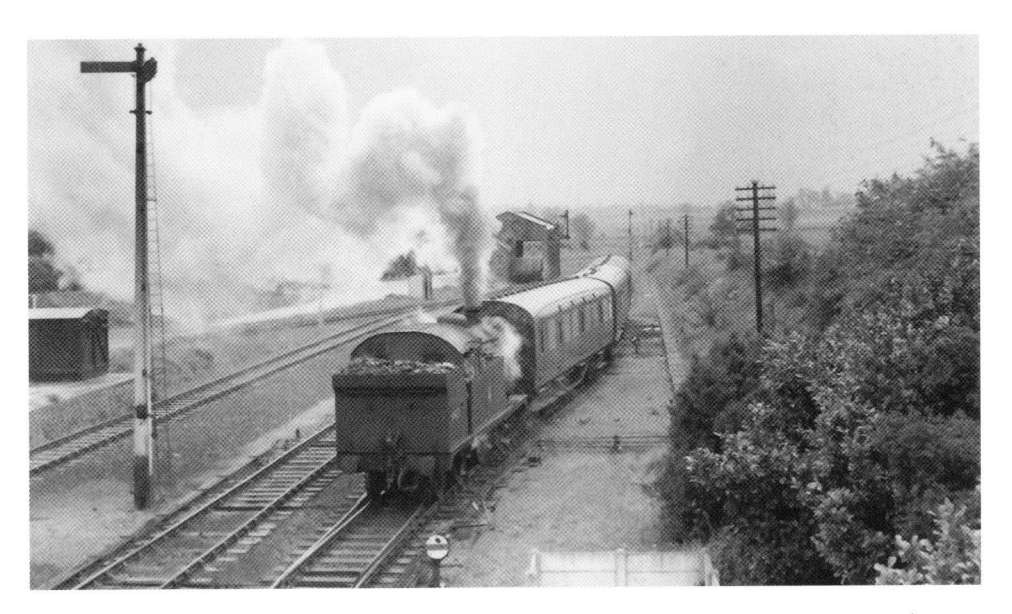

As seen from the station footbridge, N7 class locomotive No. 69620 works empty coaches out of the down siding to the platform for the next service to Bury St Edmunds. This view is dated 18 May 1957. (R. C. Riley/Transport Treasury)

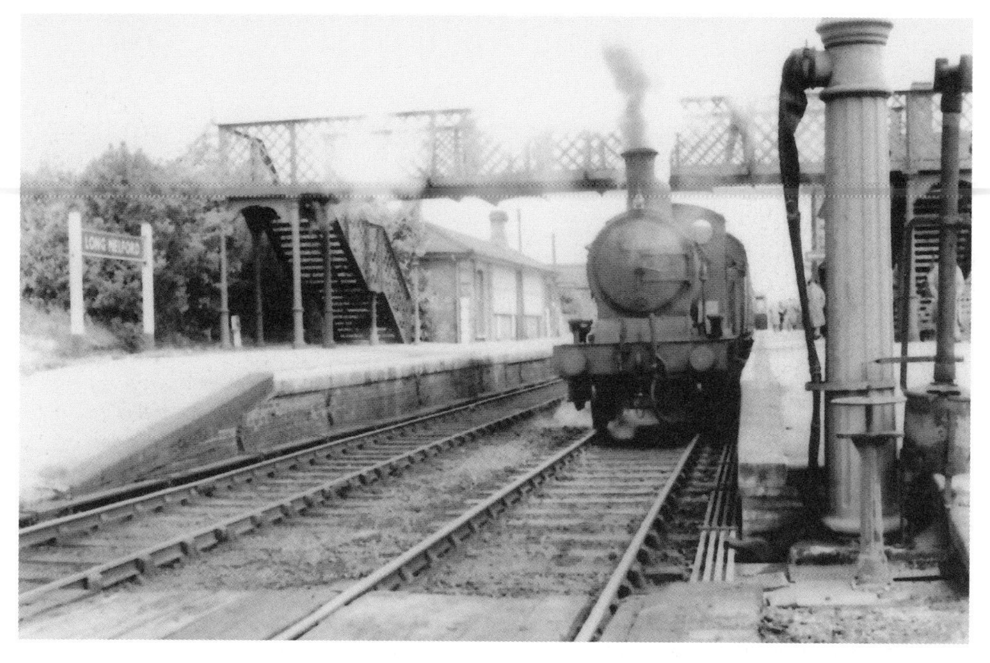

E4 class loco No. 62792 standing at the Up platform with a service for Marks Tey and Colchester; these veteran locomotives could be seen working on the branch lines in and around Cambridge. This view is dated 9 June 1956. (Historical Model Railway Society/ACE103)

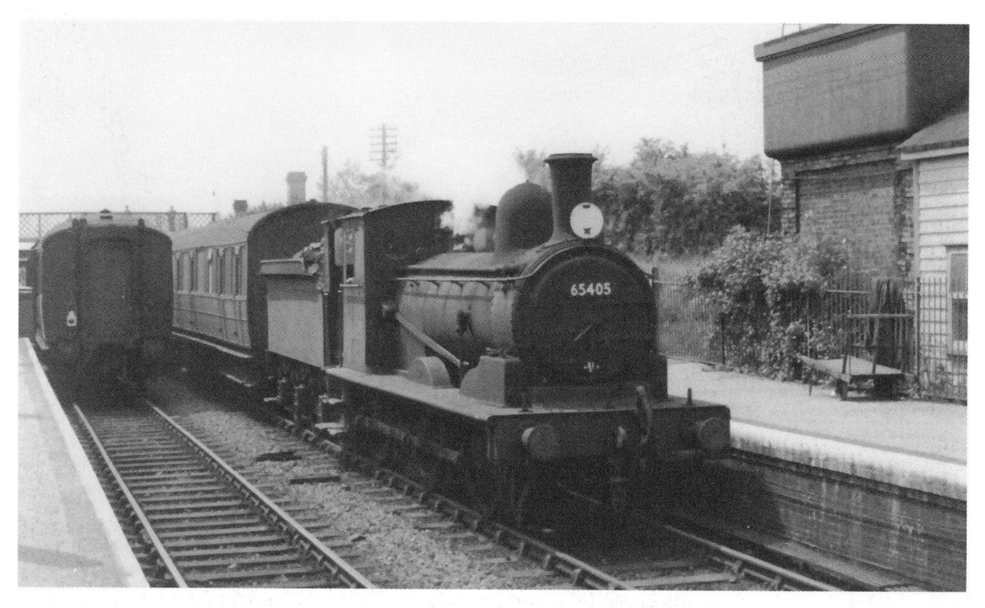

One of the tender cab-fitted J15 class locomotives, No. 65405, arrives in the Down platform with a local passenger working on 9 June 1956. During the 1950s and early 60s you could be guaranteed to see a crossing movement on the single line at this station. At this time this locomotive was allocated to Bury St Edmunds depot; during its last fourteen months of service it spent time allocated to Kings Cross and Neasden sheds before being withdrawn from service. (R. C. Riley/Transport Treasury)

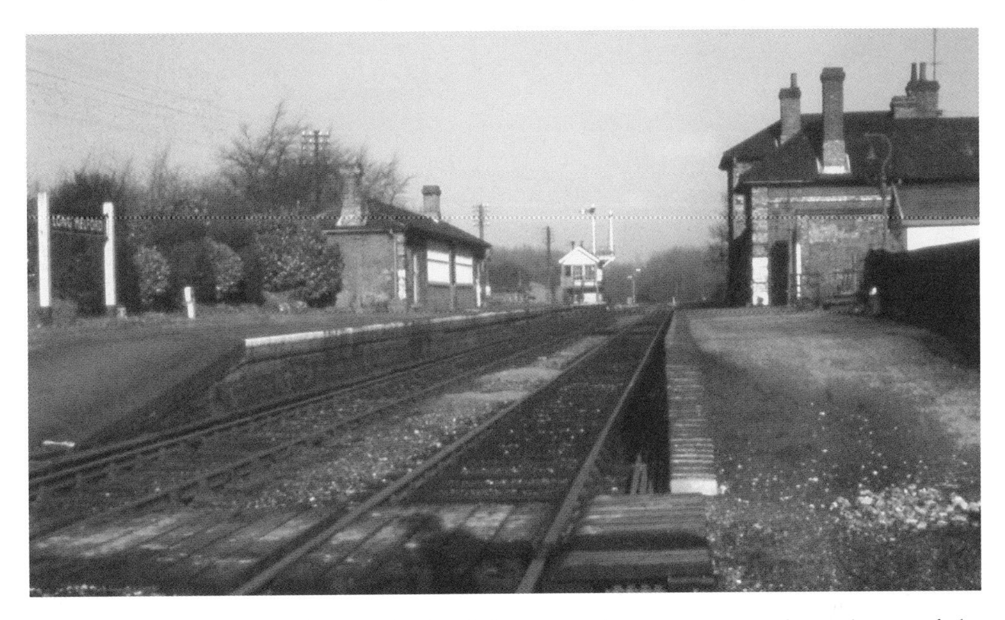

On a bright and sunny February day in 1967, just a few weeks away from closure of the station, we see the general view of the station looking towards the junction signal box. The fine bracket signal had been stripped of its Bury branch arm as the branch had been lifted towards Lavenham in the summer of 1962. (D. J. Plyer)

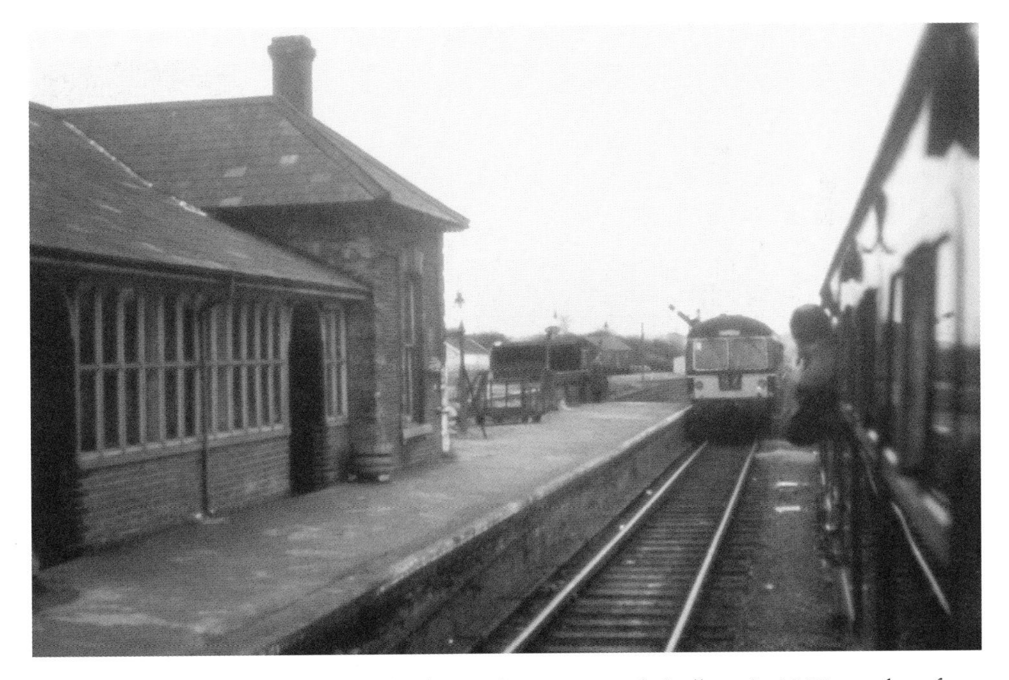

A Class 105 Cravens-type diesel multiple unit departs towards Sudbury in 1967, seen here from leaning out of the window of a Down service to Cambridge. The station had lost its passenger booking facilities in January 1963, all fares being collected on the train. The station buildings survived closure and are now a lovely home. (Brian Pask)

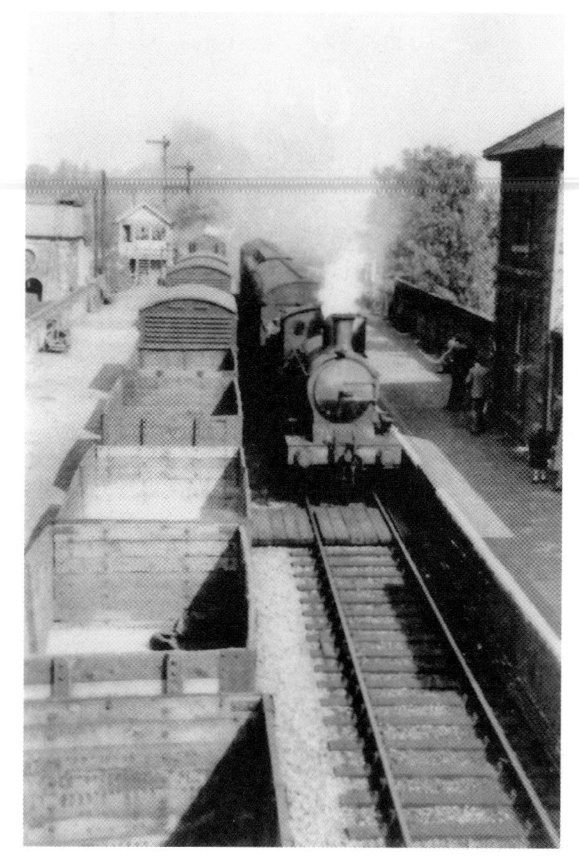

Left: A view taken from the footbridge of an E4 class locomotive and a local passenger train arriving in the Up platform; in this 1947 photograph the engine is in LNER livery with its number, 2784. A long empty freight train stands in the Down platform; also note the original lower-quadrant semaphore bracket signal, which was replaced with a tubular steel example by British Railways. (Historical Model Railway Society-ABD120)

Below: B12 class loco No. 61549 runs into the station with a branch passenger working, as seen from the footbridge. In the Down siding waits the connecting service to Bury St Edmunds with a C12 class tank engine. The date is 16 August 1957. The tall wooden lower-quadrant Up starting signal on the left was replaced by a 12-foot tubular steel example a few years later. (Brian Pask)

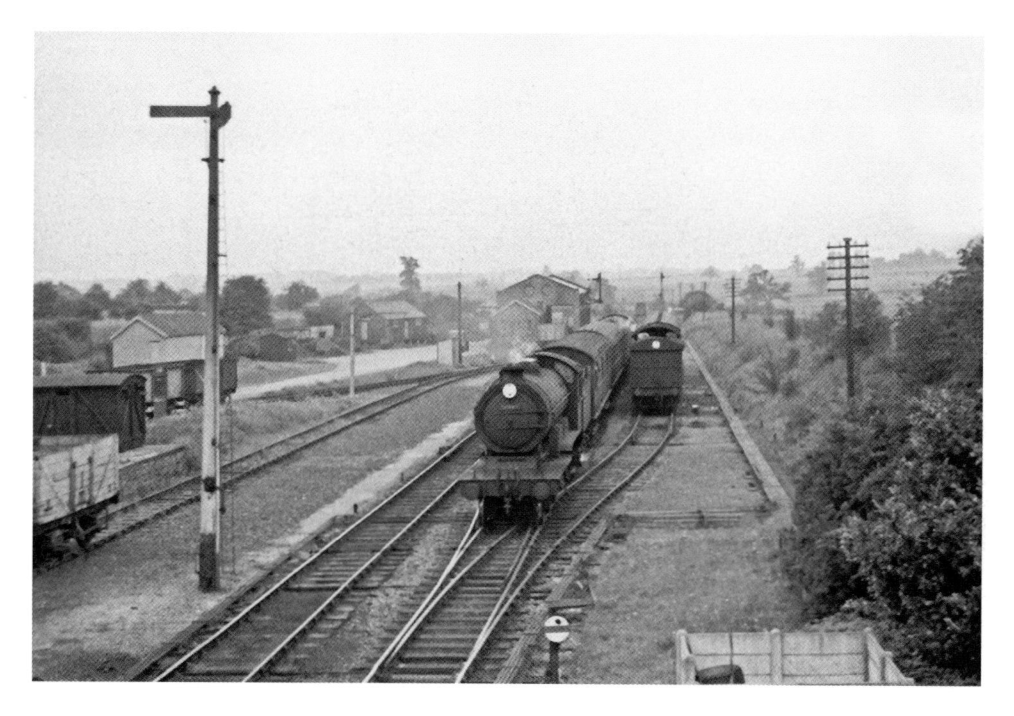

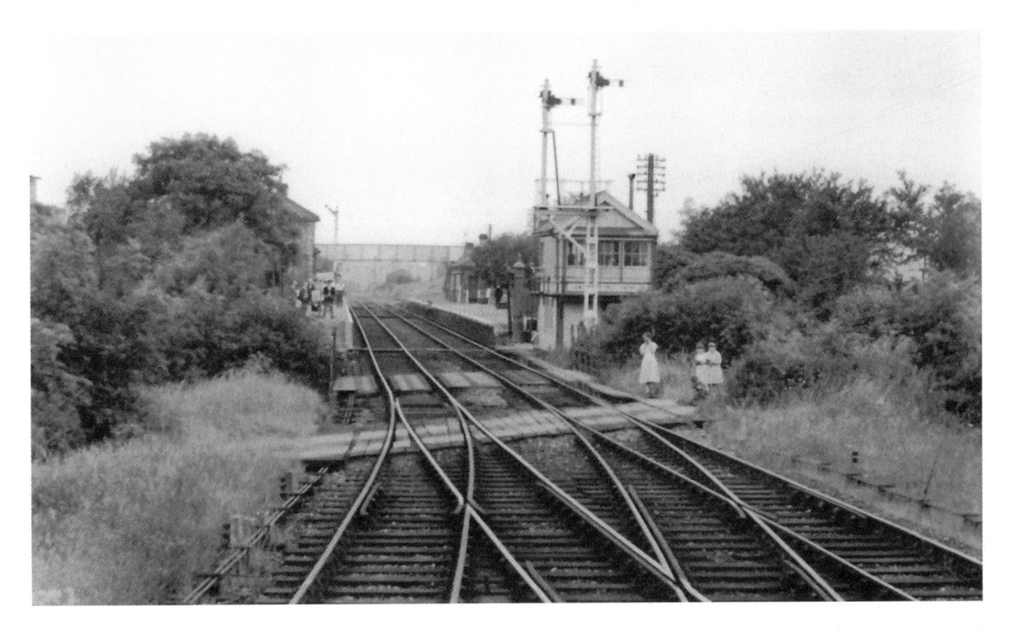

View from the cab of a Class 31 diesel locomotive as it arrives at the station with a special working from Bury St Edmunds: the last through working to travel over the whole of the Bury line, on 4 June 1961. This train had originated at Liverpool Street and had travelled to Marks Tey, then on to Bury St Edmunds via Sudbury and Long Melford; the passenger service over the Bury branch had been withdrawn on and from 10 April 1961. The track between Lavenham and Long Melford was lifted during the summer of 1962. (A. E. Bennett/Transport Treasury)

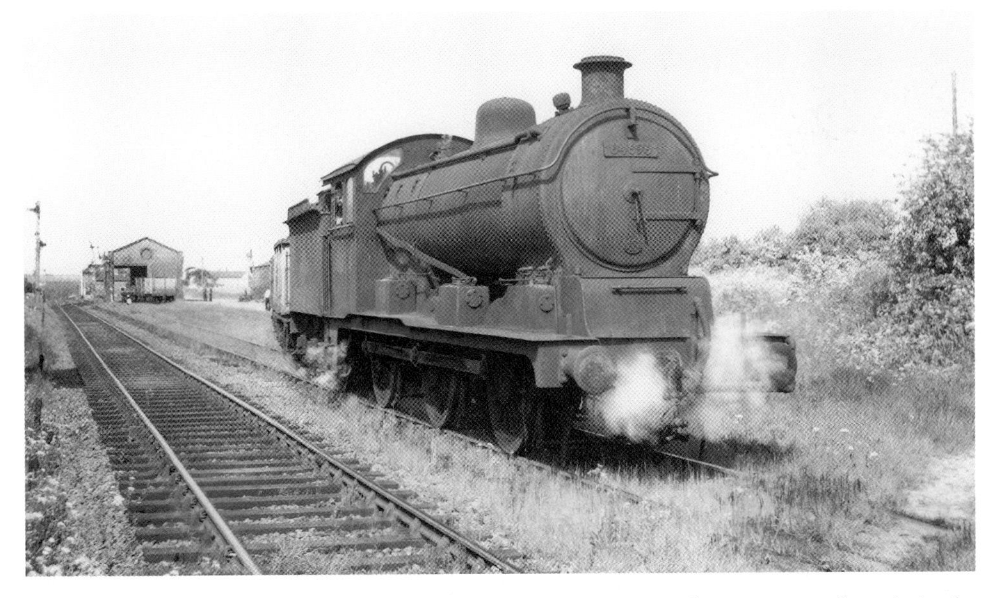

A close-up undated view of a J20 class locomotive, No. 64696, shunting a goods train in the station yard. The main single line is in the foreground and the goods shed and station can be seen in the background. This is taken looking in the down direction looking towards Haverhill and Bury St Edmunds. (Dr I. C. Allen/Transport Treasury)

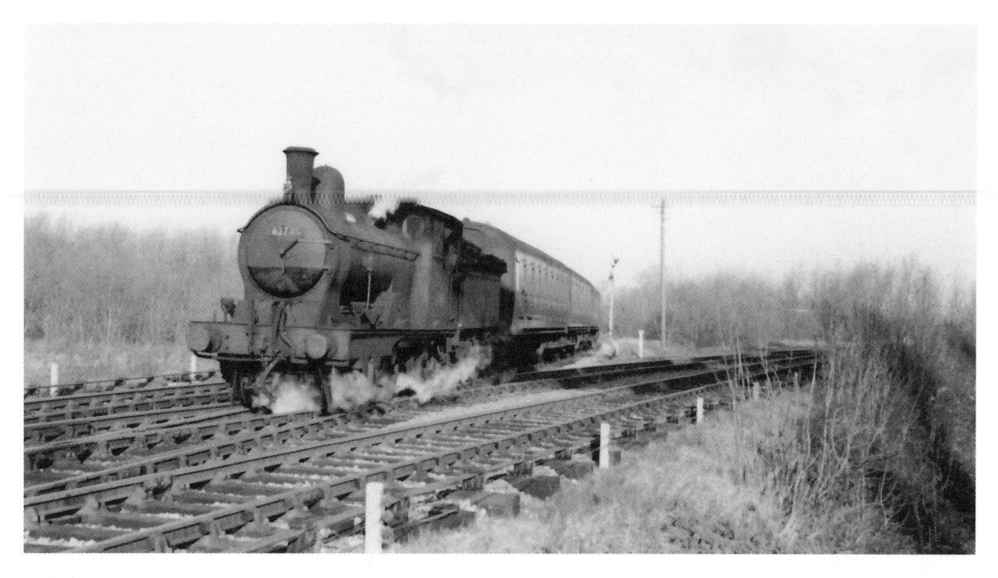

At the other end of the station an E4 class, No. 62785, is arriving at the station, passing over the junction point work from the Haverhill direction; the line to Bury St Edmunds is in the foreground. This locomotive survived until being withdrawn from traffic in December 1959; it was then restored and is now part of the national collection and can be seen at Bressingham Steam Museum near Diss. (Dr I. C. Allen/Transport Treasury)

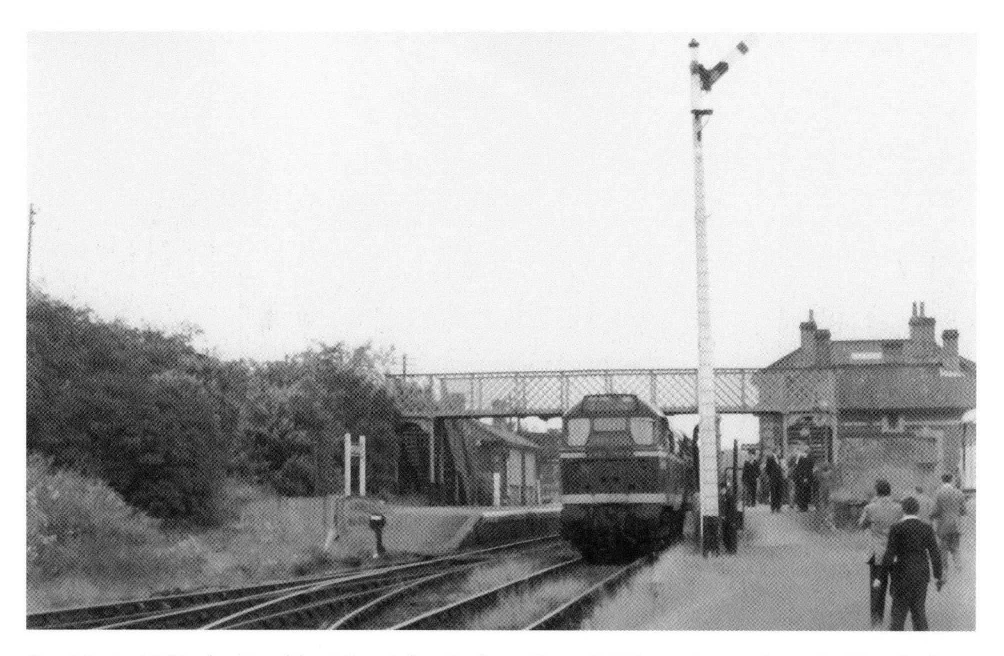

On 4 June 1961, the Ramblers' Special train from Bury St Edmunds stands at the Up platform with its 'Last Train' headboard visible on the front; the tall Up starting signal is off for the train to proceed onwards to Sudbury. After the passing of this service no more passenger trains would pass over the Lavenham to Long Melford section; the next trains would be the demolition trains, which commenced their job in the summer of 1962. (A. E. Bennett/Transport Treasury)

Glemsford

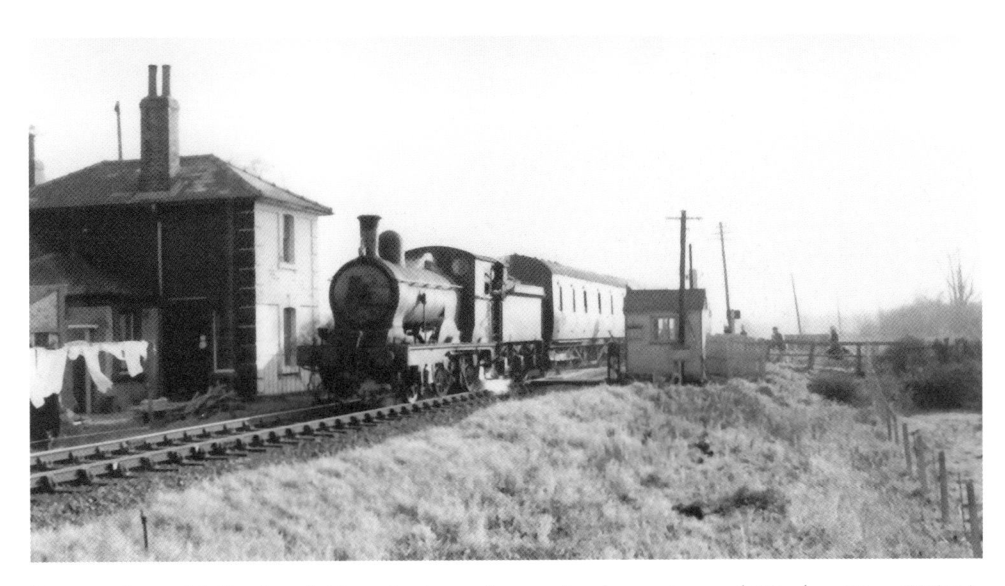

Between Long Melford and Glemsford was Lyston level crossing and E4 class No. 62797 is seen passing with a Cambridge-bound service. Although undated, this view is pre-March 1957, when the locomotive went for scrap. Note the standard GER-type station building on the left as the crossing keeper's cottage; this building still stands today. (Dr I. C. Allen/Transport Treasury)

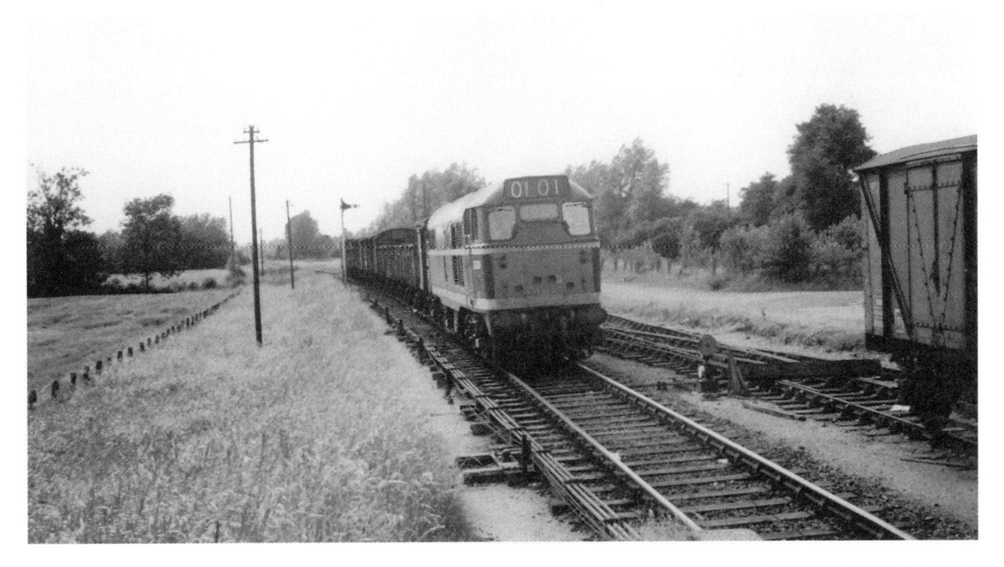

An undated and unidentified view of a Class 31 diesel locomotive working a branch freight entering Glemsford station; a point timber and red flag has been placed across the siding road to prevent wagons being shunted over the track beyond this point. The locomotive's head code is a bit suspect. The porter signalman had already put the home signal to danger. (Dr I. C. Allen/ Transport Treasury)

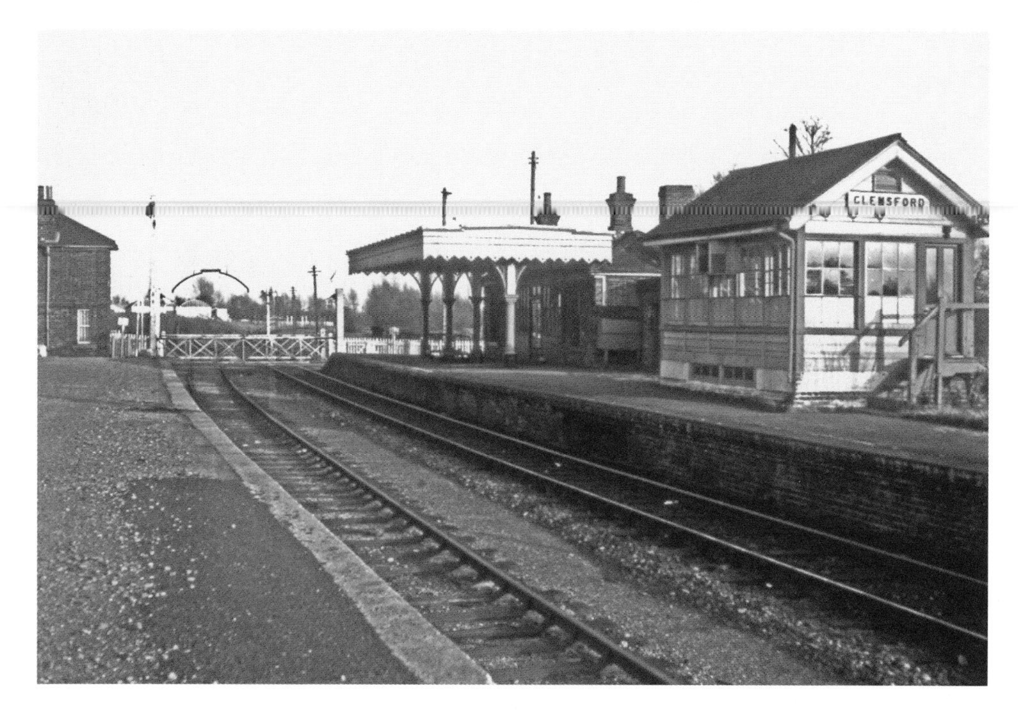

A view dating from the day after the passenger service had been withdrawn and the line closed completely in March 1967. The track would not be lifted until early 1970; the signalling was dismantled not long after closure. (Brian Pask)

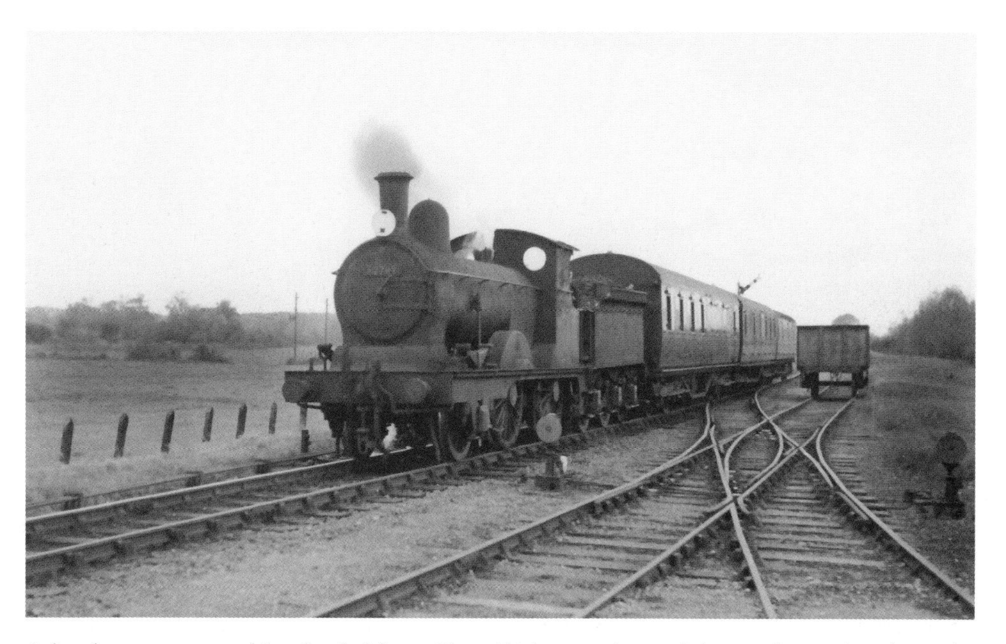

A local passenger working hauled by a Class E4 locomotive arriving at the station from the Clare direction; a solitary empty wagon can be seen in the siding. (Dr I. C. Allen/Transport Treasury)

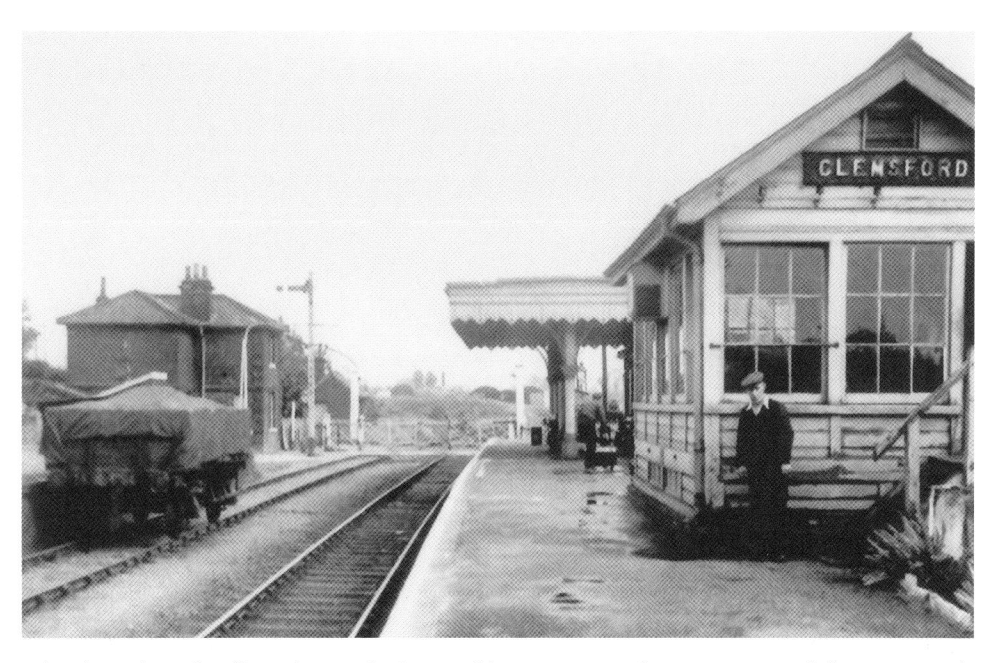

A local member of staff stands outside the signal box in a September 1950 view; a full wagon stands in the loop siding. The signal box was fitted with a twenty-two-lever Saxby & Farmer lever frame with seventeen working and five spare levers, later sixteen working and six spare. The station was never a block post and the porter signalman required the Long Melford to Cavendish tablet to unlock the facing points to access the sidings. (Historical Model Railway Society – ABC424)

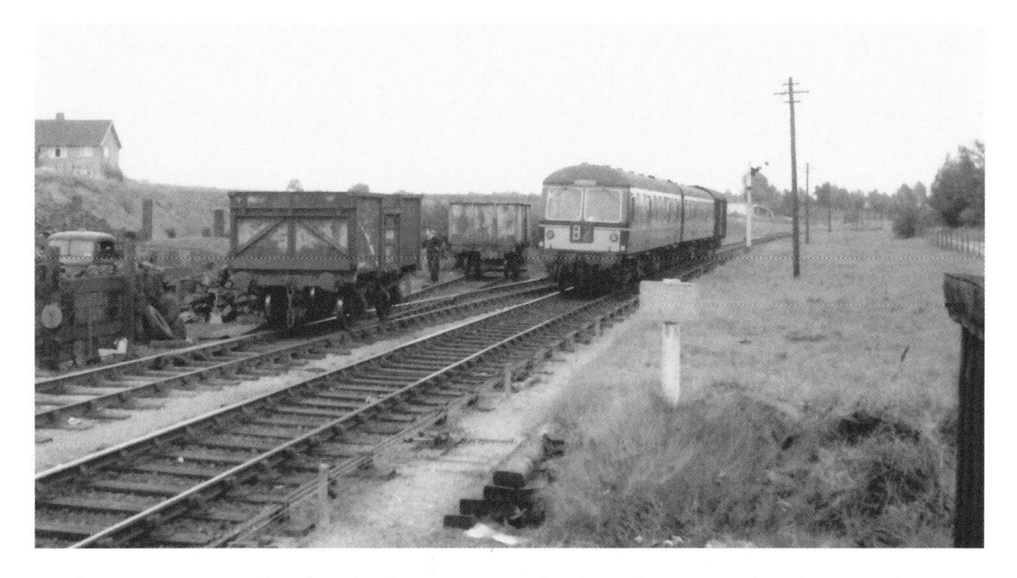

A Class 105 Cravens diesel multiple unit passes the down home signal and two coal wagons being unloaded onto the coal stacking ground on the left. The DMU is hauling a parcels van and although this view is undated it would be between 1 January 1959 and closure in 1967. The train is approaching the station from the Sudbury direction; the station would retain its freight handling facilities until 12 September 1966. (Dr I. C. Allen/Transport Treasury)

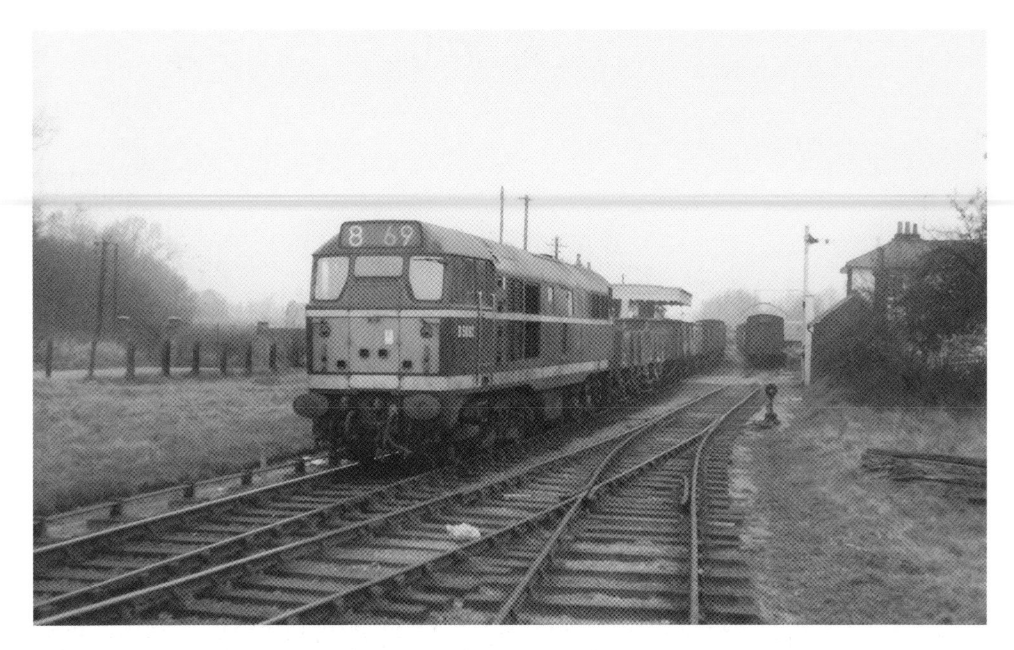

The branch freight 8_69 arrives with the daily service from the Cambridge direction and will pause in the platform line before being split and then shunting any traffic for the station into the loop siding. In the right foreground is a short head shunt which served the coal stacking ground. (Dr I. C. Allen/Transport Treasury)

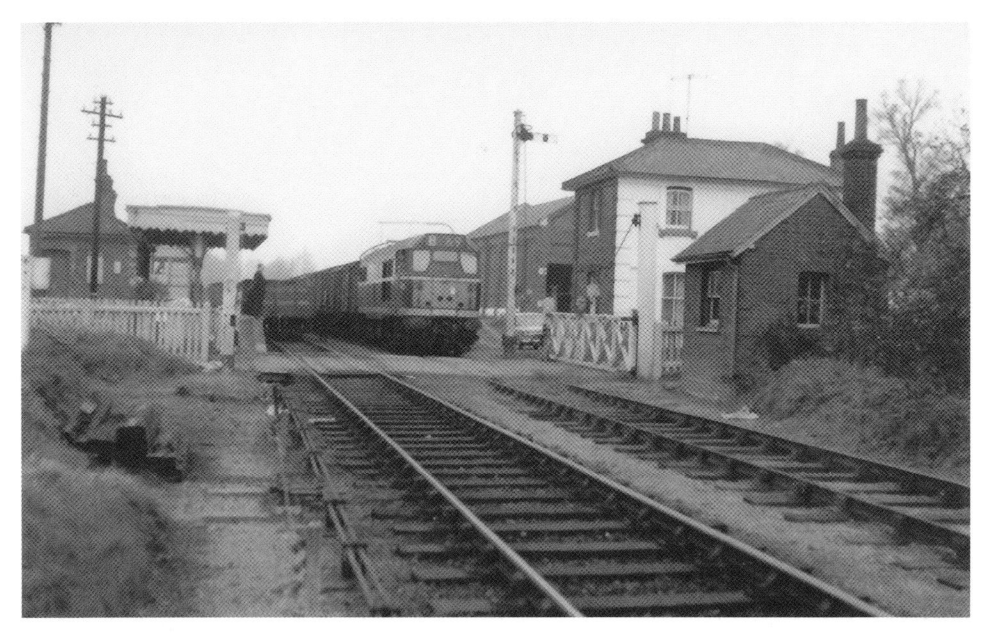

Another undated view of the same train, this time taken from the down cess as the Class 31 diesel, No. D5692, shunts wagons and vans into the loop siding. Part of the train remains in the platform line while these manoeuvres take place; the level crossing is closed to road traffic. (Dr I. C. Allen/Transport Treasury)

Cavendish

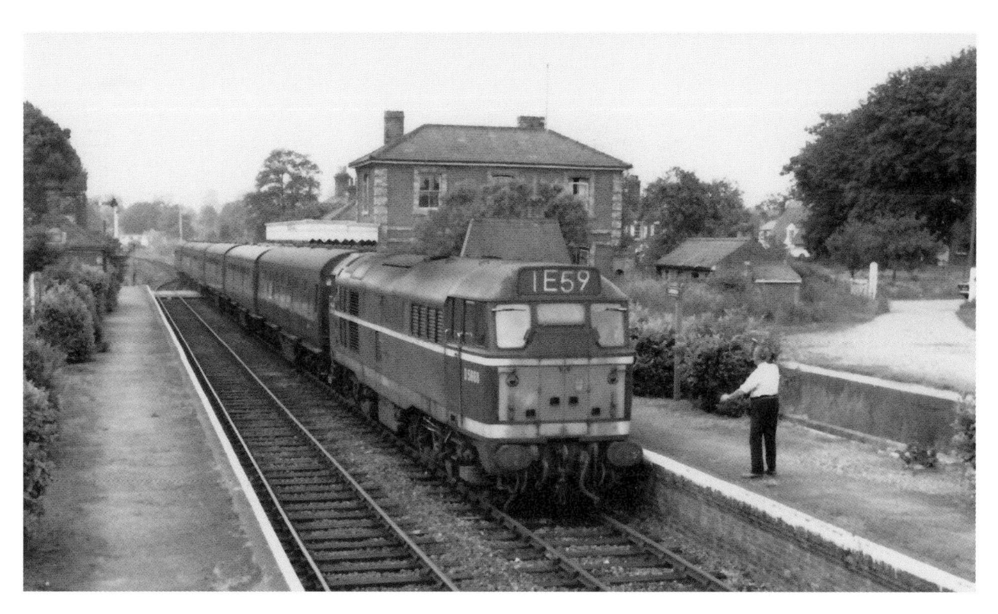

Class 31 diesel D5668 working a cross-country passenger express train from Leicester to Clacton via the Stour Valley line; this ran on Saturdays during the summer and had previously been steam-hauled. The signalman is seen preparing to exchange tokens; this view was taken from the signal box. (Dr I. C. Allen/Transport Treasury)

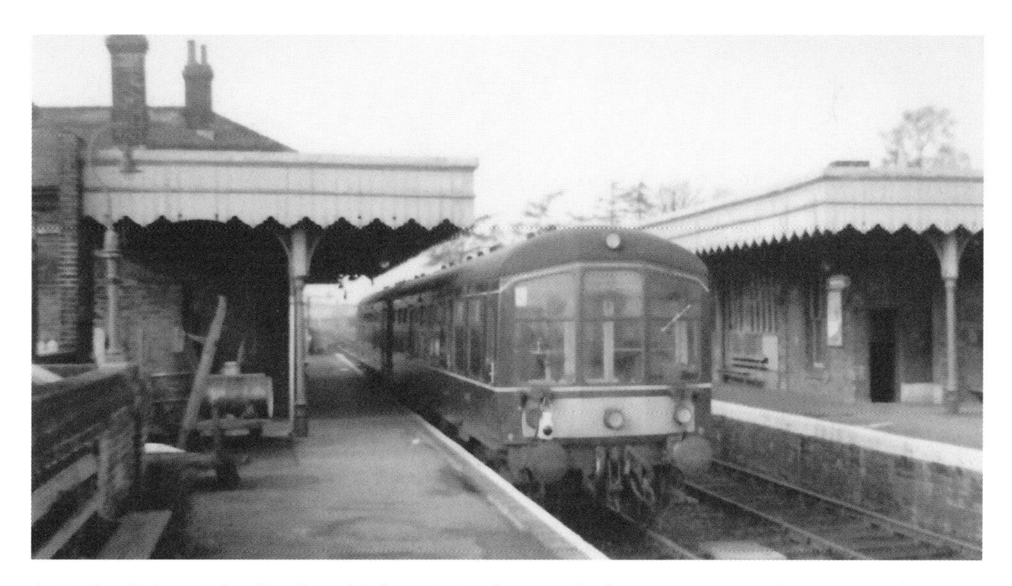

A Derby lightweight diesel multiple unit in the up platform as seen in the 1960s. The main station buildings were on the up side and a waiting room and other facilities can be seen on the opposite platform, long canopies being provided to keep any passengers dry. (Railway Correspondence and Travel Society Archive)

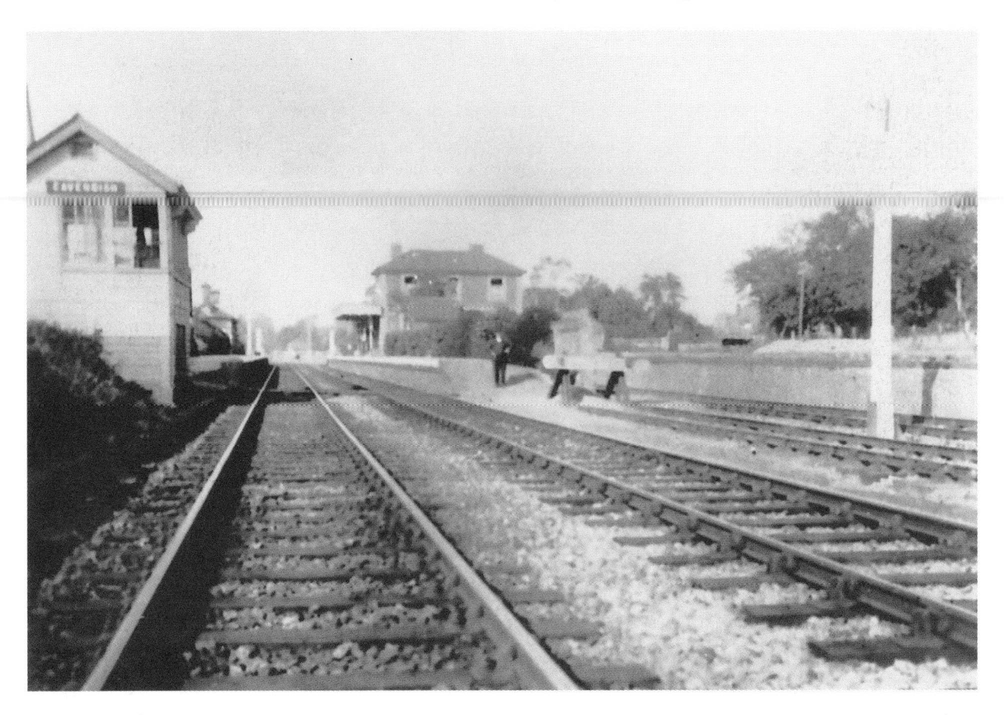

A general view of the station and signal box, looking west towards Haverhill; a member of staff stands looking at the photographer. The original Up starting signal can be seen between the two sidings. This view was taken in 1950. (Historical model Railway Society – ABC413)

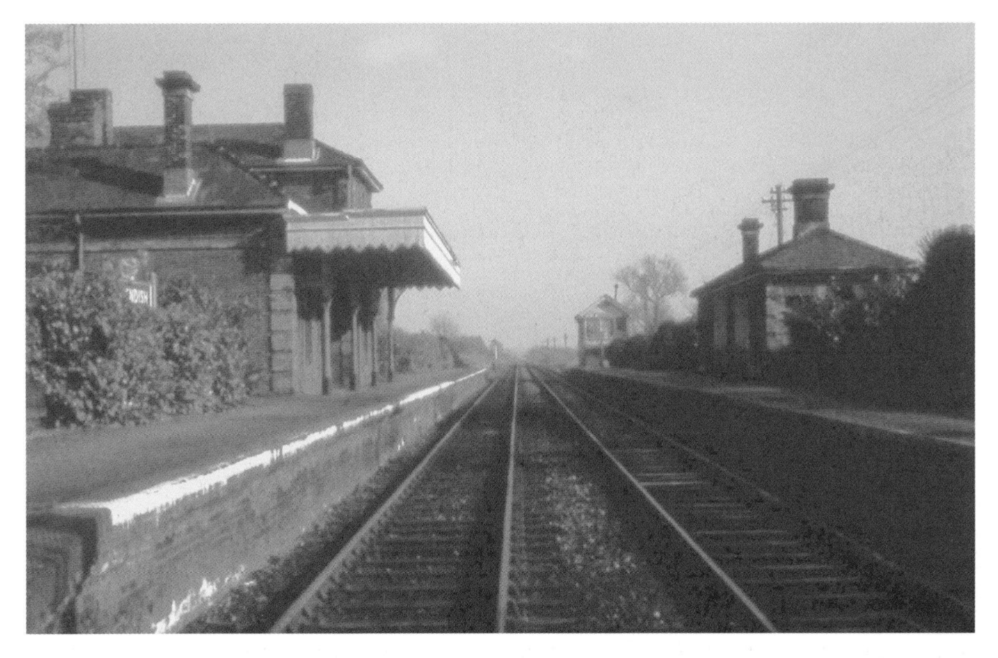

A general view taken on 18 February 1967, looking from the station level crossing at the station buildings and signal box; this view is looking towards Sudbury. (D. J. Plyer)

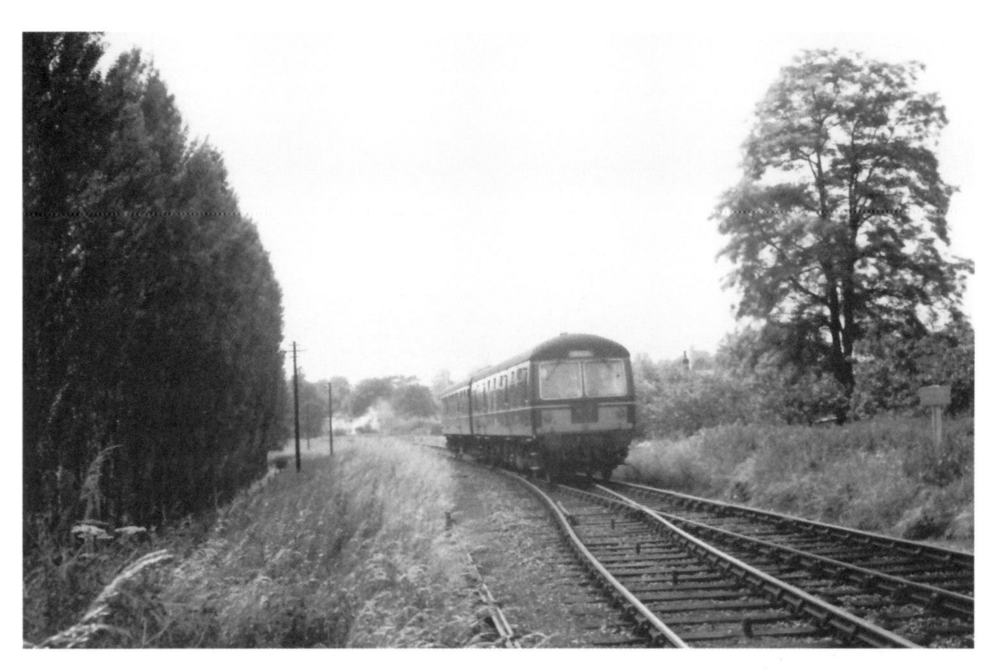

Class 105 Cravens-type diesel multiple unit approaching the station with a train from Cambridge to Colchester; although undated, this view can be dated to between 1959 and closure of the line in 1967. (Dr I. C. Allen/Transport Treasury)

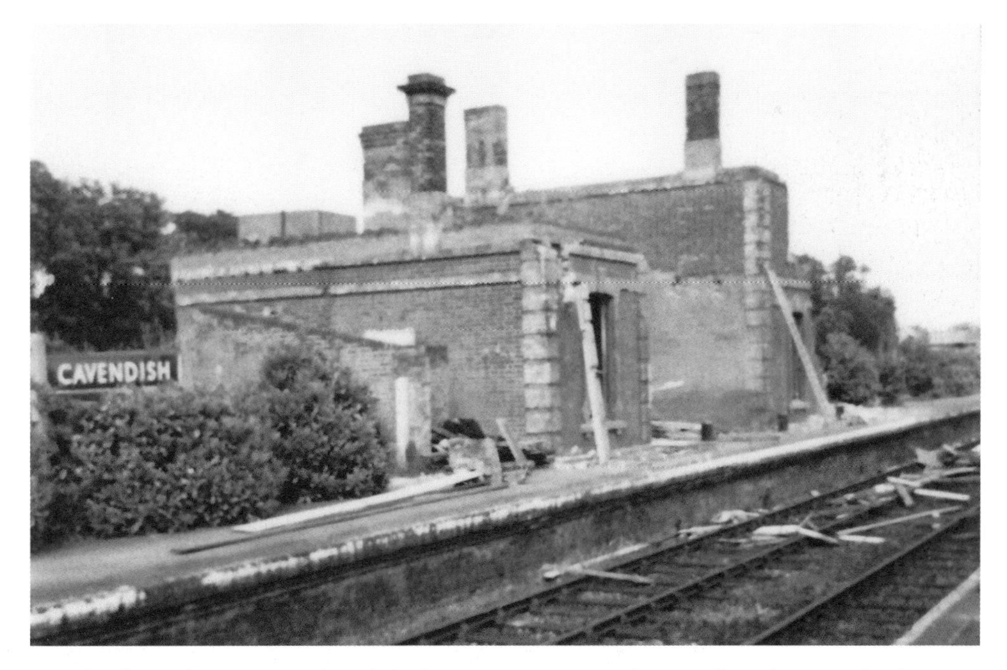

A sad sight as the station is demolished in June 1967 to make way for a housing development on the old station and goods yard land. The rails were to remain *in situ* until 1970, when the track was lifted for scrap. (Railway Correspondence and Travel Society Archive)

Clare

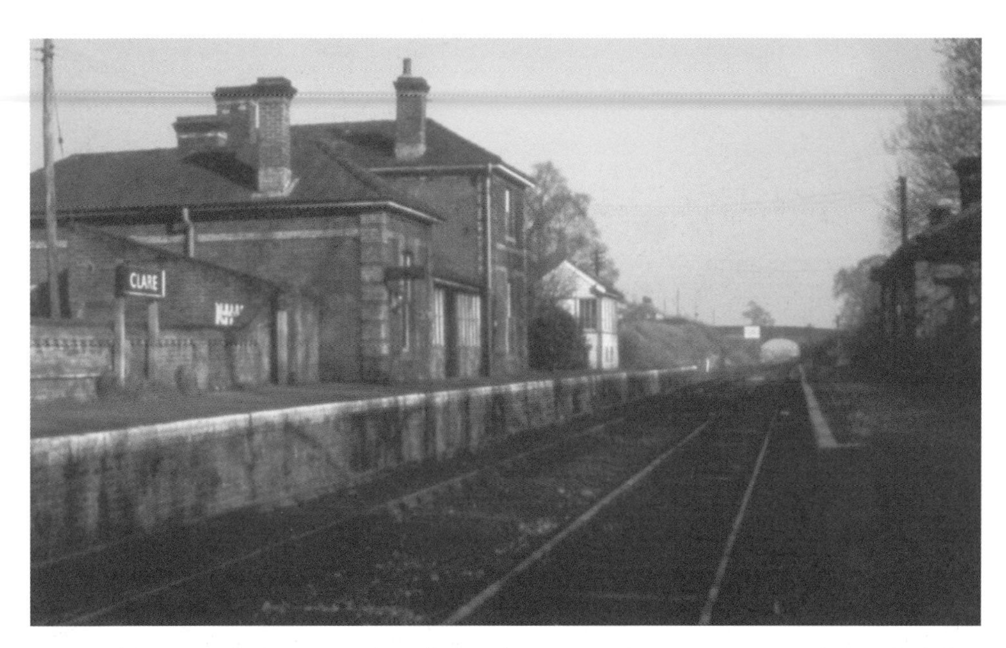

A view of the station looking towards Sudbury taken on 18 February 1967, just a few weeks before final closure. By this date the signal box had closed and all trains used the Up direction platform adjacent to the main buildings; freight facilities had been axed the previous September. (D. J. Plyer)

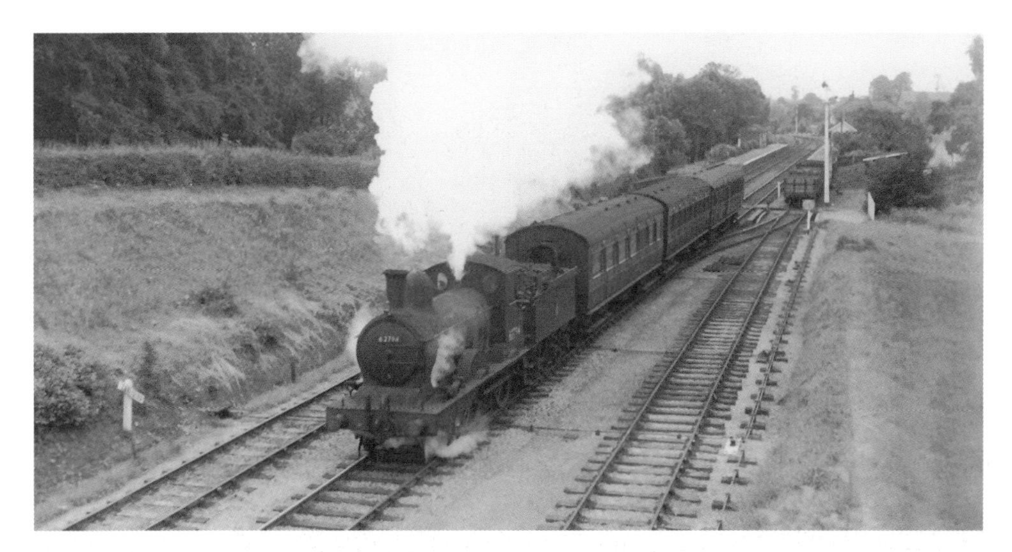

A pre-August 1955 view taken from the bridge seen in the distance in the previous picture. This view features veteran E4 class locomotive No. 62794 as it departs towards Sudbury with a local passenger working. These engines had once numbered 100 examples when first built and eighteen survived into British Rail ownership; withdrawals for scrap commenced in the 1950s. (Dr I. C. Allen/Transport Treasury)

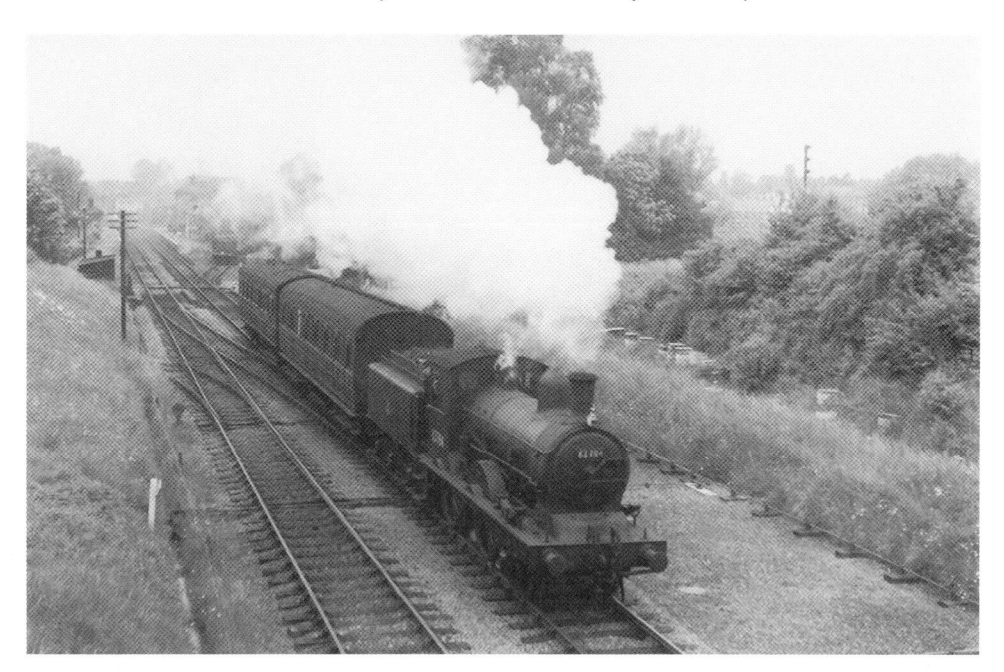

Another view taken from the same over bridge looking back towards the station and once again featuring another member of the E4 class: this time it's No. 62784. This view was taken sometime before its withdrawal in May 1955; the locomotive is working local passenger consisting of just two coaches. (Dr I. C. Allen/Transport Treasury)

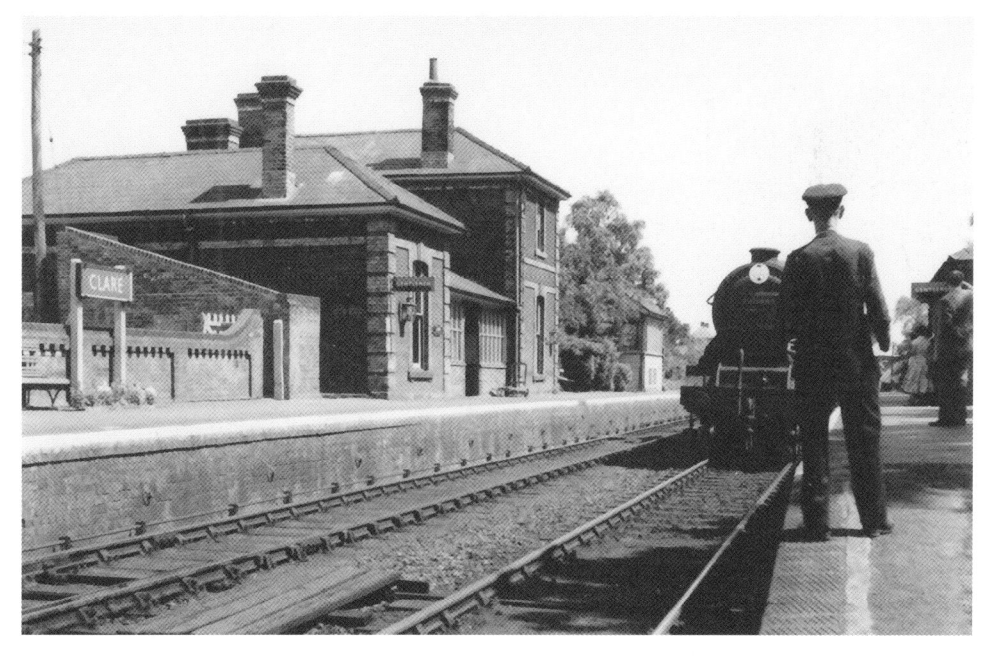

B17 class locomotive No. 61666 is seen arriving at the Down platform with the signalman waiting to transfer tokens for the next section to Haverhill; this view is dated 1 August 1955, many years before the purges of the 1960s. (Brian Connell/Photos from the Fifties)

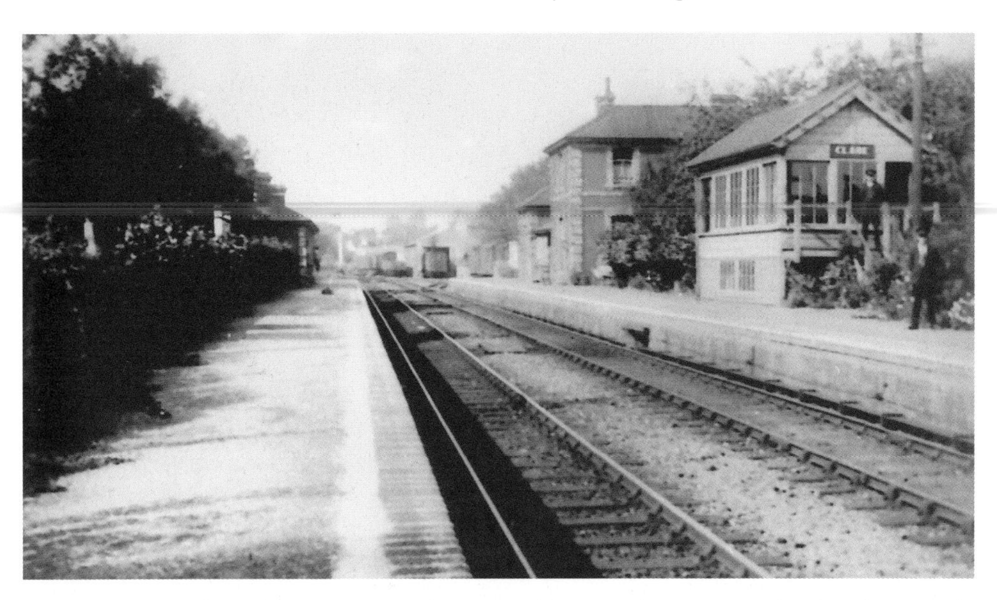

A general view of the station and signal box with the signalman posing for the photograph; this was taken during 1947, in the last year of LNER control. Clare signal box was equipped with a twenty-two-lever Saxby & Farmer frame with fifteen working and seven spare levers; in the 1932 alterations, when key token working was introduced between here and Haverhill, the frame was enlarged to twenty-five levers with nineteen working and six spare levers. The signal box closed on 20 January 1967, a couple of months before the station closed completely. (Historical Model Railway Society – ABC423)

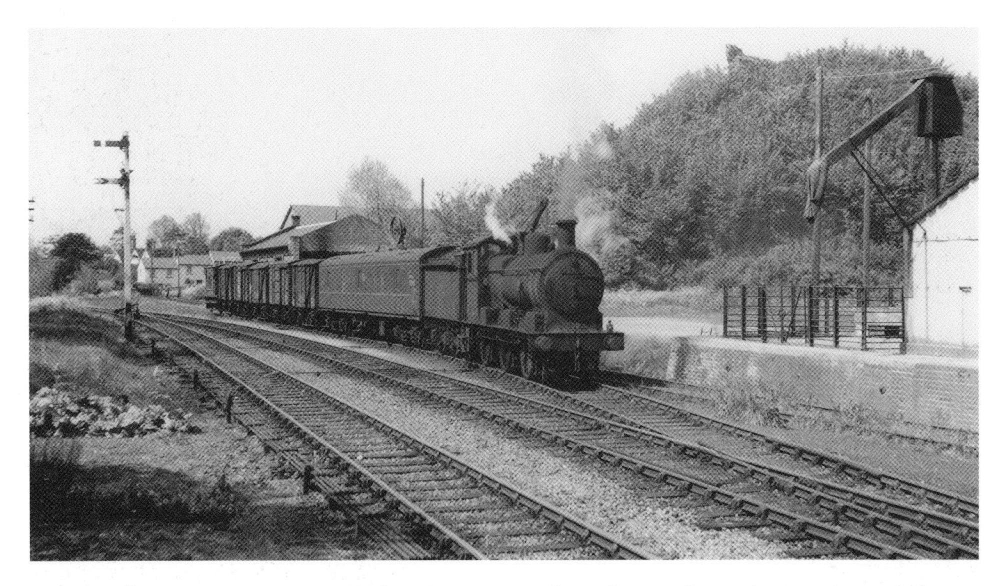

J17 class locomotive No. 6557X shunting wagons into the goods yard; note the parcels van marshalled behind the locomotive. The station, goods shed and surrounding area is now designated Clare Country Park, and until recently the warden lived in the old station house; it is now boarded up due to budget cuts as the post was withdrawn by the local authority. (Dr I. C. Allen/Transport Treasury)

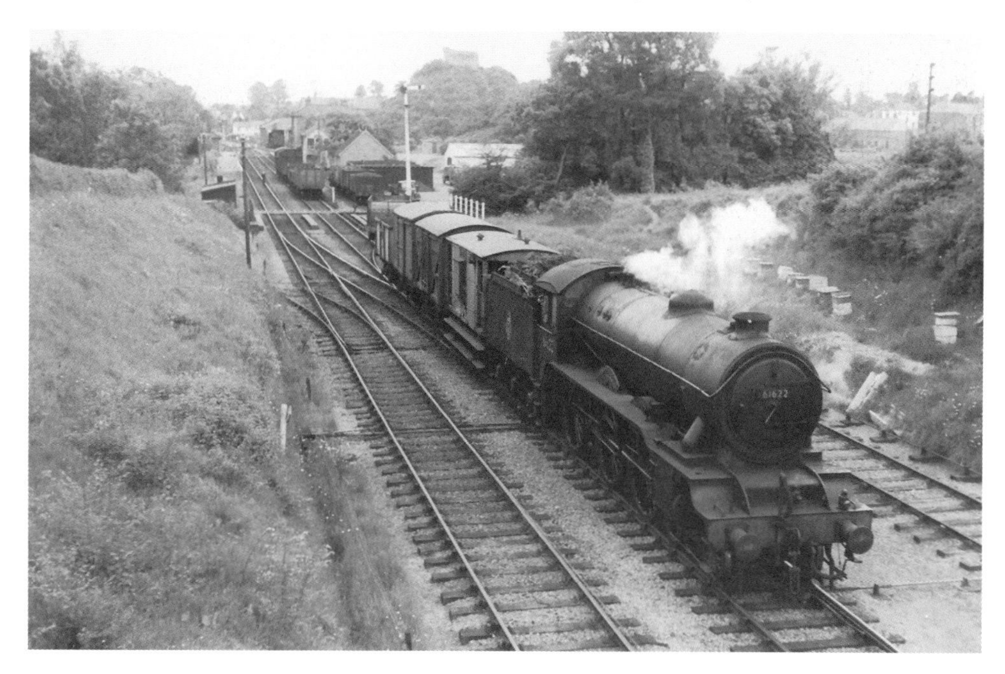

B17 class No. 61622 is seen shunting the Up siding at the Sudbury end of the station; part of the train had been left standing in the platform line during this manoeuvre. (Dr I. C. Allen/ Transport Treasury)

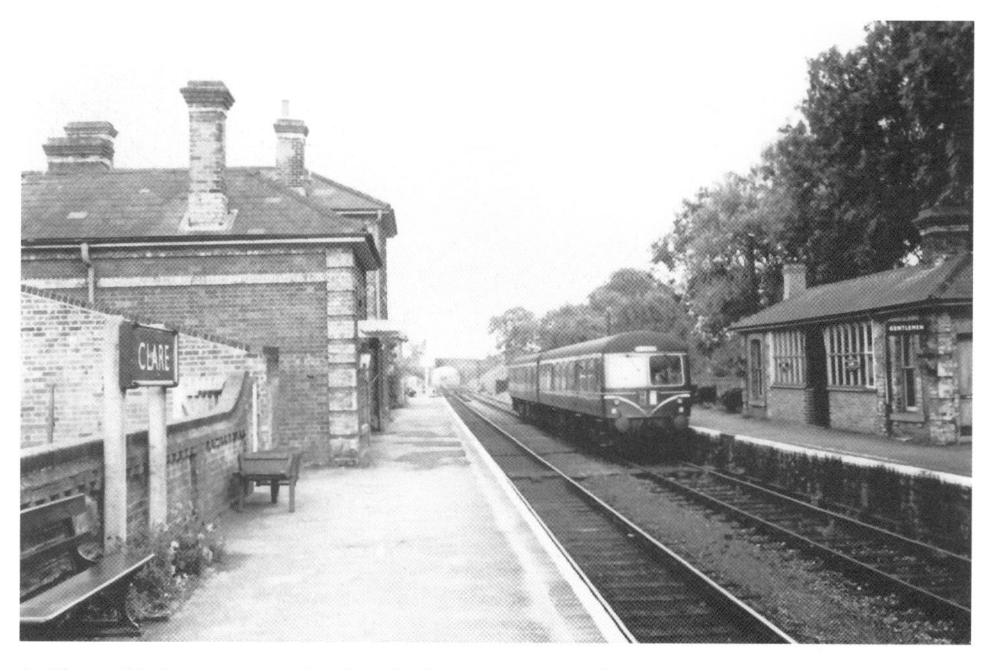

A Class 105 Cravens-type diesel multiple unit is seen calling in 1960 at the Down platform; these modern units had taken over the passenger service from 1 January 1959. In the early years a wide variety of DMU types could be seen on the line. (Stations UK)

Stoke

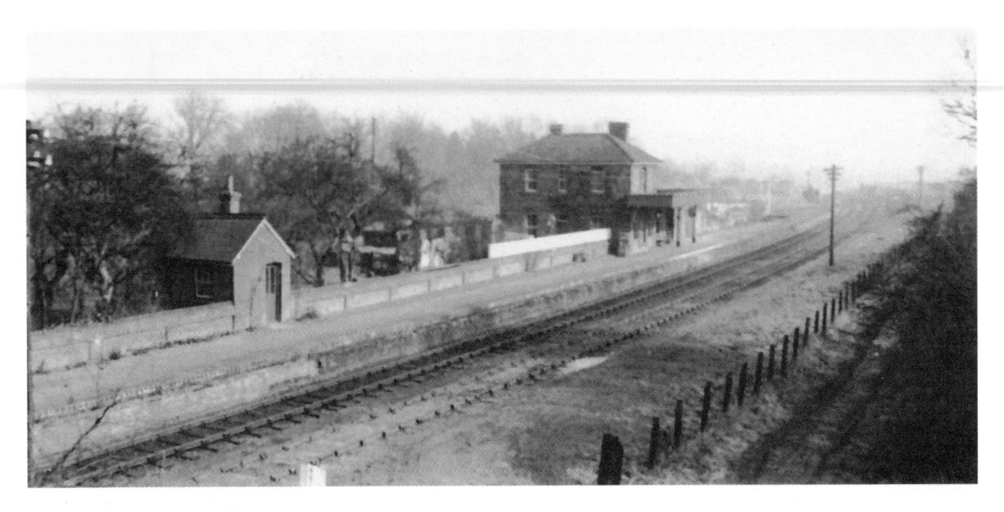

A general view taken in 1953 of the station as seen from the road bridge adjacent to the station, looking east towards Sudbury. The station had lost its signal box in 1932, it being replaced with two ground frames to work the connections to the loop and sidings; an intermediate key token machine was provided from this time for freight trains to be shunted clear of the main single line. (Stations UK)

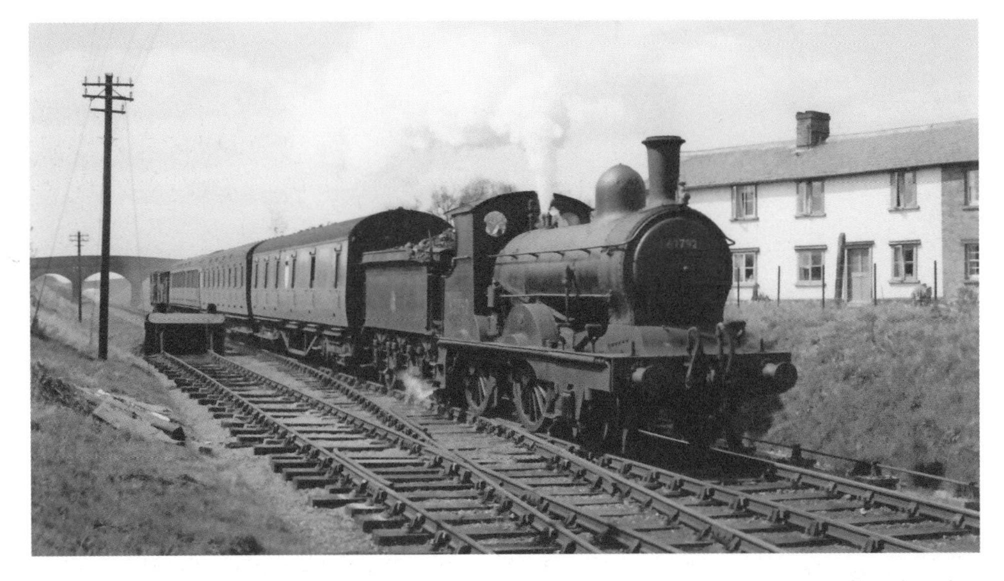

A track-level view of E4 class No. 62792 entering the station from the Haverhill end with a three-coach and van passenger train; the loop line points in the foreground were worked by the previously mentioned ground frame. I was told a tale by a local resident who lived in the house seen in this view: on schooldays the shortcut to school involved crossing the railway on the crossing adjacent to the photographer and walking down the loop line cess instead of going the long way round by road. (Dr I. C. Allen/Transport Treasury)

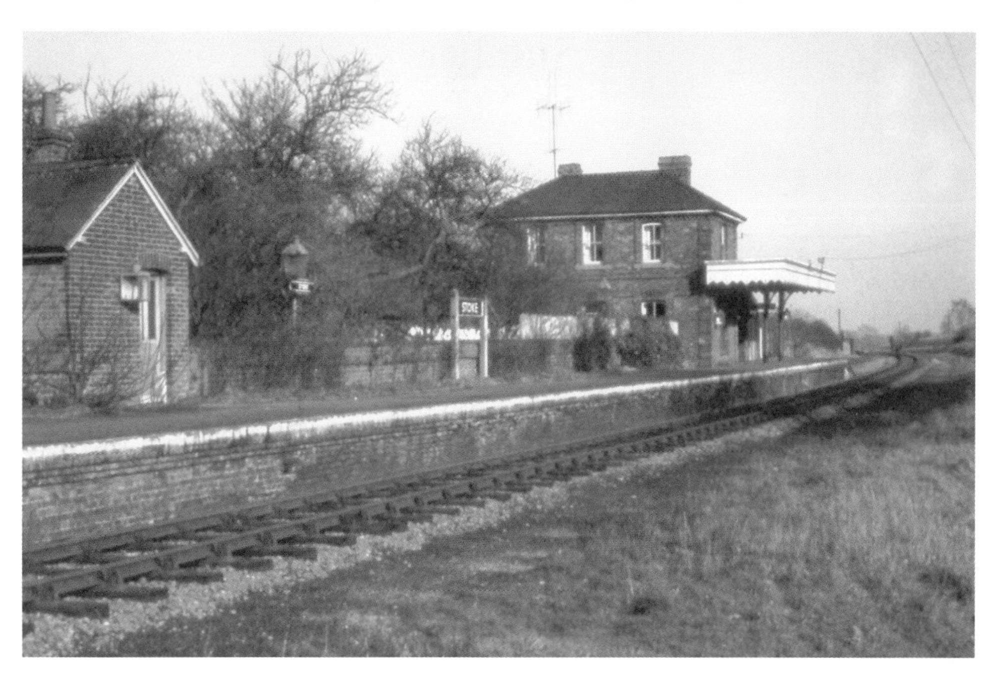

By 13 February 1967, the date of this view, the loop line and sidings in the small yard had been closed and lifted, leaving just the single platform line which would see trains only for a few more weeks. The station still stands today and has been turned into a private house. (D. J. Plyer)

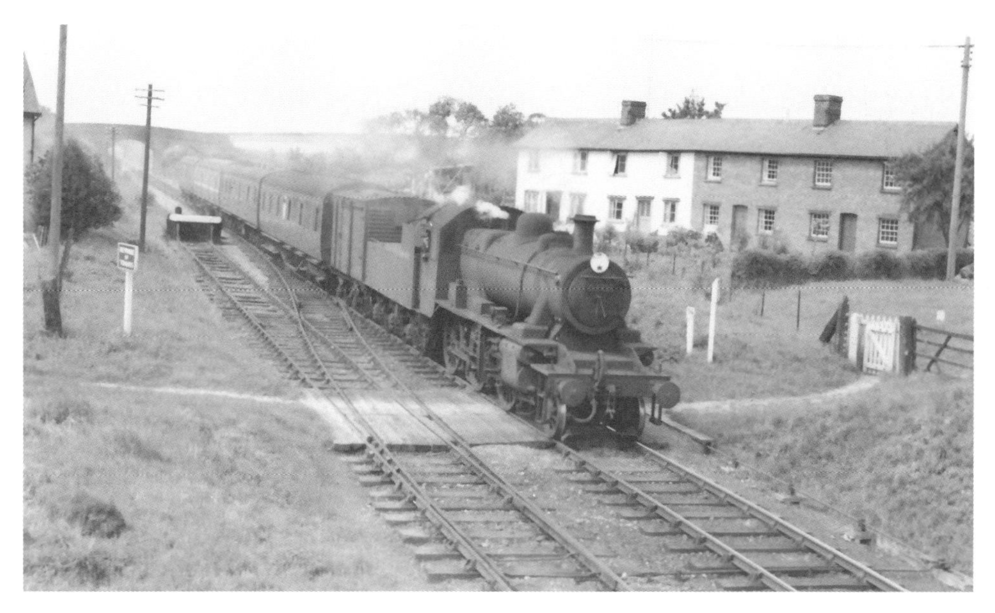

Although I have used this view before, it features one of five Ivatt-designed 2MT class locomotives that were allocated to Colchester and Cambridge for work over the local lines in the area. They replaced some of the veteran J15s and E4s, which were all getting on in age. The foot crossing mentioned earlier can be seen as locomotive No. 46469 approaches the station. (Dr I. C. Allen/Transport Treasury)

Sturmer

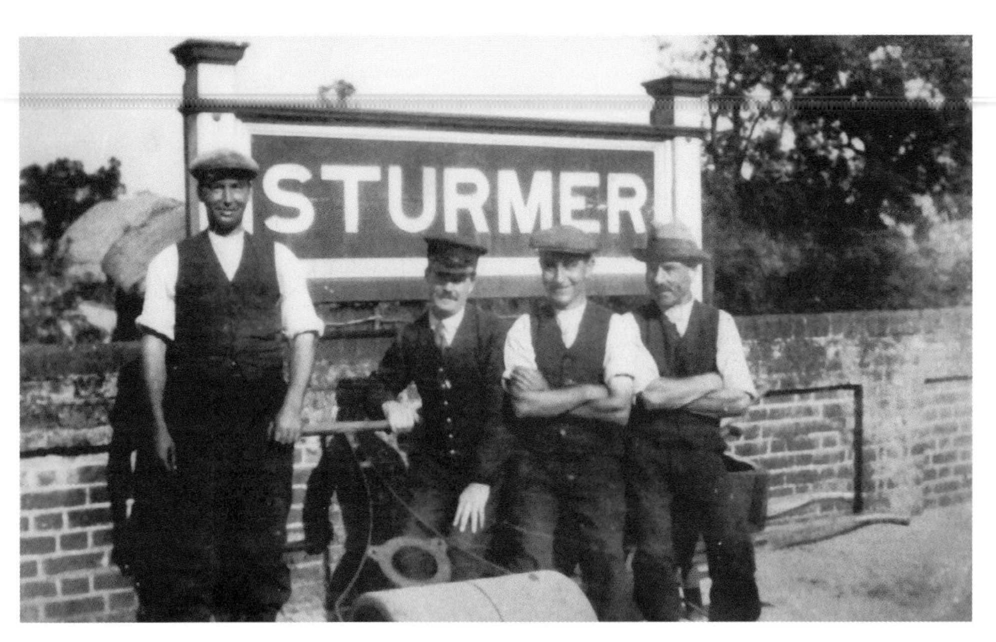

An undated view of a member of the station staff and probably local permanent way men sitting on a barrow with a large roller adjacent to the station name board; note the flat caps and collarless shirts. (CVRPL Collection)

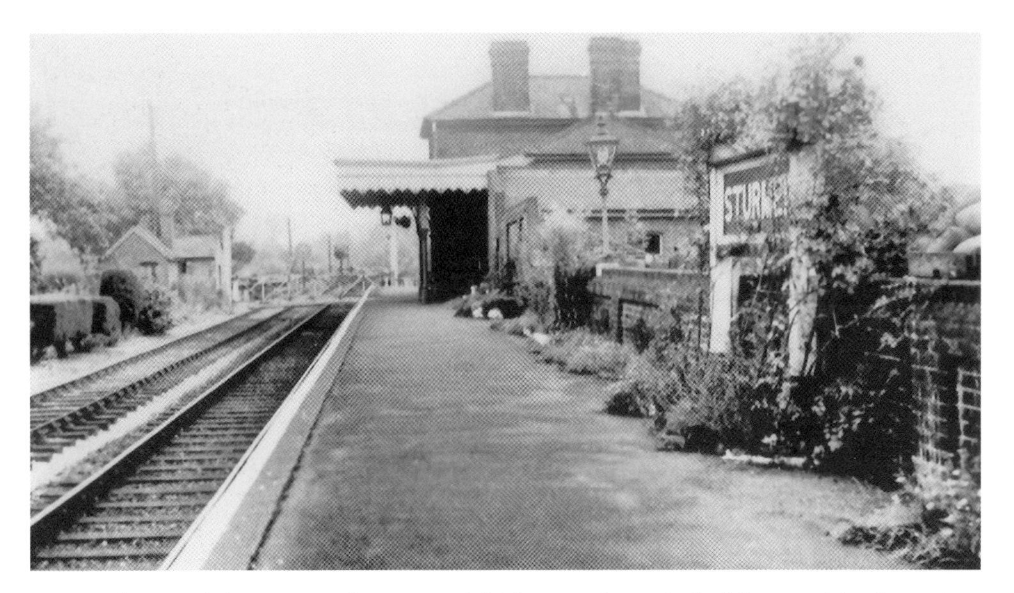

A general view of the station taken in 1950 looking at the main buildings and level crossing; the gates are fitted with large targets with a red light at night for a clearer view by drivers. Following the 1932 signalling alteration, the crossing was protected with working distant signals worked from an adjacent ground frame. (Historical Model Railway Society – ABC930)

Haverhill GE (North)

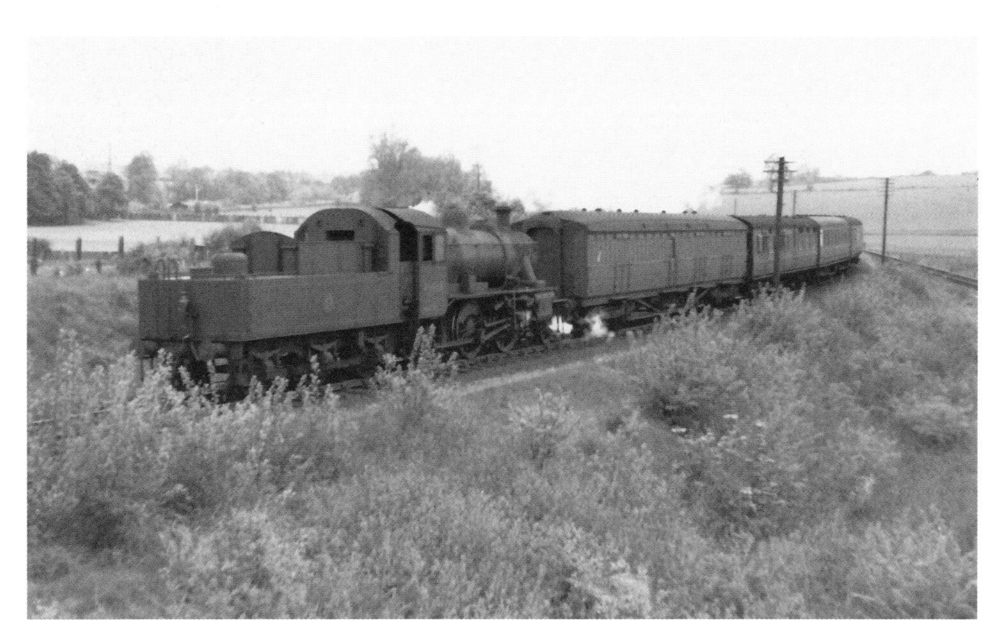

2MT class locomotive No. 46468, running tender first, diverges from the Stour Valley line onto the connecting line that leads to Colne Valley metals at Colne Valley Junction. The Stour Valley line can be seen on the extreme right of the picture. (Dr I. C. Allen/Transport Treasury)

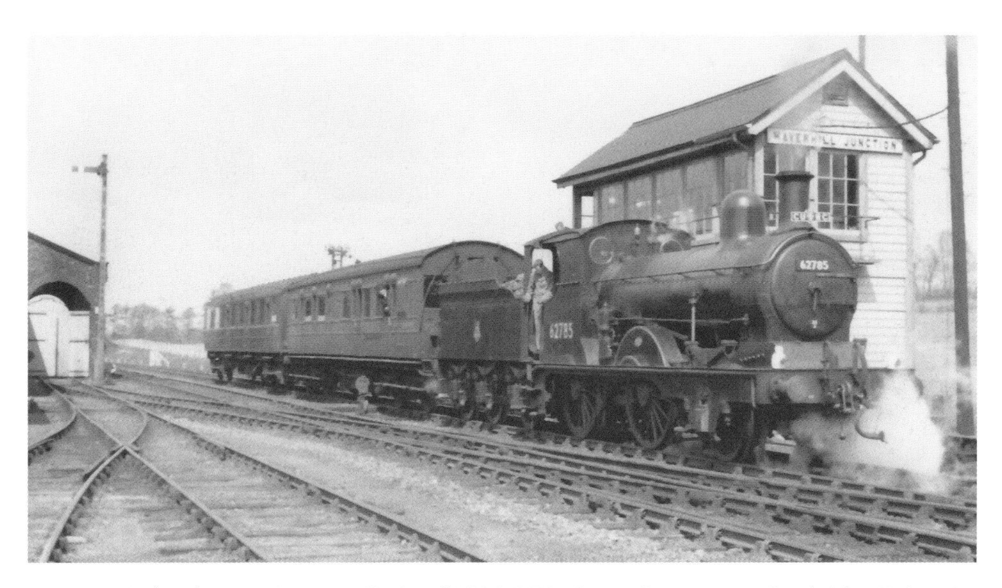

Veteran E4 class locomotive No. 62785 of 1894 GER vintage is seen on a Cambridge University Railway Club driving special outside the junction signal box with a short two-coach coaching set usually seen on the Mildenhall branch; the date is 27 April 1958. Haverhill Junction signal box survived until closure of the line in March 1967. (R. C. Riley/Transport Treasury)

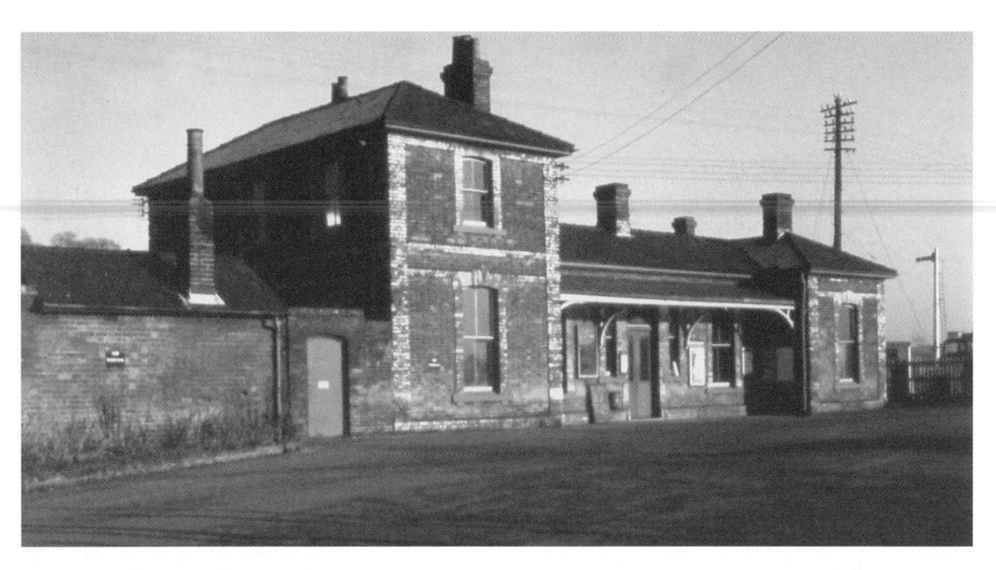

An exterior view of the station taken from the station forecourt. This view was taken in December 1966, when the station was probably at its lowest ebb. The train service had continued to run in 1966 due to a subsidy being paid; when British Rail doubled the amount required in January 1967, the local authorities withdrew their objection to closure and the line closed a few weeks later. (D. J. Plyer)

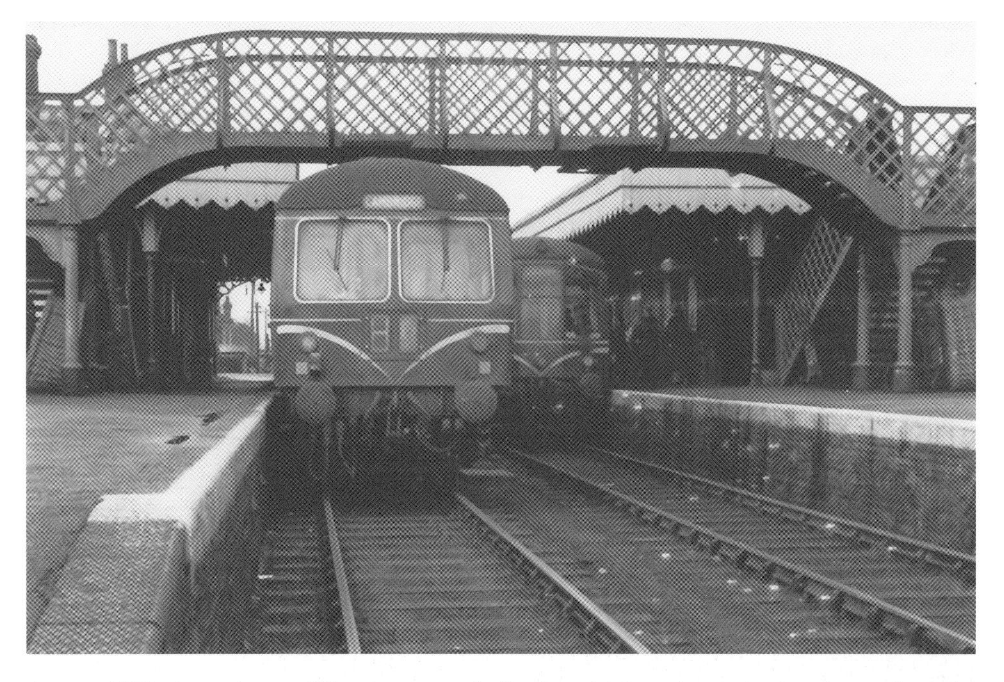

A post-1959 view of two different types of diesel multiple unit passing at the station; the Cambridge-bound service is formed of a Class 105 Cravens unit, and the Sudbury-bound service is formed of a Derby lightweight unit. At this time the platforms were connected by a fine footbridge; this was dismantled during the 1960s and passengers had to cross the line on a foot crossing at the end of the platform. (D. Lawrence/Photos from the Fifties)

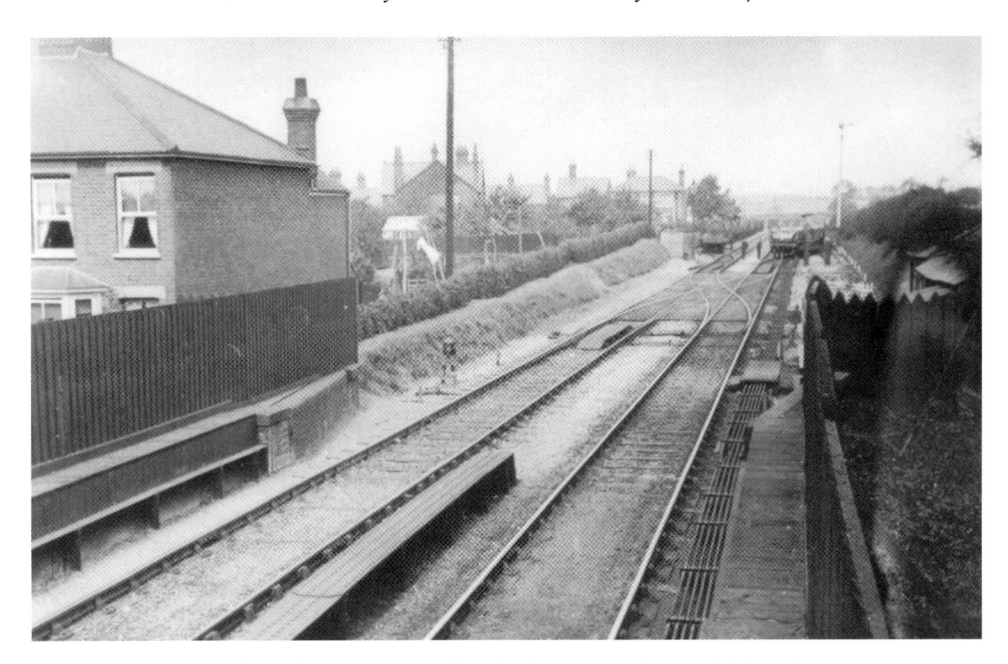

A view taken *c*. 1911 from the station signal box looking towards Cambridge; the scissors crossover survived right up to the 1960s when they were removed and replaced with a single lead once the sidings had been removed. The signal box closed on 16 July 1933 and was replaced by two ground frames, one had five levers and the other had eight levers; these were operated by the station staff when released by the junction signal box. (Historical Model Railway Society – ABB311)

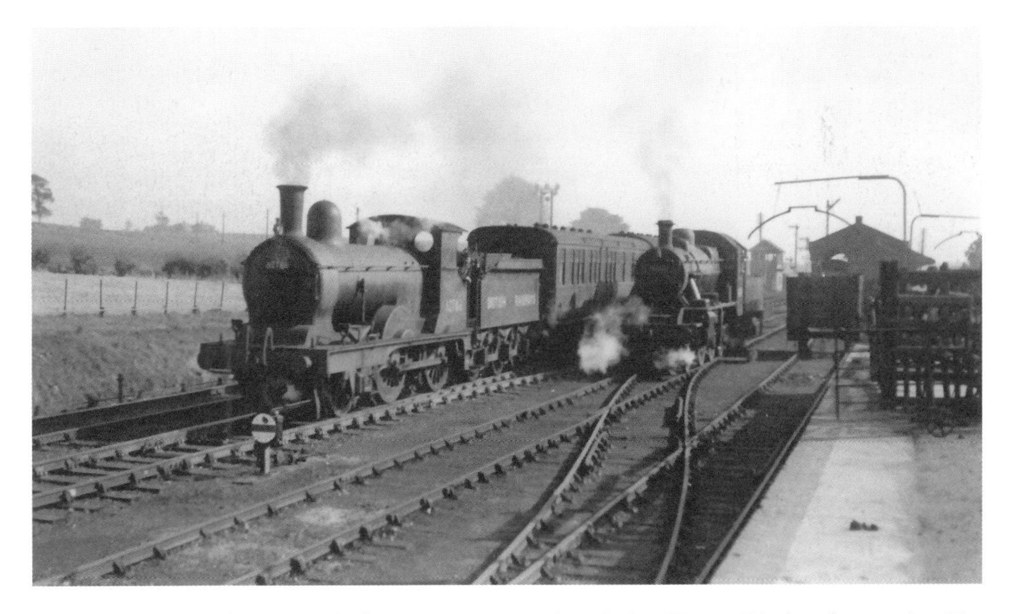

An undated image but certainly from sometime in the 1950s. We see E4 class locomotive No. 62786 arriving on a local passenger train while 2MT class engine No. 46465 waits in the sidings for its next working; in the background can be seen the junction signal box and on the right is the goods yard and sidings, complete with a loading gauge. (Dr I. C. Allen/Transport Treasury)

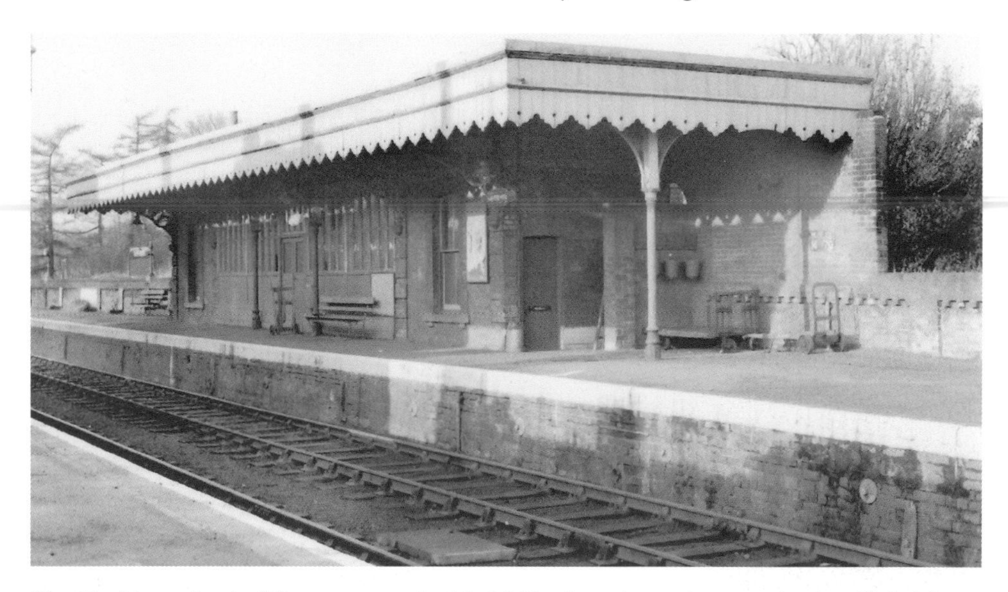

The Up side station buildings are seen in this 1960s view; the station remained staffed right up to August 1966, which meant the station was kept in a clean and tidy condition. After that date tickets had to be bought on the train from the conductor/guard; tickets could only be issued to a limited range of destinations and passengers making longer journeys would have to rebook at Cambridge or Colchester. (Railway Correspondence and Travel Society Archive)

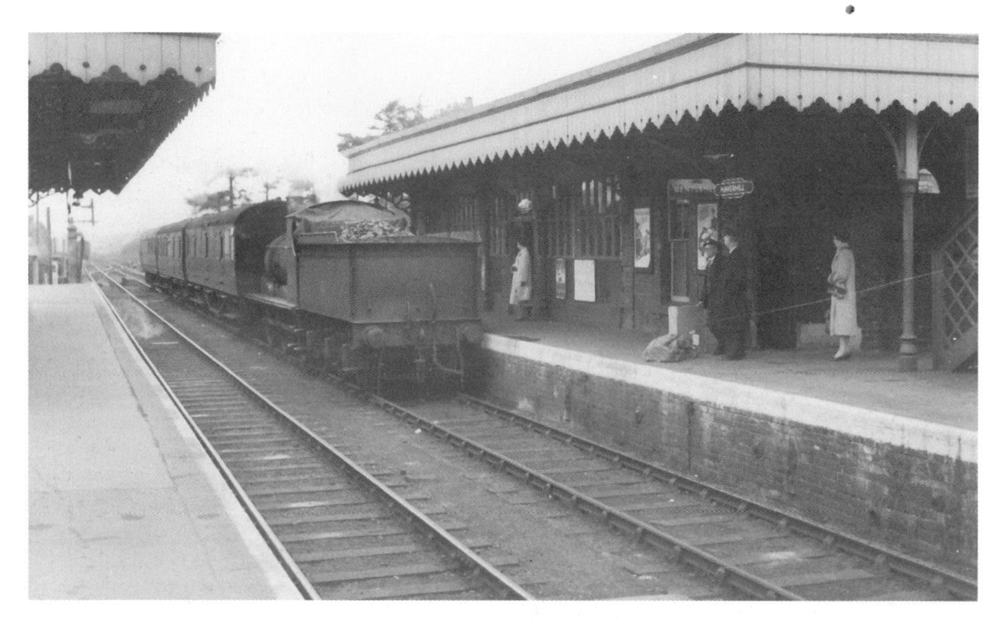

Haverhill seen in happier times with a J15 class locomotive arriving in the Up platform with a three-coach train in 1956; the station porter is waiting to help load a couple of parcels together with the postman with a couple of sacks of mail. This station was the interchange point with the Colne Valley line, the branch trains departing after the Stour Valley service only to get to Chappel & Wakes Colne first, the journey via the Colne Valley line being the shorter of the two routes. (R. S. Carpenter)

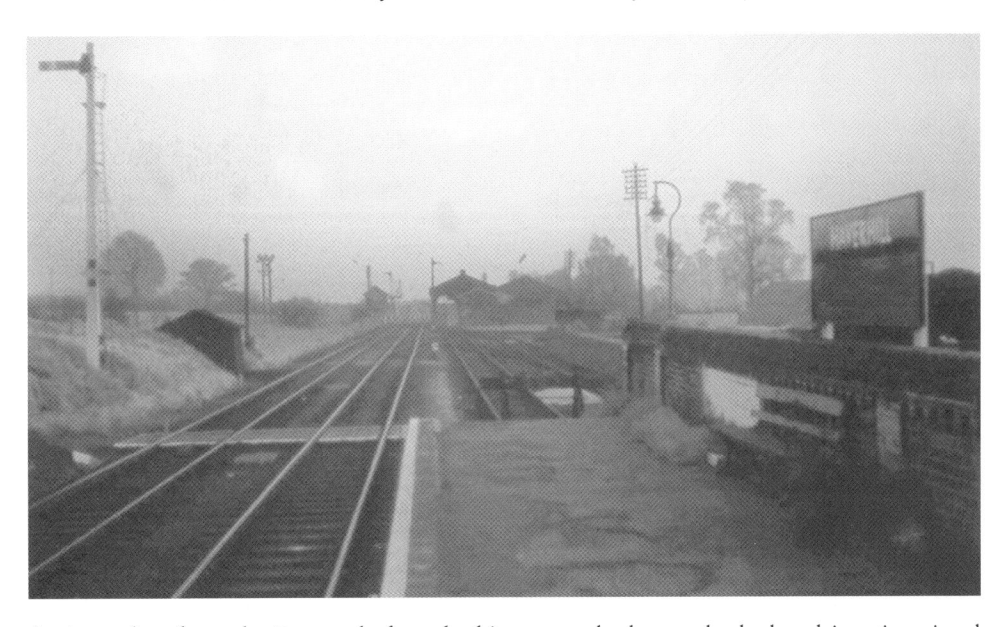

A view taken from the Down platform looking towards the goods shed and junction signal box, taken on 3 December 1966; goods handling facilities had been withdrawn on and from 31 October, leaving just the passenger service to continue for the remaining weeks prior to closure in the following March. (D. J. Plyer)

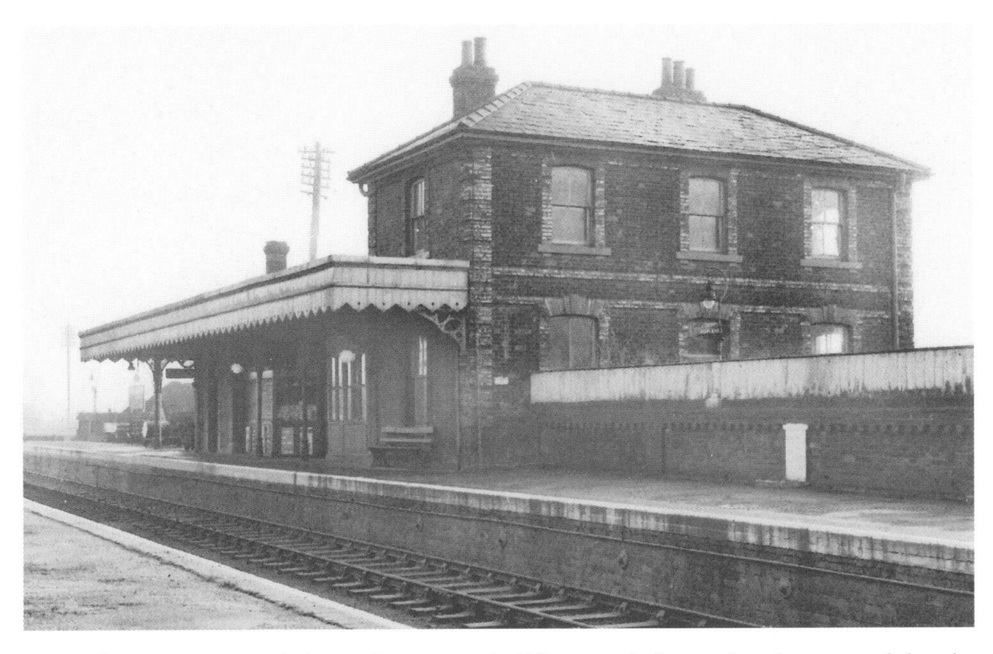

An early 1960s view of the main station buildings and the station house used by the stationmaster as his accommodation. The station was built in the 1860s and opened with the line from Shelford on 1 June 1865; it would reach its 100th birthday in June 1965, only to close in March 1967. The station buildings were all demolished prior to the track being lifted in 1970. (Railway Correspondence and Travel Society Archive)

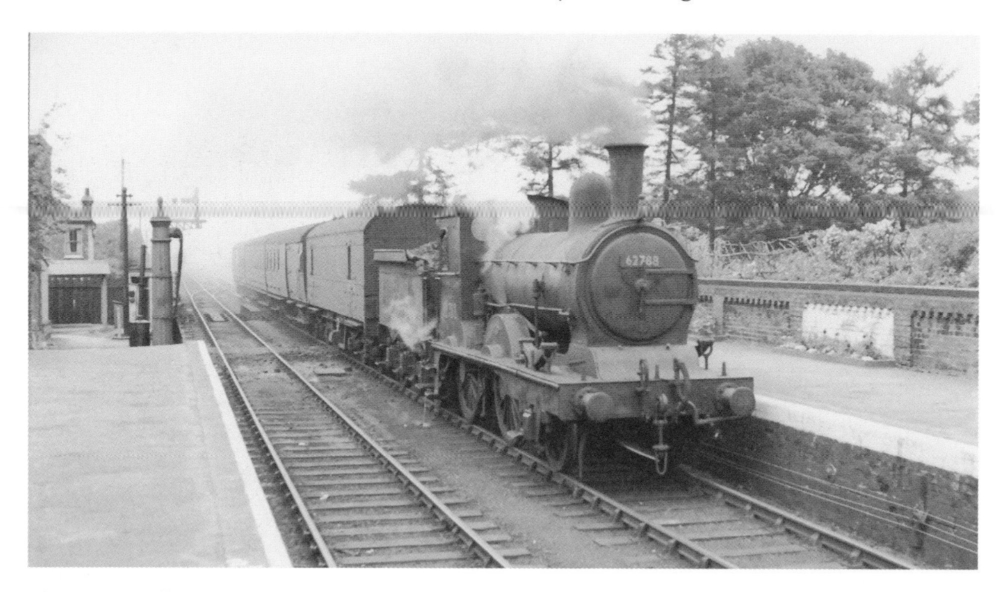

The Stour Valley line was home for the veteran E4 class engines; this one, No. 62783, is seen arriving at the station with a local passenger working from Cambridge sometime before March 1958. Station staff would collect the single line tablet and place it in the auxiliary machine at the station to clear the section to Bartlow; staff would then issue a tablet to the next Down line service on the signalman's instruction. (Dr I. C. Allen/Transport Treasury)

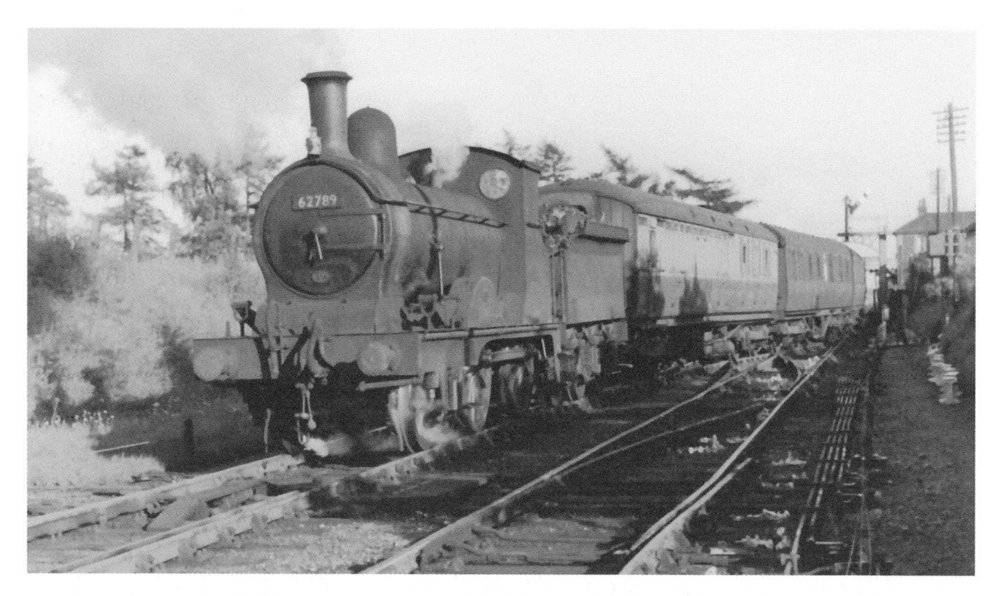

E4 class No. 62789 departs with a Cambridge-bound service. This view was taken from the carriage siding looking back at the station. The starting signal was control by lever six in the junction signal box and was also slotted by the station ground frame by lever five. The point rodding in the foreground was worked by the eight-lever ground frame, which worked the Down carriage sidings points and traps as well as the up refuge siding and part of the scissors crossover from the carriage sidings to the up main platform line; this ground frame remained in use until the sidings were abolished in the early 1960s. (R. C. Riley/Transport Treasury)

Bartlow

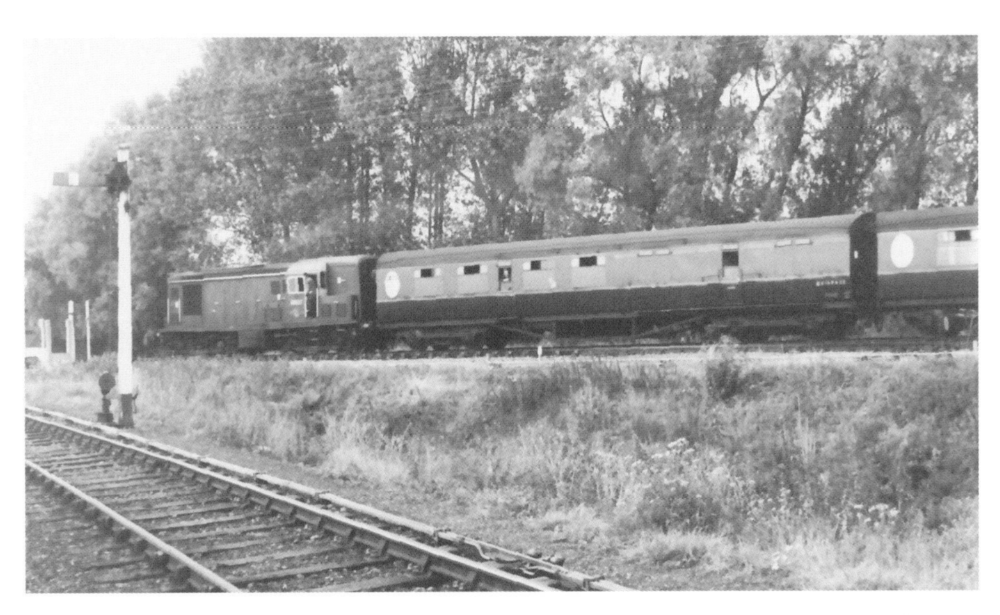

An unusual working captured from near to the signal box: a Type 1 diesel, D8227, plus two coaches and a van passing through the station on 5 September 1964. The signal in the foreground is the branch starter, which allowed movements out onto the Stour Valley line. (D. J. Plyer)

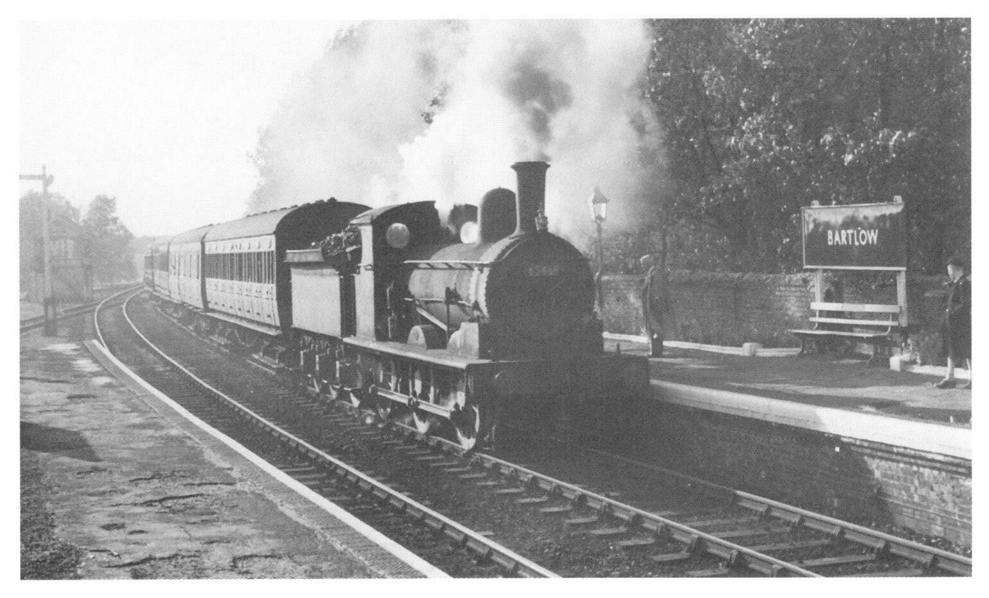

J15 class locomotive No. 65468 arriving with a Colchester-bound service on 28 August 1956 in the Up direction platform; the J15s were the stalwart of the line, giving long service ably assisted by the E4s, C12s and later the Ivatt-designed 2MTs. Diesels came to the branch fully in 1959. (A. E. Bennett/Transport Treasury)

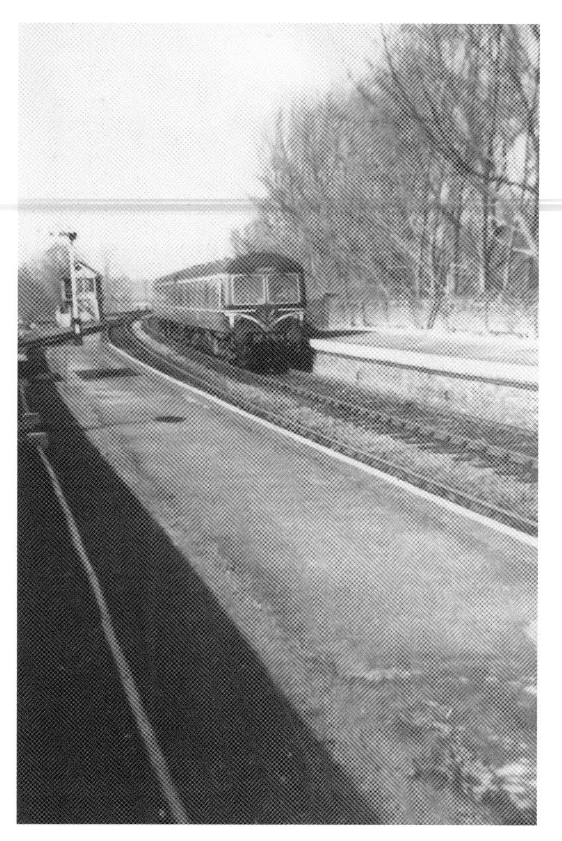

Left: A Cravens-type DMU arrives in the Up platform at the station. This view is undated; the signal box can be seen on the left. The station and platforms survive to this day and have been turned into a very nice private residence. (Paul Smith)

Below: A view taken from the Down siding showing the Down platform starting signal on the right and the branch starting signal on the left with the junction signal box in the centre of this view; the signalling on the line had a mixture of equipment and in this view there is a Great Eastern lower quadrant signal. The station signal box had been closed in 1926; all the signalling was then concentrated on the junction signal box, which was enlarged by one lever. In 1939 the junction was simplified from a double junction to a single lead, and from this time it had thirty-three working and six spare levers. The signal box closed on 17 April 1966; all traffic was then worked over the Down platform loop until the line closed. (A. Swain/Transport Treasury)

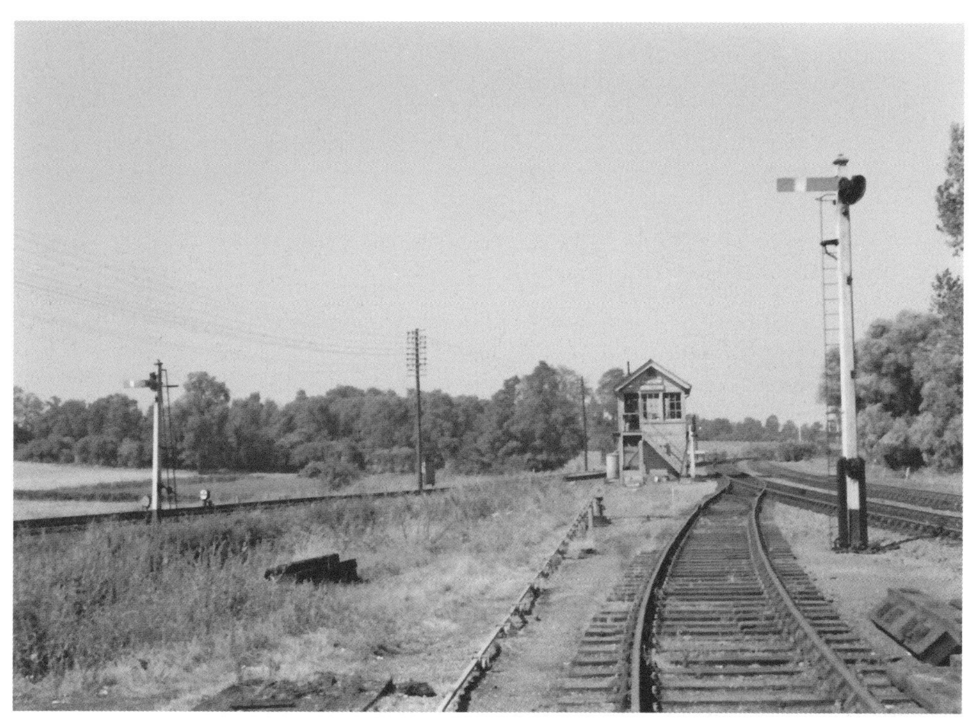

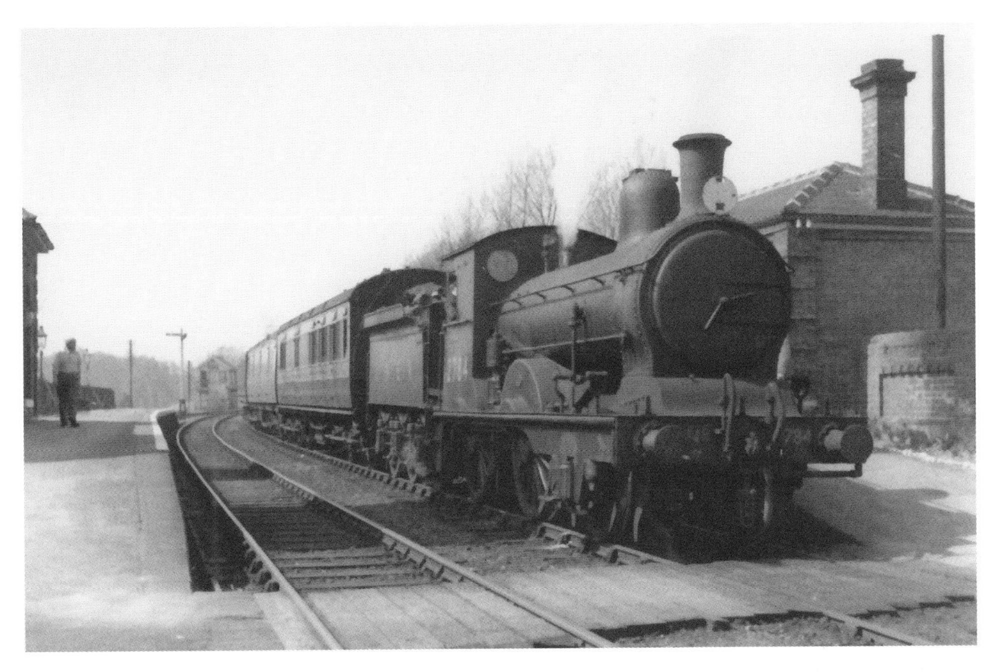

An E4 class in LNER livery as No. 2784 stands at the station with a Colchester-bound service on 16 April 1947. The days of the LNER were numbered as from 1 January 1948 the former GER line would become part of the new British Railways. (Stephenson Locomotive Society – 28653)

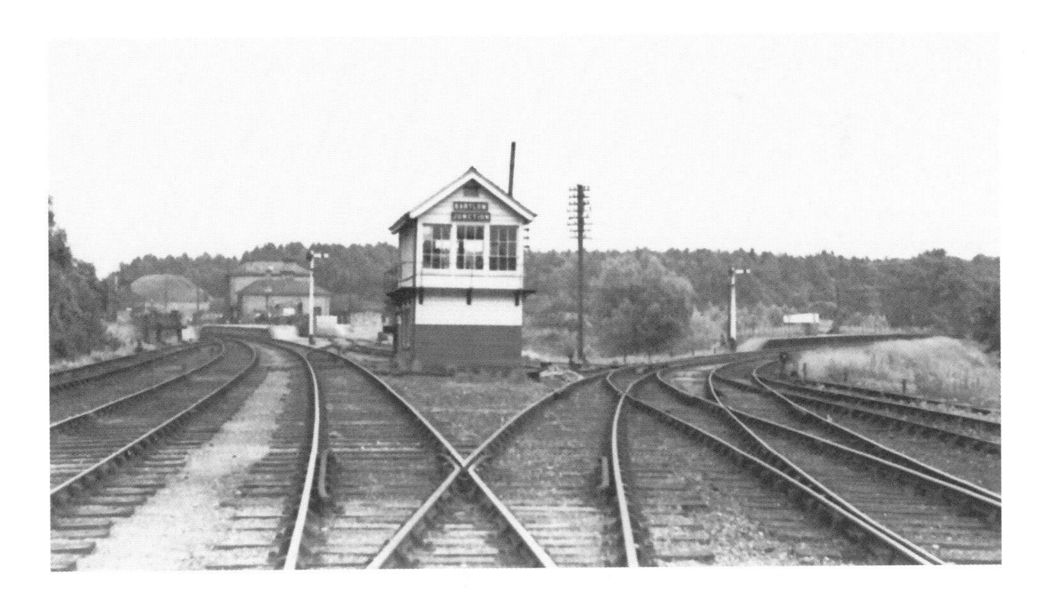

A general view taken in 1937 looking back at the main and branch platforms; the two parts of the station were connected by a footpath. Since closure, the station and its surrounds have been turned into a nice residence; the shell of signal box stood for many years before the roof collapsed in on itself. (Stations UK)

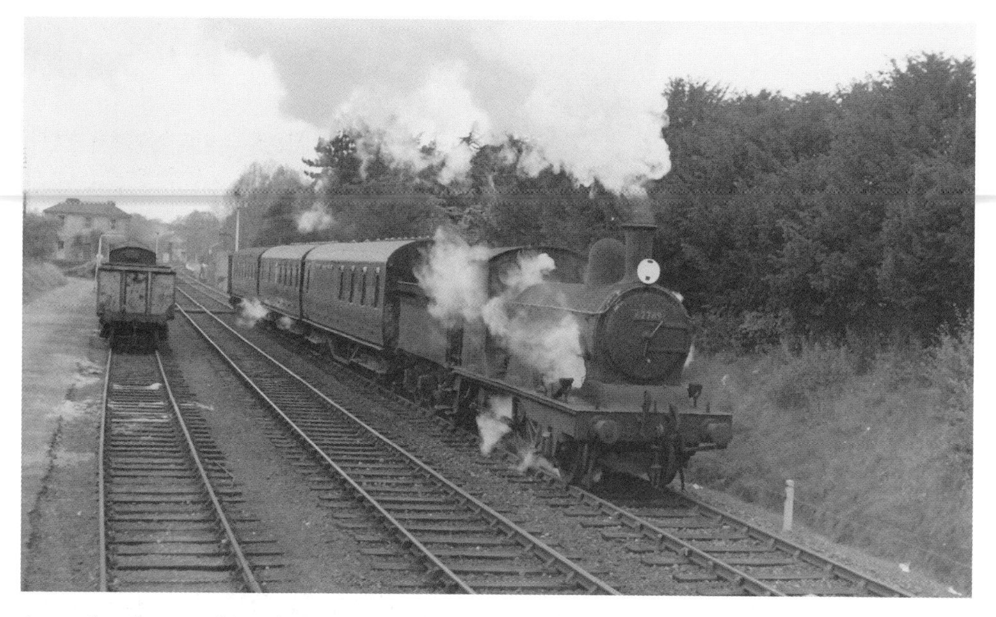

An undated view of E4 class No. 62789 departing with a two-coach passenger train heading towards Haverhill and Sudbury; as this locomotive was withdrawn from traffic in December 1957, this helps date the picture. On the Haverhill side of the station there were two sidings: the first can be seen in the picture; the second, located behind the photographer, was worked by a ground frame released from the signal box. Also, at this point the double track became single, the points being worked by an electric point machine. (Dr I. C. Allen/Transport Treasury)

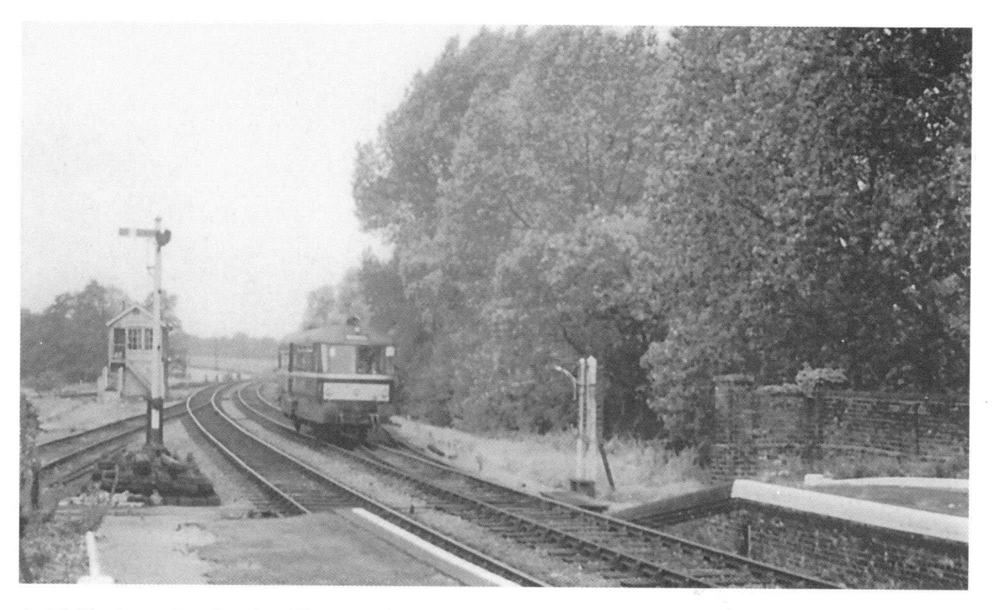

A 1964 view of a diesel railbus working into the station. Two of the Audley End to Bartlow services were extended to and from Haverhill, which required a reversal at the station; these services ceased with the withdrawal of the Saffron Walden branch passenger services on and from 7 September 1964. (Historical Model Railway Society – ABB597)

Linton

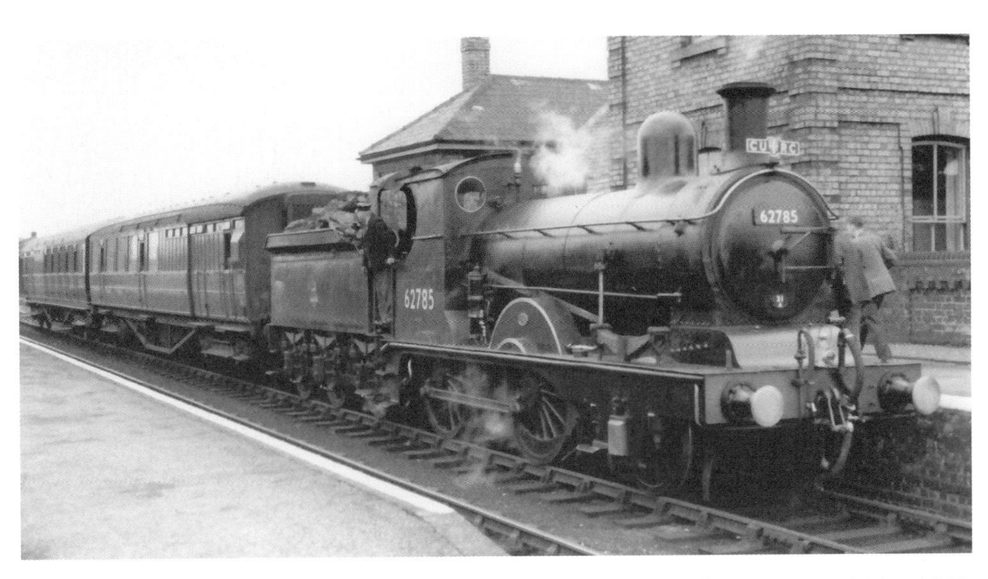

E4 class No. 62785 on a Cambridge University Railway Club special at Linton on 3 May 1959. For some reason the engine came off here to be replaced with B17 No. 61616, which then continued onto Haverhill. (R. C. Riley/Transport Treasury)

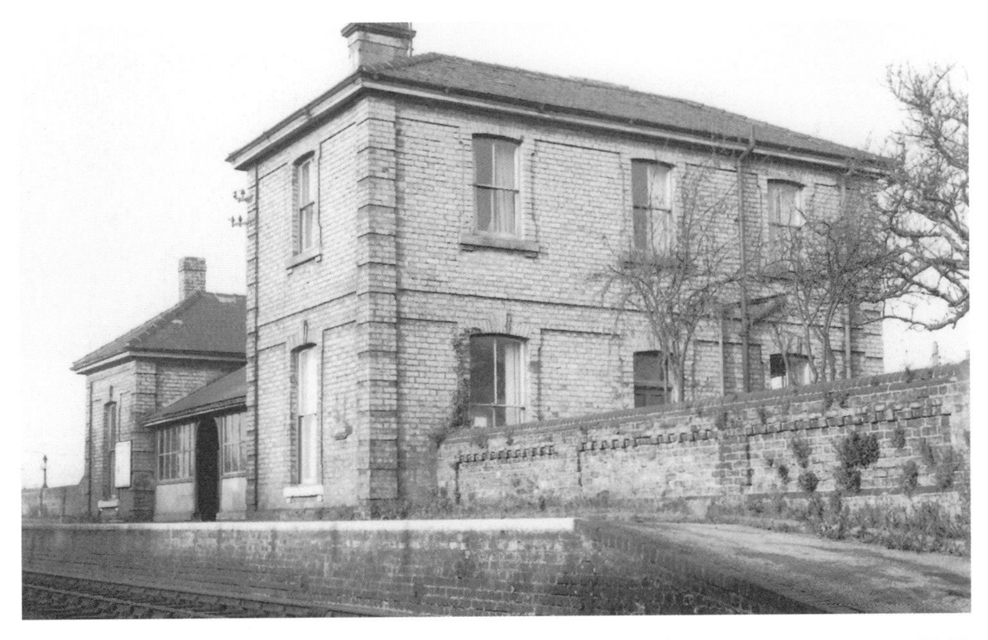

The station was equipped with standard GER buildings dating from its opening in June 1865; the accommodation was usually provided for the stationmaster. Remarkably, the station still stands nearly fifty years after it closed; the former goods yard and the surrounding land has all been redeveloped. (Railway Correspondence & Travel Society/CHO5682)

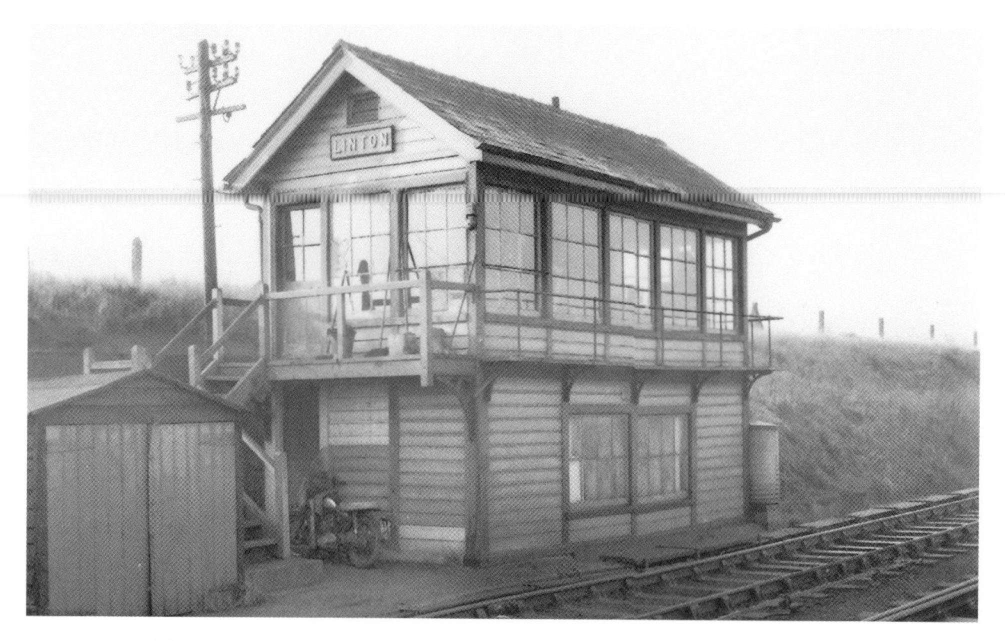

Linton signal box, seen in the 1960s, was fitted with a Saxby & Farmer thirty-lever frame; it remained in use until the line closed in March 1967. The signal box was of all wood construction with a slated roof and dates from the 1889 resignalling of the line. (Railway Correspondence & Travel Society Archive)

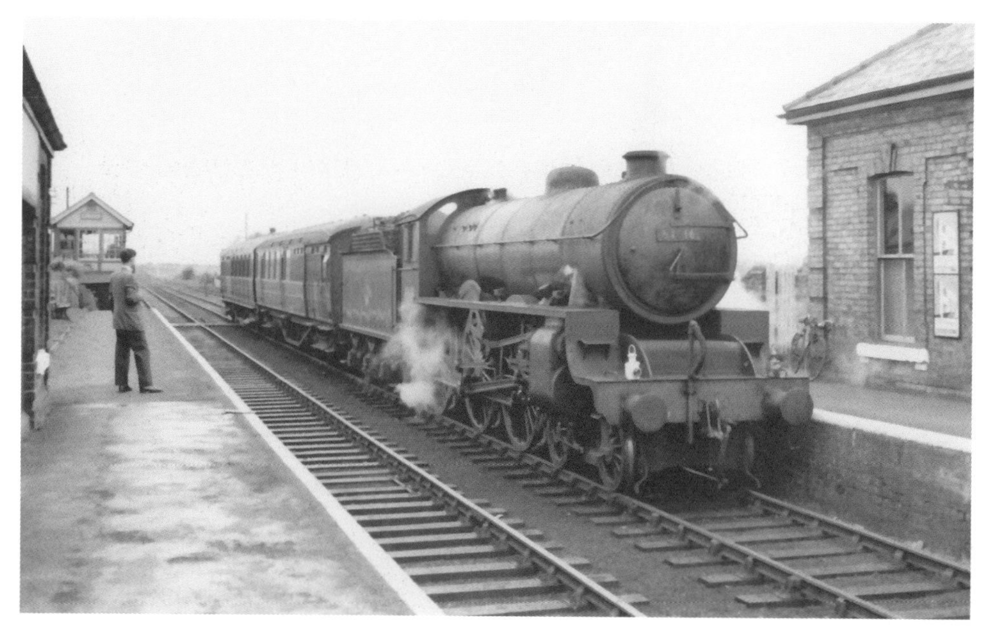

B17 class No. 61616 arrives at Linton as a replacement engine for the CURC driving trips. It would eventually continue on to Haverhill; the trips would shuttle between Bartlow and Haverhill until all the club members had had a driving turn. This view was dated 3 May 1959. (R. C. Riley/Transport Treasury)

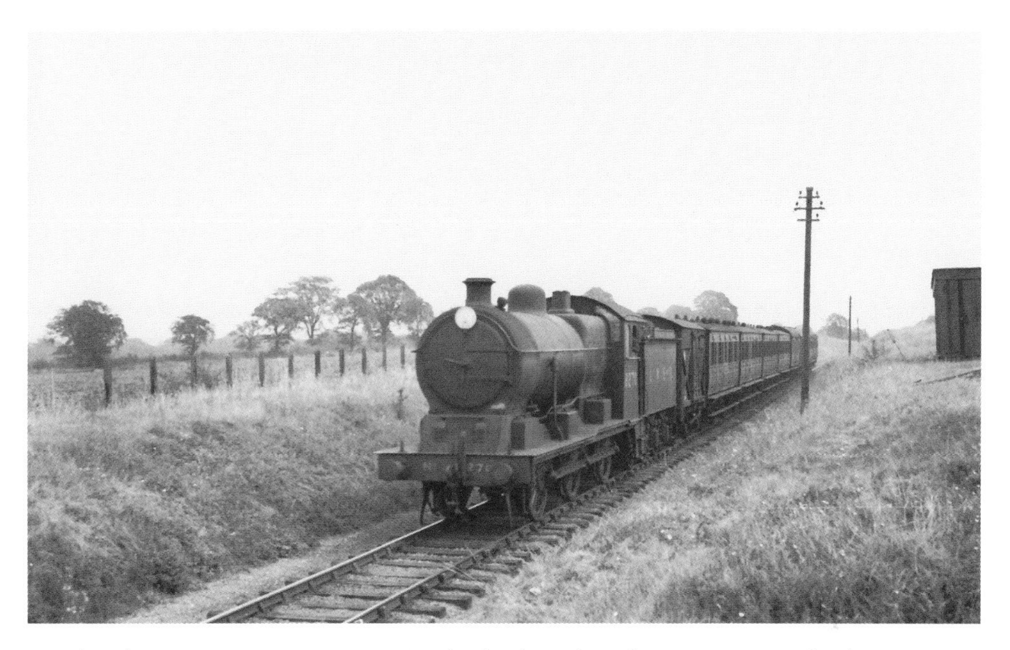

J20 class locomotive No. 8270 on a Cambridge-bound working near Linton hauling a vintage rake of mostly GER coaches. These powerful locomotives would not normally be working passenger trains as they were a freight engine normally seen on heavy coal trains or something similar. This view is dated August 1934. (Dr I. C. Allen/Transport Treasury)

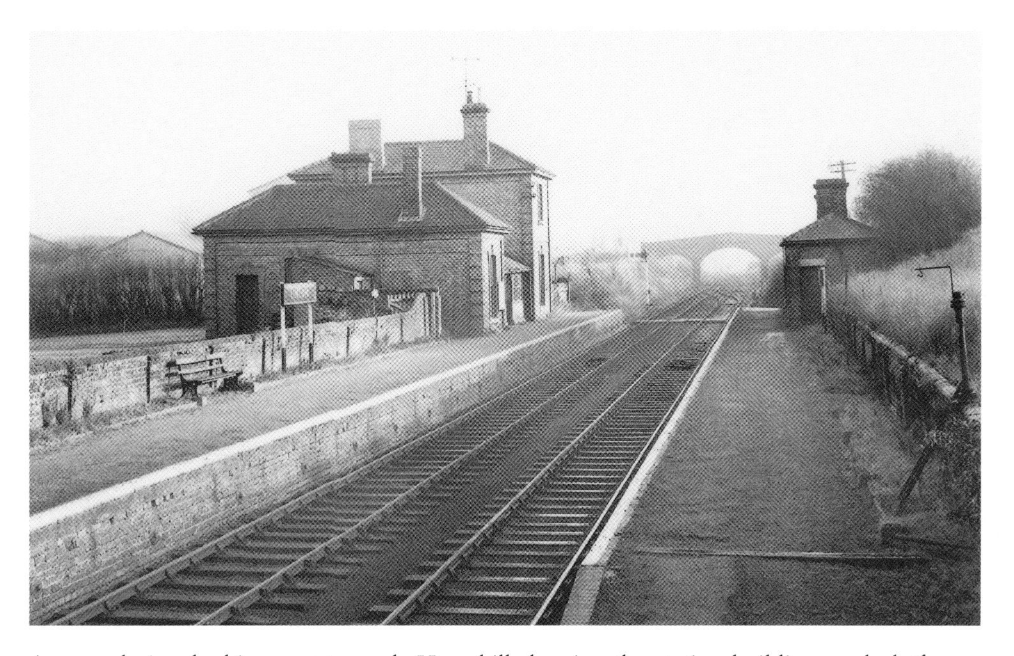

A general view looking east towards Haverhill showing the station buildings and platforms. The road over bridge has long since been removed and part of the old railway land has been developed into a business park, although the old station buildings have been retained. (Railway Correspondence & Travel Society Archive)

Pampisford

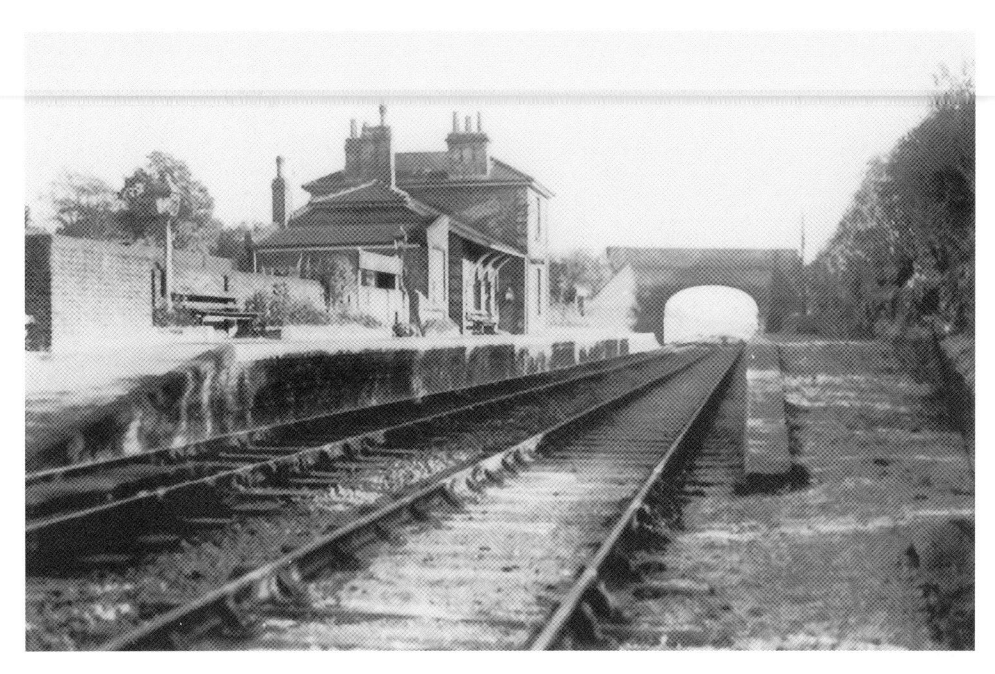

A general view of the station as seen in 1950, looking east towards Bartlow. The former Down platform can be seen on the right; this was taken out of use when the signal box was closed and replaced by ground frames as an economy measure – from that date it was used as a loop siding. (Historical Model Railway Society/ABC800)

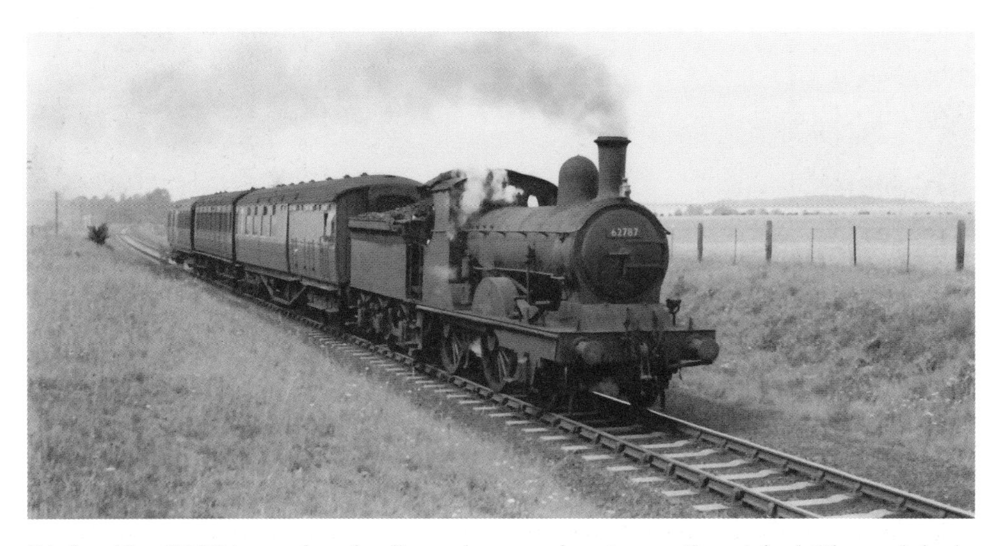

E4 class No. 62787 is seen here hauling a three-coach train near Pampisford. The track looks to be in good condition having been re-laid with concrete sleepers with bull-headed rails. (Dr I. C. Allen/Transport Treasury)

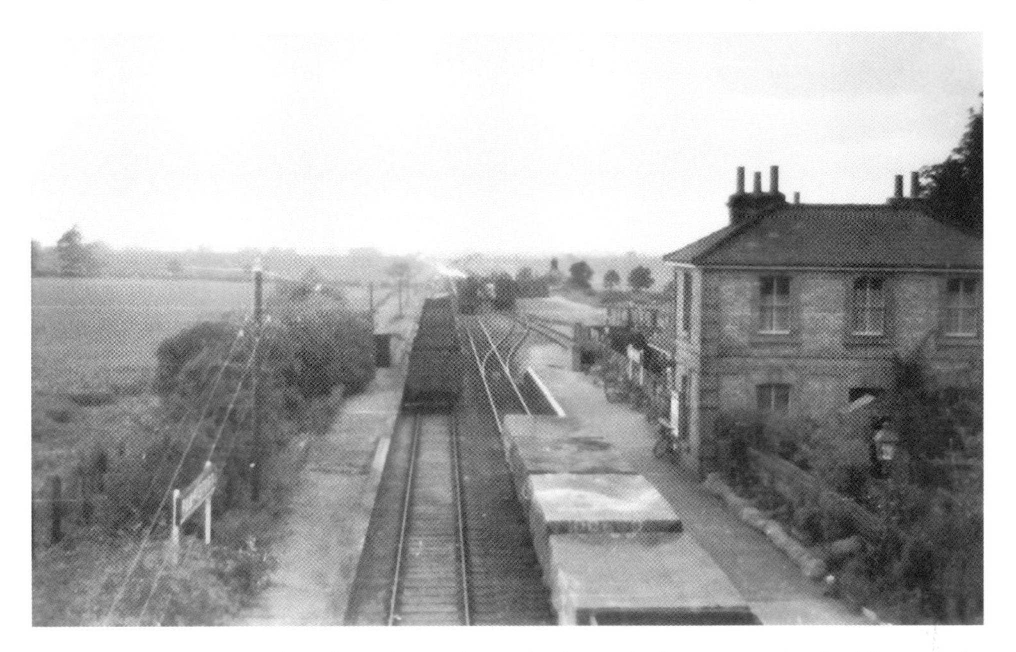

A busy shunting scene taken from the road over bridge with the main station buildings on the Up side; an engine is seen shunting wagons in the sidings as well as on the main line. Freight handling facilities survived here until April 1965; the yard and loop siding track was then recovered. (Stations UK)

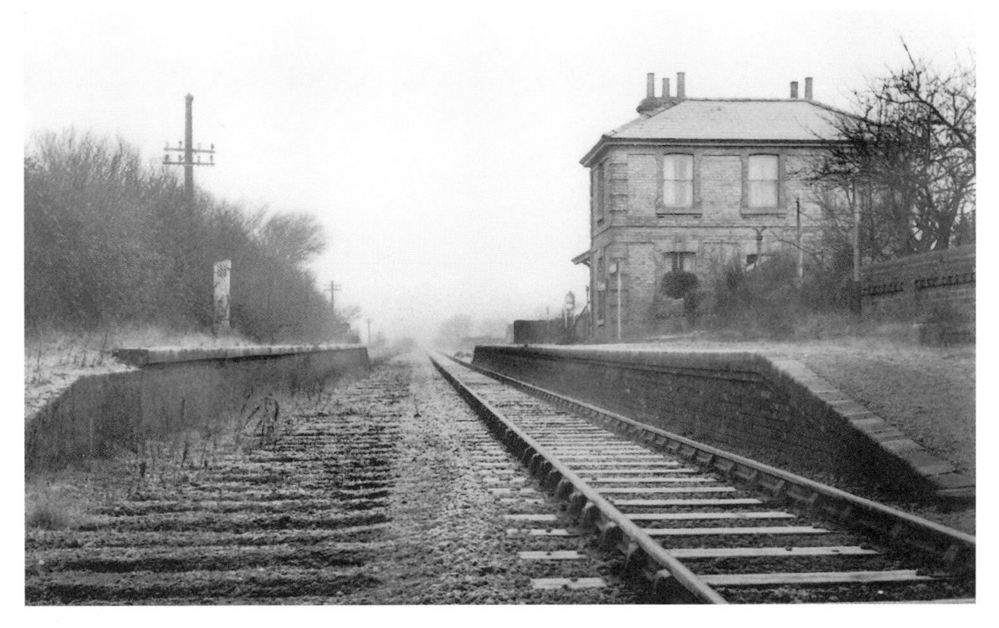

A desolate scene photgraphed just before final closure, with the loop siding and the goods yard closed and lifted. By this time the station was unstaffed although the house was still lived in. The station site saw further use as a building materials recycling centre before part of the site was used for building of the A11 dual carriageway. (Railway Correspondence & Travel Society Archive)

Shelford

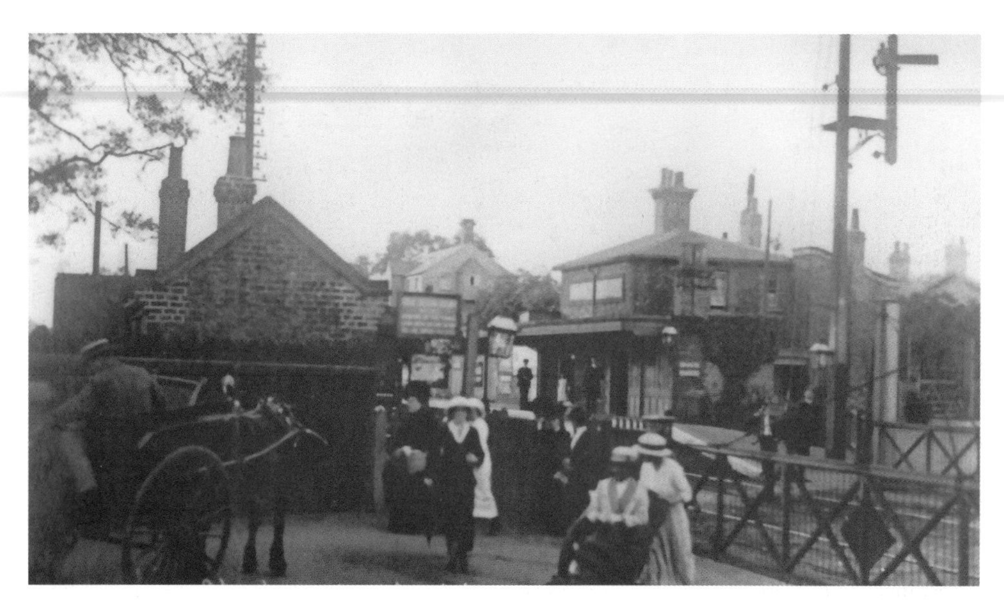

A Great Eastern view of the station and level crossing with a pony and trap and people in period dress; the branch starting signal can just be seen on the right of the view. The station building still stands today although not used for railway purposes. (Lens of Sutton Association)

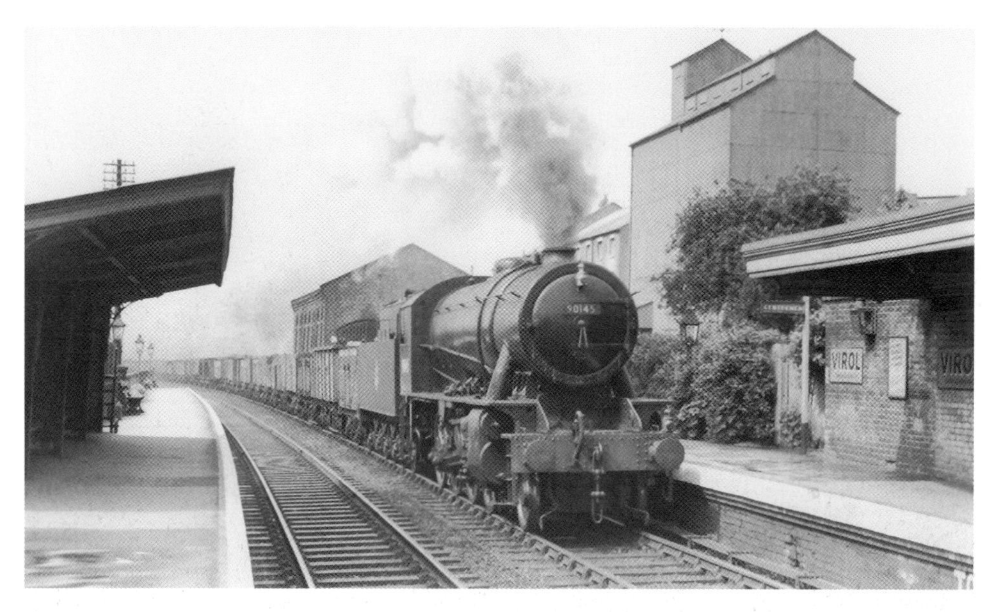

WD-type locomotive No. 90145 works a heavy mineral train through the station on 30 May 1953. This view is looking north towards Cambridge; the industrial premises on the right have long since been replaced with housing. The station is still part of the national network. (R. E. Vincent/Transport Treasury)

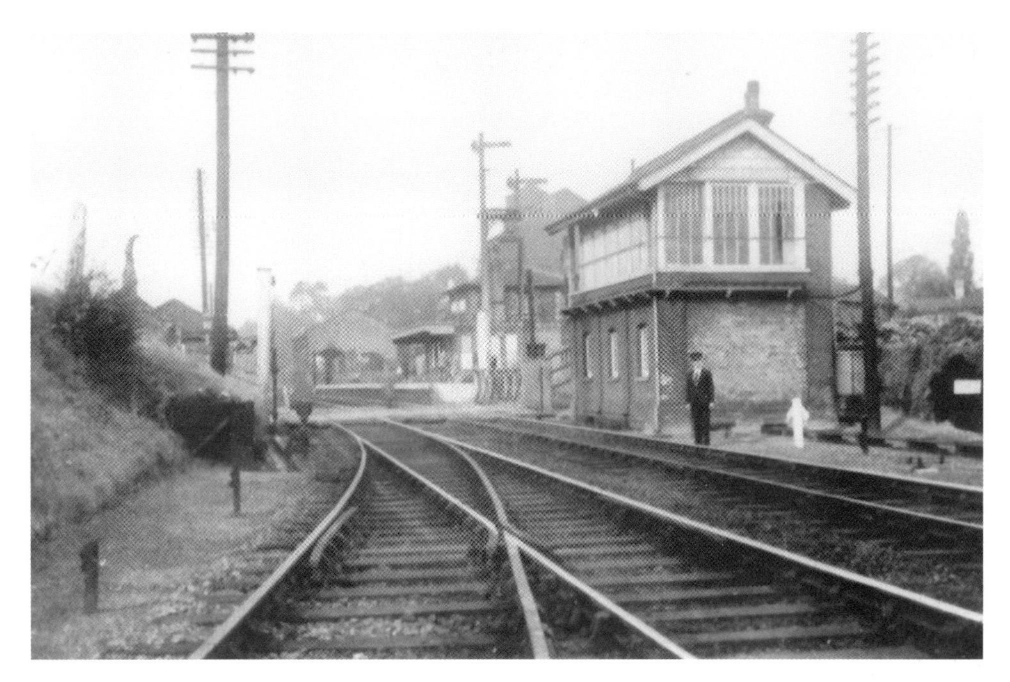

A member of staff poses for a photograph showing the station, level crossing and signal box. The signal box, in a reduced capacity, continued to give good service until it was closed with the commissioning of new signalling controlled from Cambridge power signalling centre. (Historical Model Railway Society – ABC907)

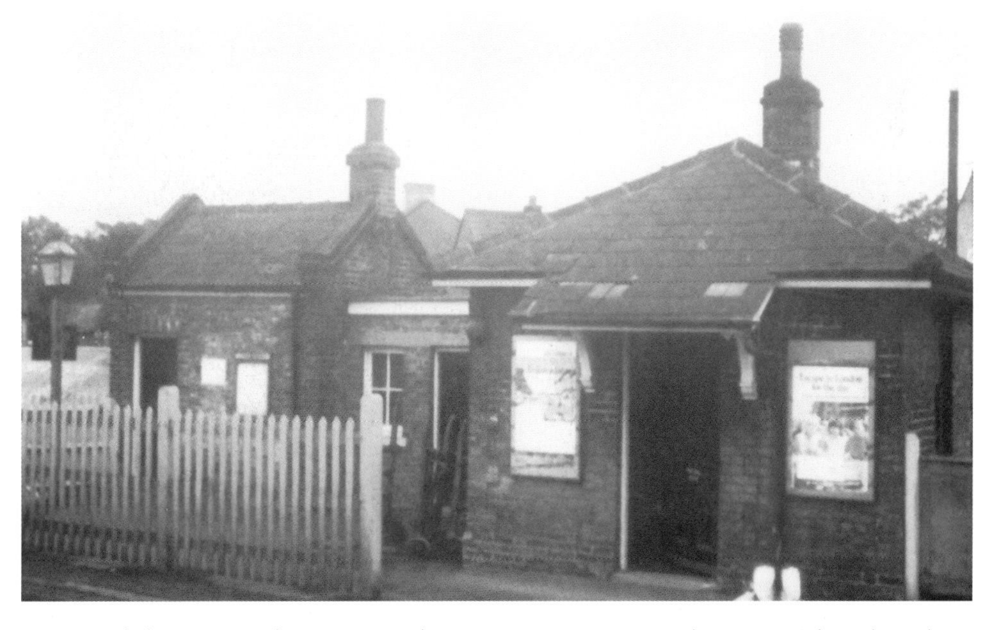

A view of the Down side waiting and porters' rooms seen in the 1960s. These have been demolished and intending passengers now have only a bus-type shelter to shelter them from the elements while waiting for their train. (Historical Model Railway Society – ACD487)

The Colne Valley Branch: Chappel & Wakes Colne to Haverhill CV (South)

By 1854, the larger Eastern Counties Railway (ECR) had taken control of the Eastern Union Railway and the good citizens of Halstead and surrounding area had their hopes raised that their branch would be built; however, the ECR was in no position to do this and so the decision to go it alone was made. Accordingly, the Colne Valley & Halstead Railway was sanctioned by Parliament on 30 June 1856.

Authorisation was given to build a railway from Halstead to Chappel with an intermediate station at Colne (later White Colne). Prior to opening, there was some haggling with the ECR as to the actual positioning of the junction; these were eventually resolved and the line opened on 16 April 1860. Not content with just the original 6-mile line, the Colne Valley Company obtained a further Act of Parliament authorising an extension from Halstead to Haverhill. This opened in stages: Hedingham was reached on 1 July 1861, Yeldham on 26 May 1862 and finally through to Haverhill on 10 May 1863.

The Great Eastern Railway (GER), incorporated in 1862, took over the majority of the lines in East Anglia, including the former ECR. Powers were renewed for all the Stour Valley extensions and the GER eventually reached Haverhill in 1865 with a connecting line to the CVR at Haverhill. From this time Colne Valley trains ran to and from the GER station; some trains still used the old Colne Valley station at Haverhill and would continue to do so until the station closed to passengers in 1924.

The story of the early years of the CVR largely consisted of financial problems. The line was declared bankrupt in 1874 and an official receiver was appointed; under his guidance things gradually got better and after eleven years and another Act of Parliament which authorised the raising of new capital, the railway continued to prosper, allowing for two new locomotives to be purchased. In 1882 a new small station was opened at Ford Gate (later Earls Colne); a new signal box was also provided. As an economy measure, the original Colne (White Colne) station closed on 1 May 1889 and the name Colne was transferred to Ford Gate station, which received an enlarged goods yard and a new twenty-six-lever frame in the signal box to control the enlarged layout.

Following the passing of the Regulations of Railways Act in 1889, the Colne Valley board were required to install new signalling and accordingly the line was signalled to modern standards.

Colne station was rebuilt and enlarged in 1903/4 and was renamed Earls Colne on completion in 1905. The old Colne station (White Colne) was reopened in 1907 to goods traffic, and the following year it regained its passenger status and a new name; a new platform was built to go with the reopening.

Like a lot of branch lines the CV&HR had reached its zenith in 1914; heavy war use and only limited repairs and renewals left the line in a poor state at the end of the First World War. Meanwhile, following the passing of the 1921 Railways Act the CV&HR was to pass into the hands of the new London & North Eastern Railway (LNER). The new LNER took over the GER and the other railways from 1 January 1923; the CV&HR was wound up and was fully taken over on 1 July of that year.

The new owners were always looking for savings: much of the former's rolling stock was withdrawn and scrapped, and three of the five CV&HR locomotives found further use for a short while with the LNER. The locomotive and carriage works at Halstead was closed, as was the locomotive running shed; the shed at Haverhill was used instead. The former CV passenger station at Haverhill closed in July 1924 and on 1 January 1925 the Colne Valley station was renamed Haverhill South, the GE station becoming Haverhill North.

The line was upgraded to electric token working between Earls Colne and Haverhill in 1925/6. This was followed by the closure of Colne Valley Junction signal box; this was replaced with a ground frame, the token sections were modified to suit and Birdbrook became a block post for the first time. Excursion traffic was run from the late 1920s, Clacton and Walton being popular destinations.

The Second World War saw another peak in traffic over the line, many special bomb trains being run to White Colne, Earls Colne and Yeldham goods yard for onward transportation to local airfields. After the war, the days of the LNER were numbered and from 1 January 1948, the former CV&HR became part of the unified British Railways.

Changes were slow in coming; some new BR-built, Ivatt-designed Class 2MT locomotives were allocated to Cambridge and Colchester sheds and were used on the Colne, Stour and Bury branches. From 1 January 1959 diesel railbuses and multiple units took over all of the local passenger workings. However, nothing could stop the state concern from making increasing losses and accordingly closure notices were posted in 1961. Objections were heard and eventually rejected and the last passenger train ran over Colne Valley metals on Saturday 30 December 1961. Birdbrook station was closed completely, but parcels and freight traffic were still handled at the other stations.

Following publication of the Beeching Report in early 1963, the remaining goods yards were closed; Sible & Castle Hedingham station closed on 13 July 1964, but remained as a public delivery siding until the end of the year. Yeldham, Earls Colne and White Colne followed on 28 December 1964, which just left Halstead and Haverhill South; these followed on 19 April 1965.

Demolition of the remaining line followed in 1966; fortunately a short portion of the railway has been rebuilt near Castle Hedingham, and many old railway artefacts have found their way to this site, which is well worth a visit for those interested.

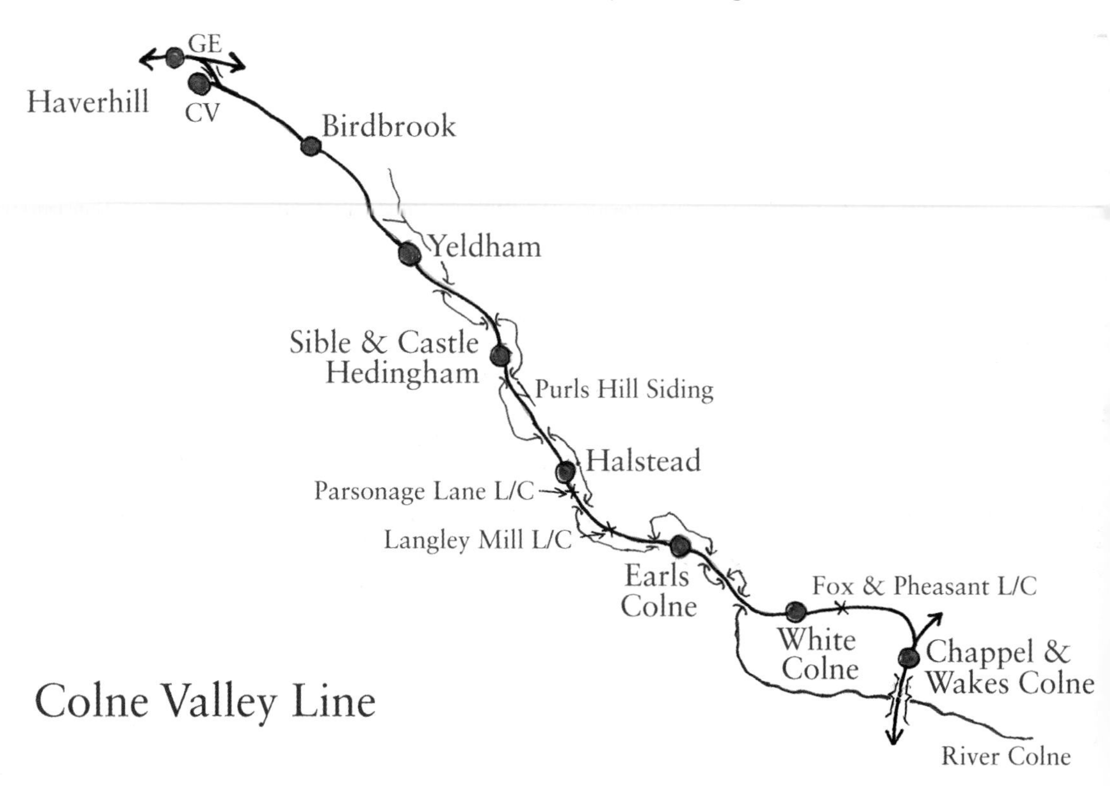
GE
Haverhill
CV
Birdbrook
Yeldham
Sible & Castle Hedingham
Purls Hill Siding
Halstead
Parsonage Lane L/C
Langley Mill L/C
Earls Colne
Fox & Pheasant L/C
White Colne
Chappel & Wakes Colne
River Colne
Colne Valley Line

White Colne

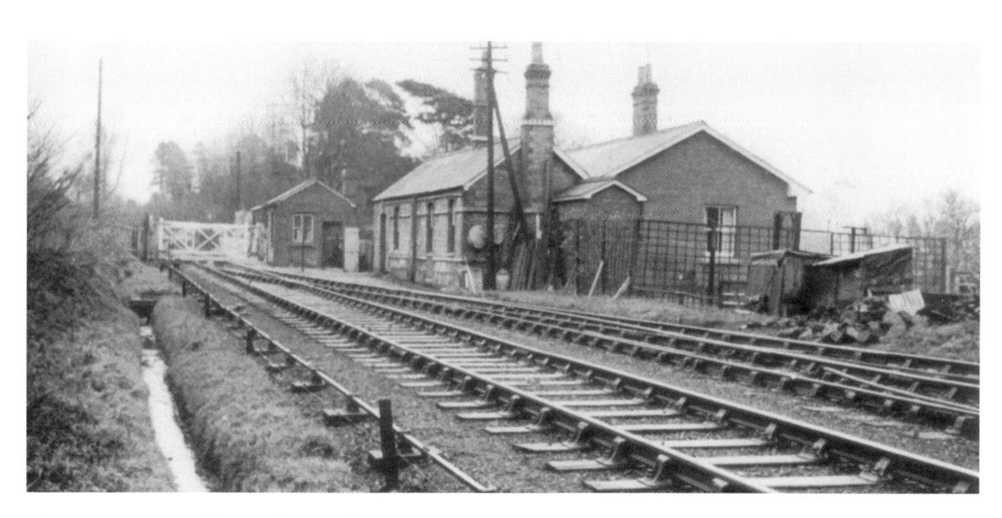

This 1960s view shows the platform, ground frame, crossing hut and original station building. The level crossing retained its manned gates and working distant signals until the very end of the freight service in April 1965. It is pleasing to know that the station building now survives as the village hall; the brick crossing hut was donated by Essex County Council to the new CVR and was duly dismantled and re-erected at Castle Hedingham. The platform coping stones were also salvaged when the old platform was demolished to make way for a small housing development. (Stephenson Locomotive Society)

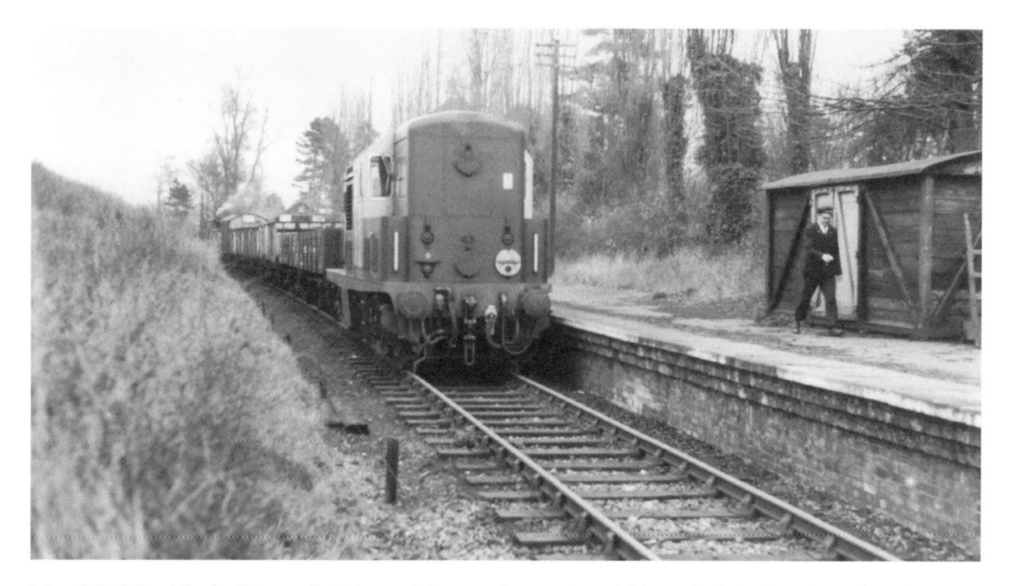

No. D8228 with the Down freight arriving at the station. Although this view is undated, it was between January 1959 and the closure of the line in April 1965; after the passenger service finished at the end of 1961, all the stations on the branch retained freight handling facilities with the exception of Birdbrook, which closed completely. White Colne finally closed to freight traffic at the end of December 1964. (Dr I. C. Allen/Transport Treasury)

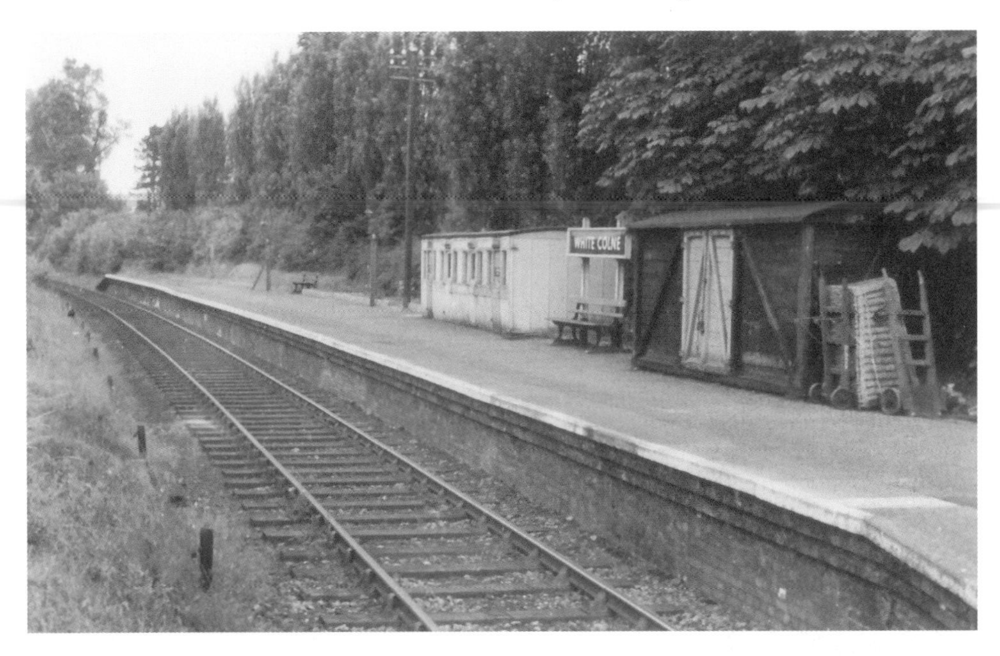

A view along the platform provided in 1908 when the station re-opened to passenger traffic; it received the name of White Colne at this time also. This view is looking towards Chappel & Wakes Colne. The old coach body provided passenger waiting facilities and the van body provided lock-up facilities for small items of freight; note the platform trolleys neatly stacked next to the van body. This picture was taken in 1954. (Lens of Sutton Association)

Opposite above: The station seen from the approach road. The original CV&HR building is the portion nearest the track; the extension was provided many years later. The little porch provided access to the ticket window – this had previously been inside the original building; the window still survives in the building today. The brick crossing keeper's hut was provided in 1907. When the station was re-opened to freight traffic it originally contained a nine-lever ground frame, later reduced in the LNER era to just four levers. After the line closed completely, the brick hut was donated by Essex County Council to the new Colne Valley Railway at Castle Hedingham; it was expertly dismantled and rebuilt as a large permanent way hut. (BR/CVRPS Archive)

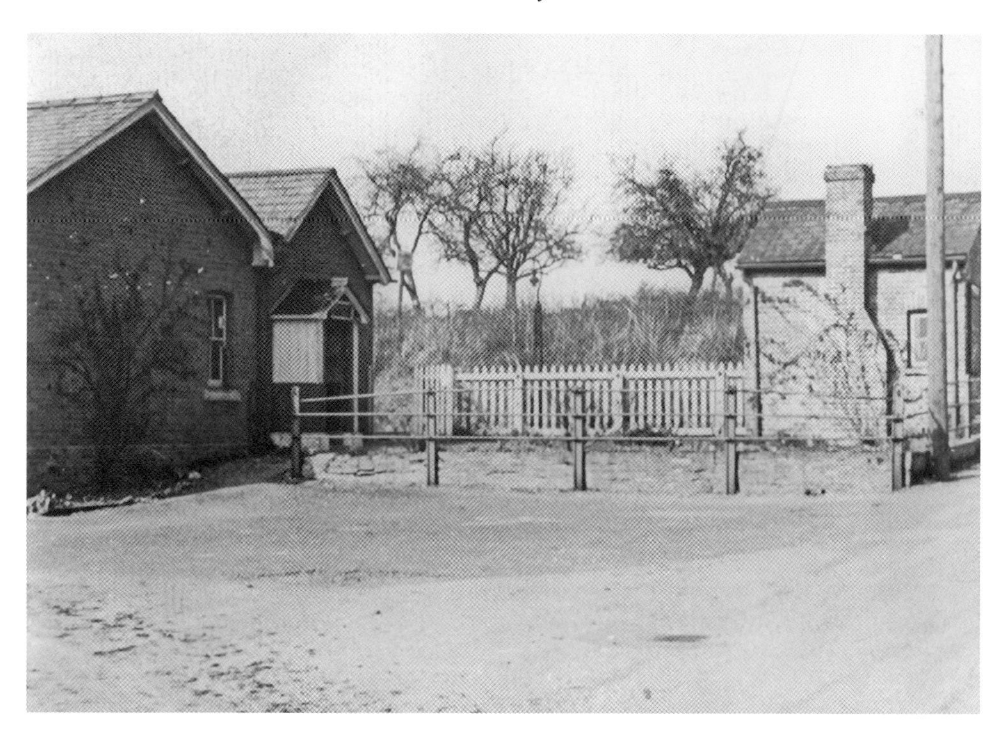

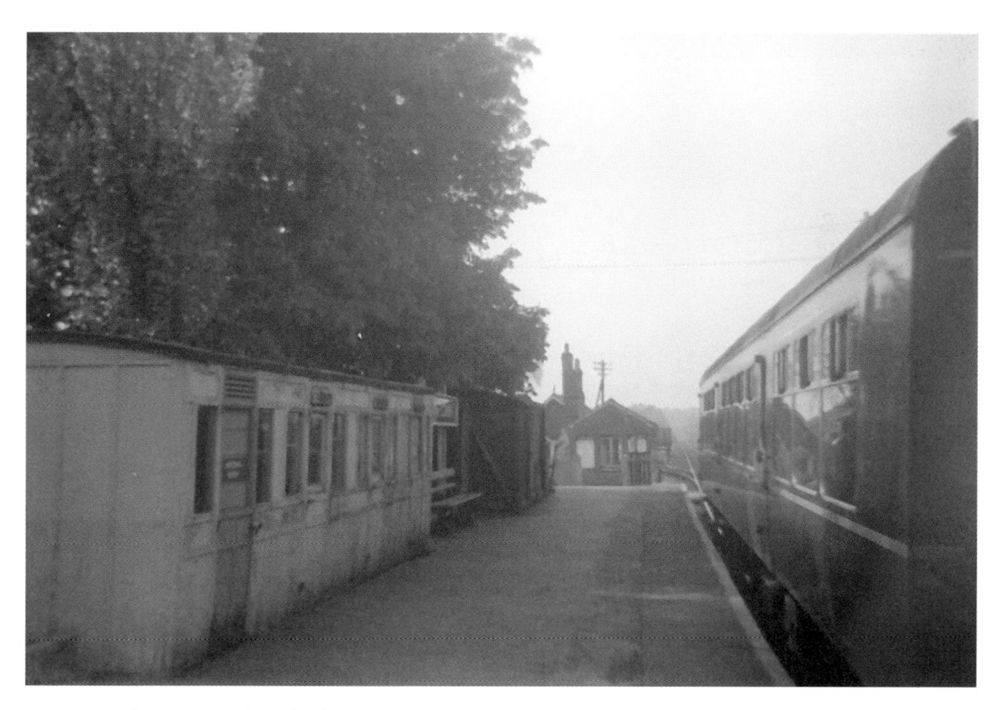

A view taken from the platform with a Down direction DMU waiting to depart from the station. The old passenger coach used as waiting room accommodation can be seen on the left; the brick hut in the middle distance was used by the crossing keeper and contained the level crossing ground frame. (Peter Berry)

Earls Colne

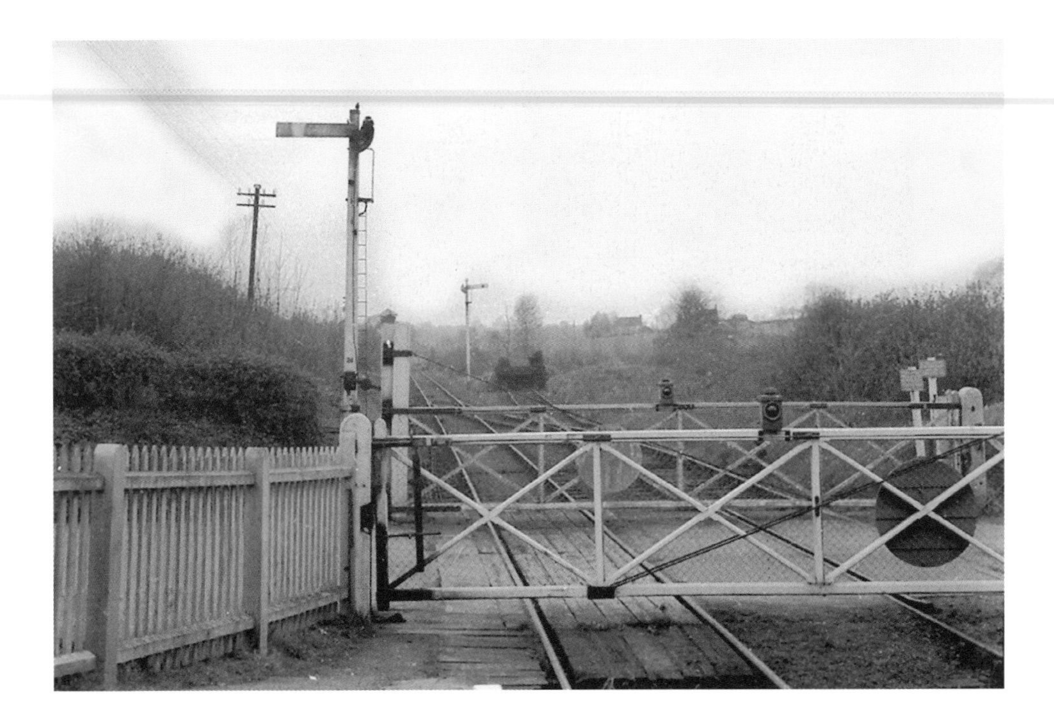

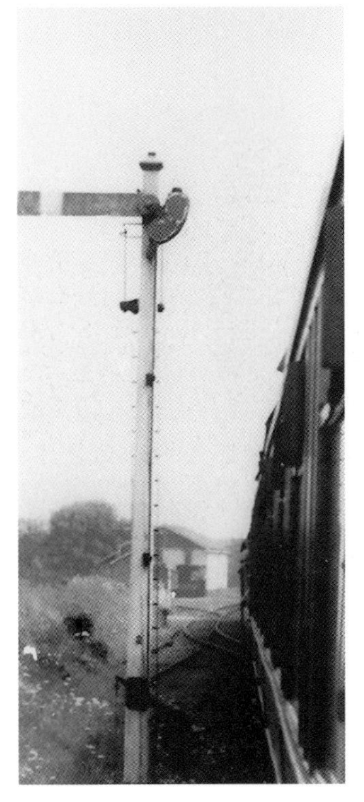

Above: View looking from the platform at the level crossing and its gates; the two signals that can be seen are the Down starter, controlled by lever twenty-four, and the Up home signal, controlled by lever two. The station had started life as an addition halt provided in 1882 with basic facilities and was called Ford Gate; in 1889, when the original Colne (White Colne) station closed completely, the name was transferred to Ford Gate. When the station was resignalled in 1889 it received a larger twenty-six-lever McKenzie & Holland lever frame. The signalling was designed to allow an addition platform adjacent to the goods shed; however, the impecunious Colne Valley never built the extra platform, and the Up starting No. 3 was destined never to signal a passenger train. The semaphore was replaced by the LNER with a shunting Dodd. (Brian Pask)

Left: A view taken from a departing train, looking back at the station with the goods shed in the background and the Up home signal in the foreground. The signal box closed on 1 January 1962; in fact, the box was disconnected and facilities dismantled on the Sunday after closure to passengers. Two of the connections to the goods yard were retained and worked from ground frames; the connection outside the signal box was abolished and eventually recovered. The signal box was eventually demolished in October 1962. (Historical Model Railway Society)

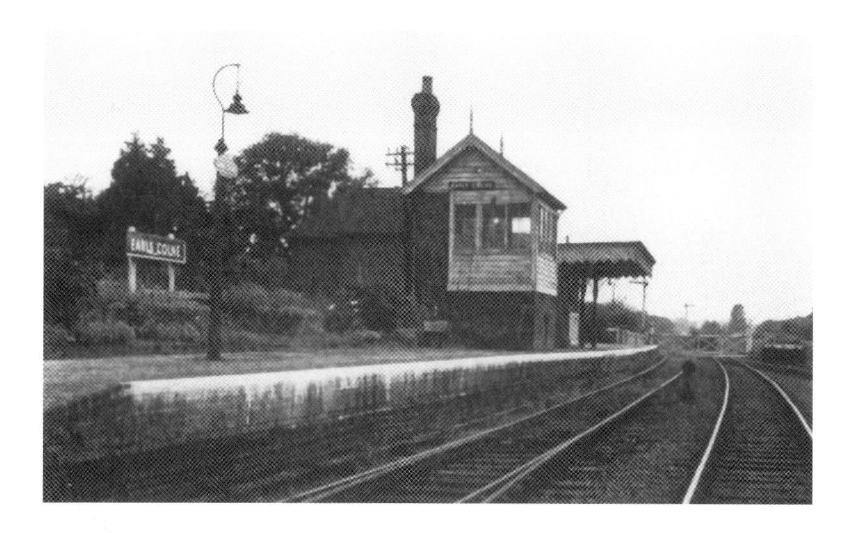

A track-level view looking at the platform and signal box with the level crossing gates in the background. This picture was taken in 1954 and is looking towards Halstead; the crossover mentioned in the previous paragraph can be seen at the bottom edge of the photograph. (Lens of Sutton Association)

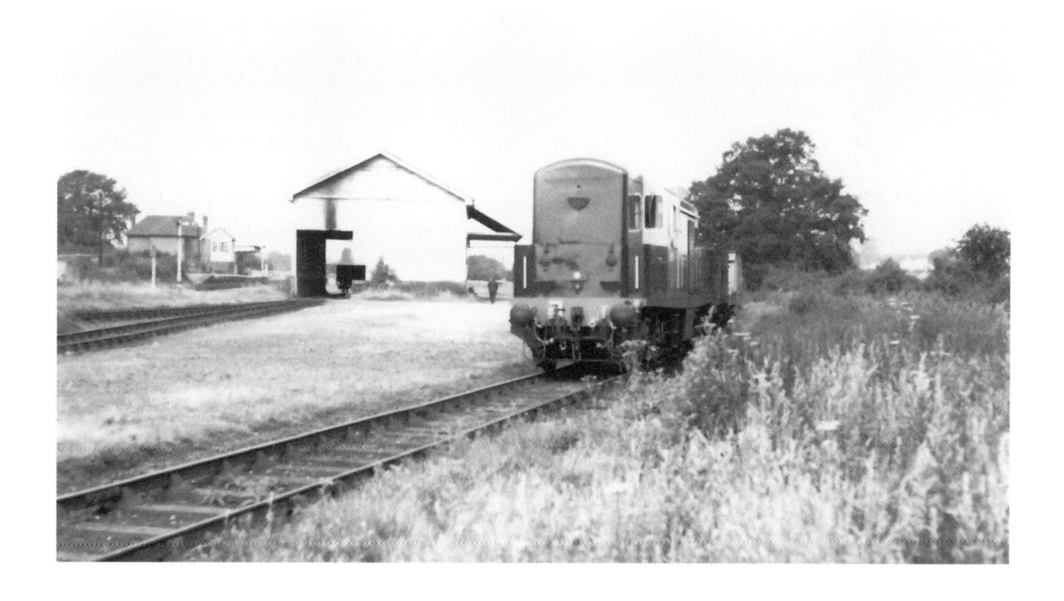

No. D8225 shunting in the goods yard. These locomotives worked most of the freight trains over the line between 1959 and 1965. Occasionally examples of the North British Type 2s, later Class 21s, could be seen in the very early 1960s working timber trains to Sible & Castle Hedingham; later, these locomotives were moved away from East Anglia. (Dr I. C. Allen/Transport Treasury)

Halstead

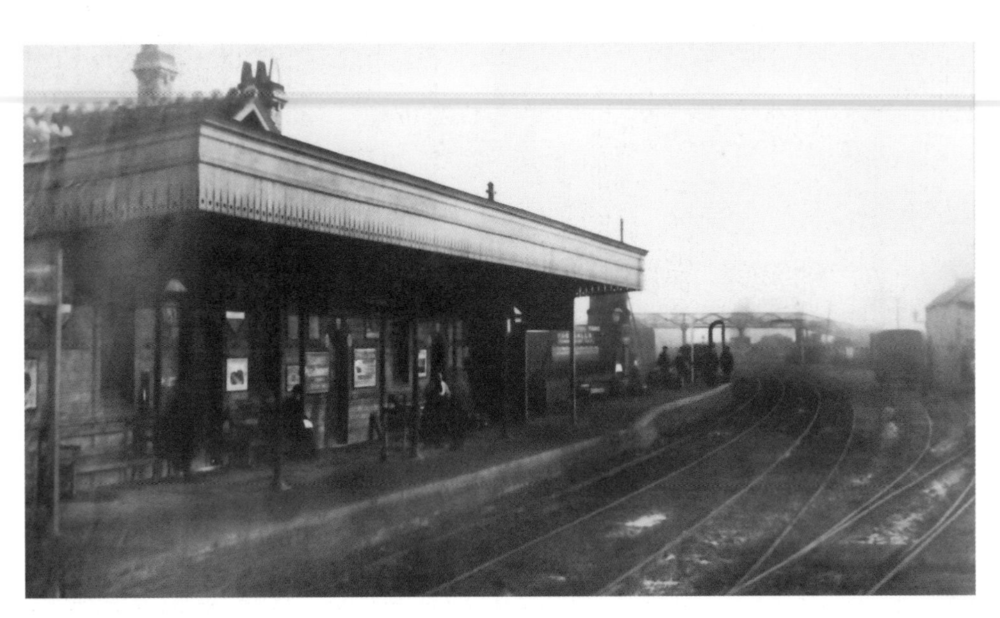

A very early view of Halstead station from around the 1880s, before the line received its first signalling. It looks like the original footbridge across the yard can be seen in the distance – this was originally made of timber only to be replaced with cast iron and steel many years later. In this view the sleepers are covered with drift gravel; many years later this practice ceased. (Michael Brooks Collection)

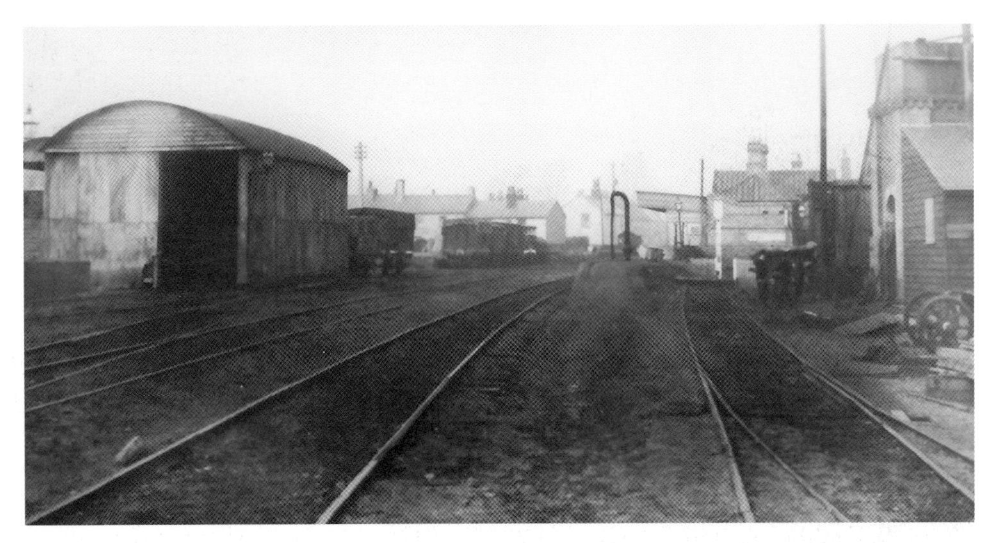

Another very early view, this time looking from the sidings back towards the station, showing the original goods shed before it was rebuilt in brick with a slate roof. This photograph is dated *c.* 1880, prior to the railway being signalled, which took place from 1889. The track looks to be of the flat-bottom type, directly spiked to the sleepers. Examples of this type of track survived in the sidings at Halstead until final closure of the line. (Michael Brooks Collection)

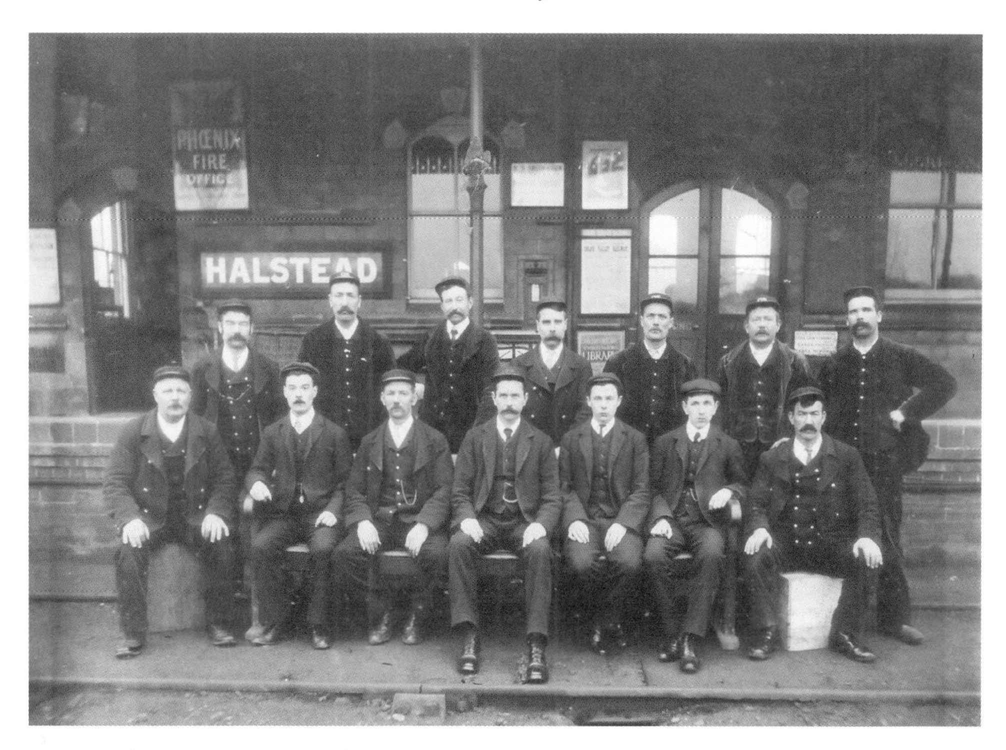

Being the busiest station on the line, the staffing was the largest, and in this view we see fourteen employees posing for the camera; apart from the two younger lads in the front row, the common feature seems to be moustaches. This view is dated 21 December 1908. (CVRPL Collection)

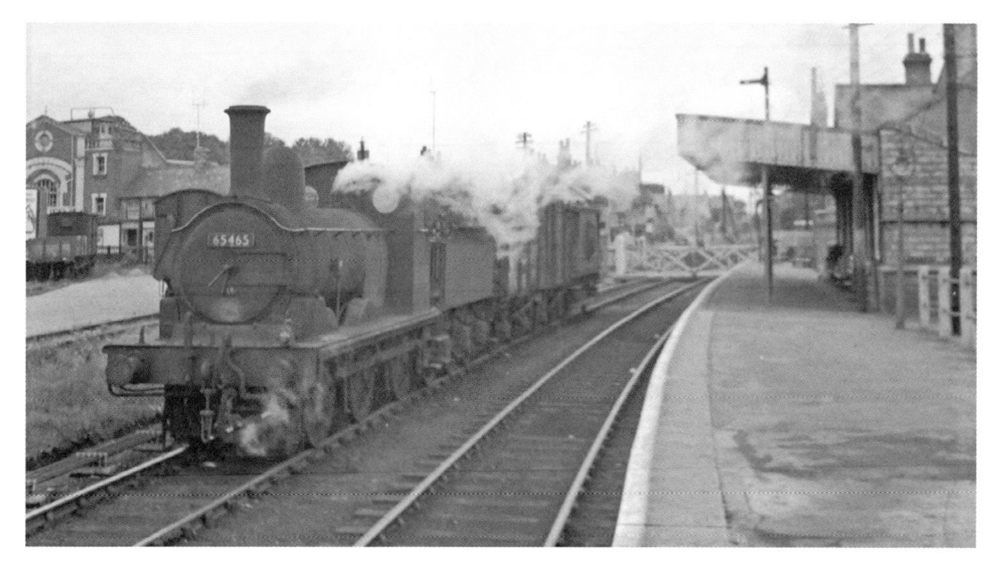

J15 class locomotive No. 65465 is seen on a short goods working, standing in the goods loop line opposite the platform, in the late 1950s. This view is looking north-west towards Sible & Castle Hedingham; the level crossing gates can be seen in the background. The signal box is seen behind the rear wagon adjacent to the level crossing. (Brian Pask)

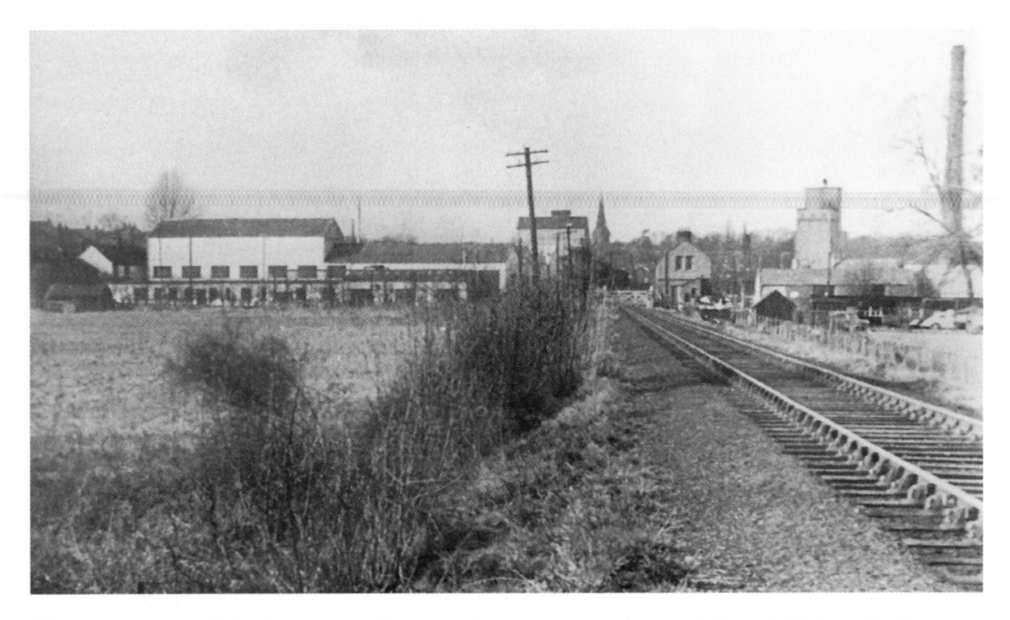

The view approaching Parsonage Lane level crossing on the outskirts of Halstead; the gates and crossing keeper's house can clearly be seen. The crossing was protected by working distant signals. For many years the old signal box had stood, becoming more derelict as the years ticked away before it was demolished in the 1950s. One of few remaining railway buildings at Halstead is the former crossing keeper's cottage. (B. A. L. Bamberger)

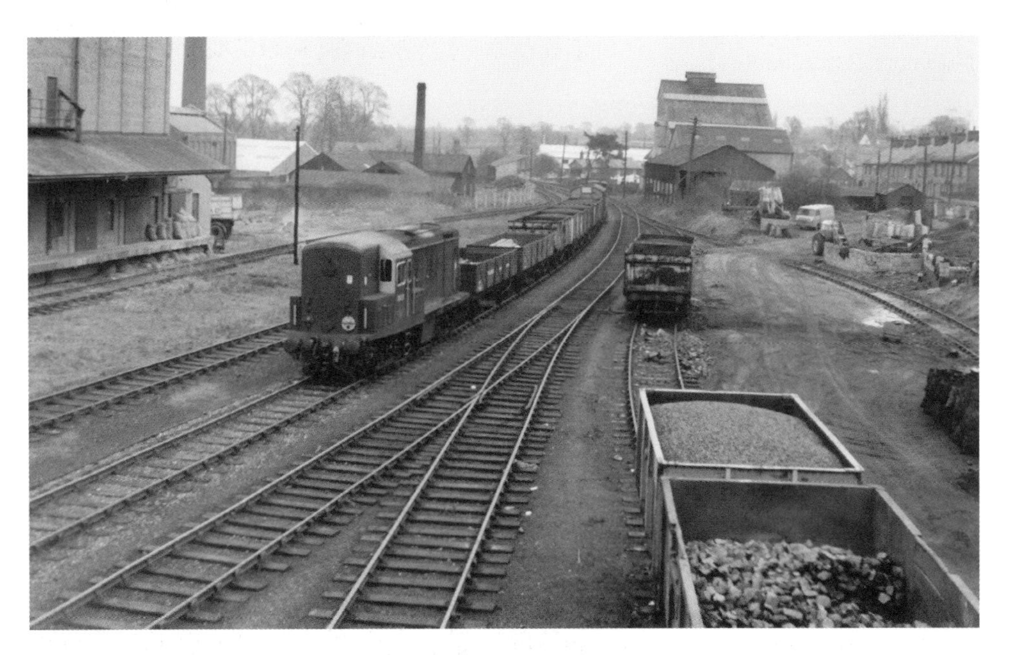

A view from the footbridge which spanned the yard at Halstead shows Class 15 diesel D8228 with a goods working. This picture can be dated to between October 1962 and April 1965 as all the signalling was removed after the line closed to passenger trains and, out of view, the old signal box was demolished in the October of the earlier year. (Dr I. C. Allen/Transport Transport)

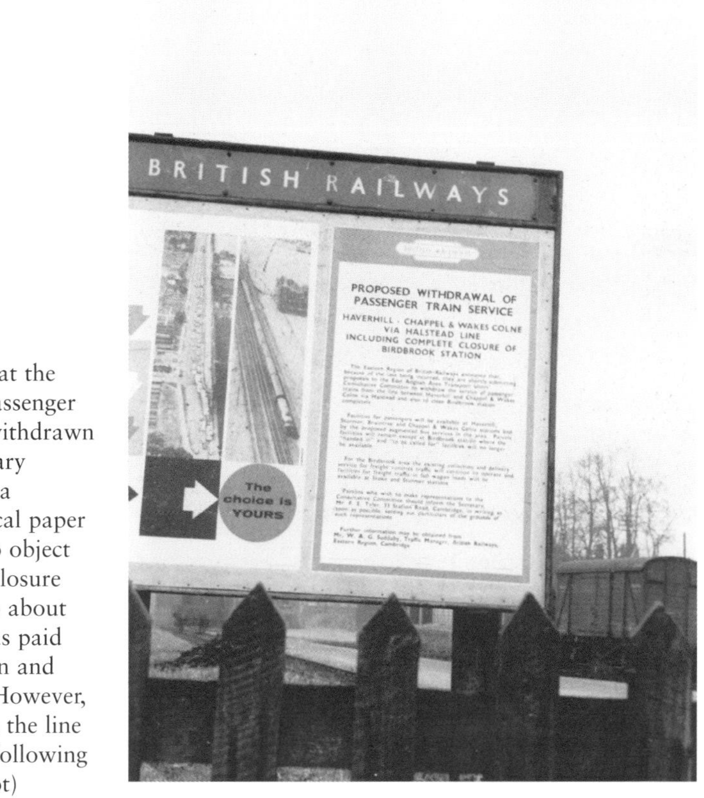

An official notice posted at the station stating that the passenger service was going to be withdrawn following the usual statuary process. I have a copy of a full-page advert in the local paper urging the local people to object to the above-mentioned closure and describing how to go about doing this. The advert was paid for by the Halstead Urban and Rural District Councils. However, it did not do any good as the line closed to passengers the following December. (Malcolm Root)

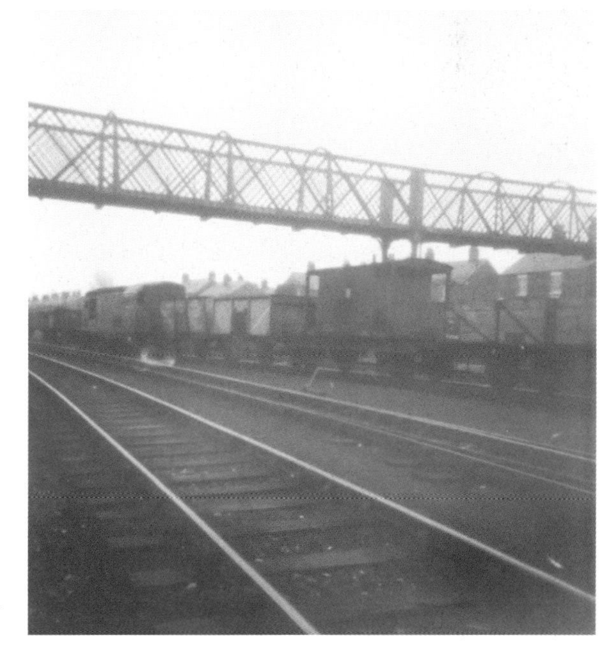

A rather grainy picture of Class 15 D82xx shunting wagons in the yard on the final day of the goods-only service which, as it was the Easter weekend, was on the Thursday before, the official closure date being Monday 19 April 1965. A sad day for the town of Halstead. (Geoff Barrett)

Sible & Castle Hedingham

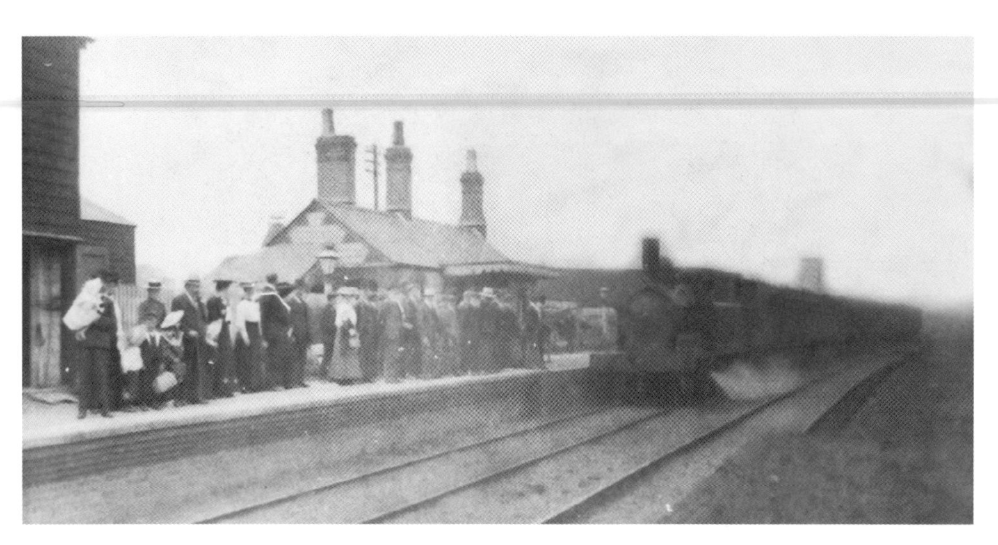

A passenger train arriving at Sible & Hedingham, *c.* 1900. There seems to be a decent crowd on the platform for the train, which was travelling towards Halstead. The small station building survived closure and now can be found at the new Colne Valley Railway, having been dismantled brick by brick and transported 1½ miles to its new home. (A. Corder-Birch Collection)

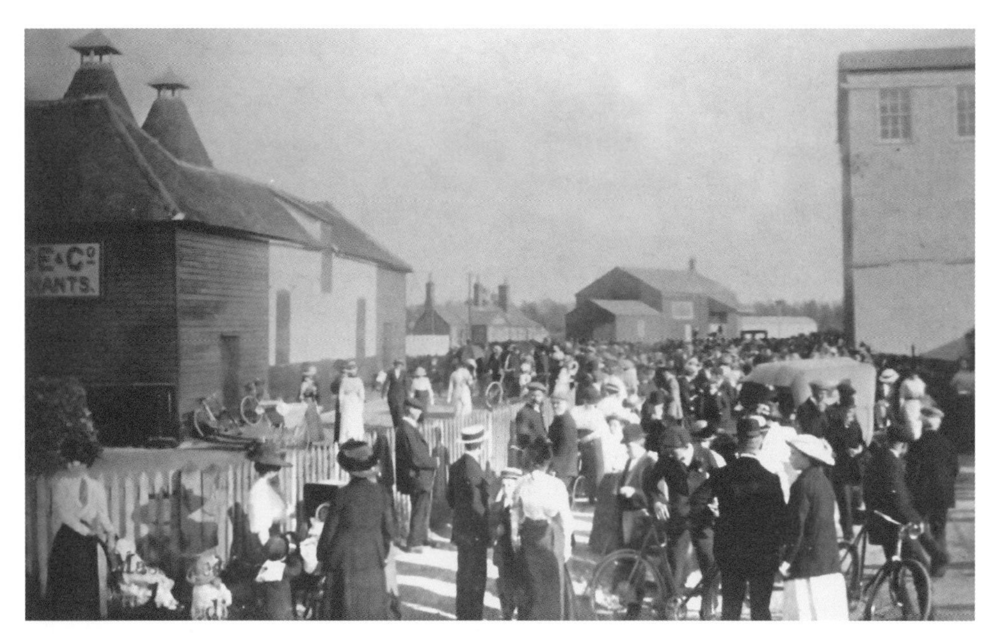

Hedingham station yard with the station buildings and goods shed in the centre background of the picture. The occasion of this gathering of so many people is not known, but we do know the date is 1914; in the CVRPS archives is a similar picture showing banners, so it could have been some sort of demonstration. (A. Corder-Birch Collection)

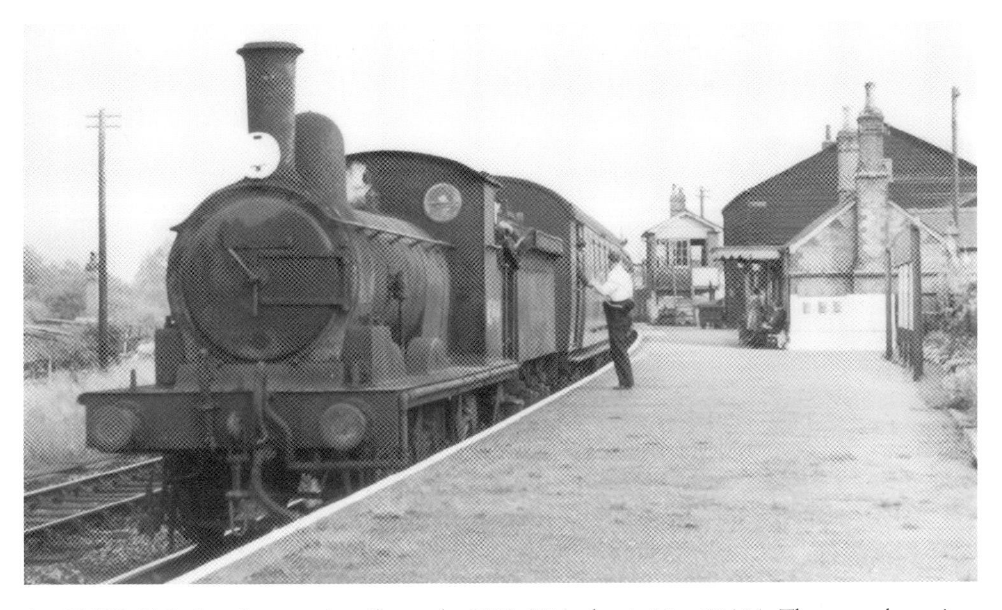

An LNER J15 class locomotive (formerly GER Y14 class), No. 65464. The crew have just exchanged tokens with the signalman as the engine hauls a Down direction local passenger train into the station. In the background can be seen the station building, large goods shed and signal box. (F. Church/Transport Treasury)

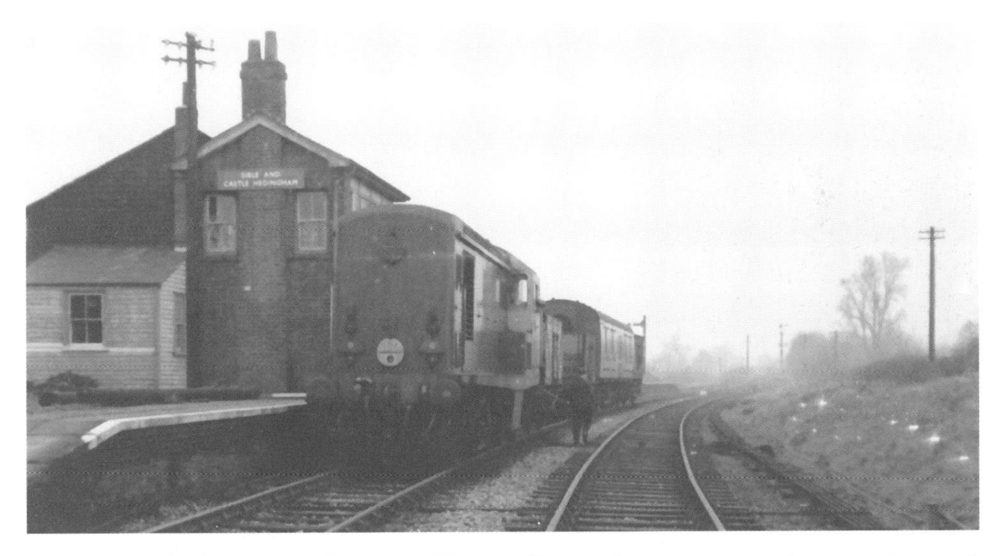

Wind forward a few years and we see a Class 15 diesel and some wagons, plus a parcel or mail coach and brake van. The brick-built signal box can be seen to the left. Right up to the end of steam workings passenger trains would cross at this station, which involved the up train being signalled into the loop while the Down train was accepted into the platform. Once tokens had been exchanged the Down direction train would depart, and when he was clear the train in the loop would be shunted back onto the main line so passengers could join or alight and then it would go on its way. No second platforms were ever built on the Colne Valley line. (D. Lawrence/Photos from the Fifties)

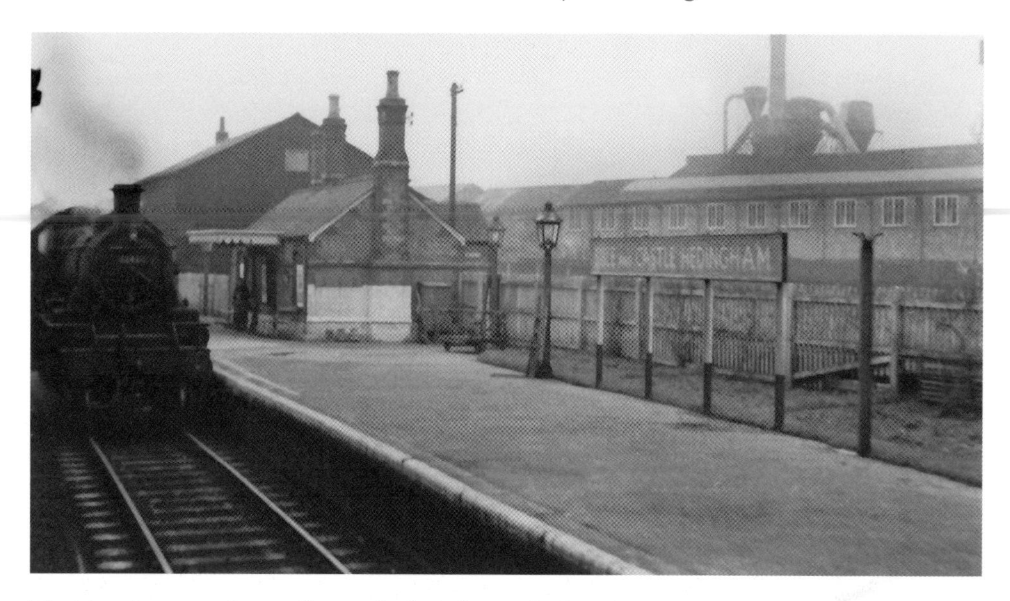

The view from a train standing in the loop line. Whether this was a passenger or freight train is not known, but the train arriving in the platform is hauled by 2MT class No. 46466. Note the long running-in board giving the station its full name. The industrial activity in the background was the local wood-working business, which provided much traffic for the railway until it was given over to road transport. (D. Lawrence/Photos from the Fifties)

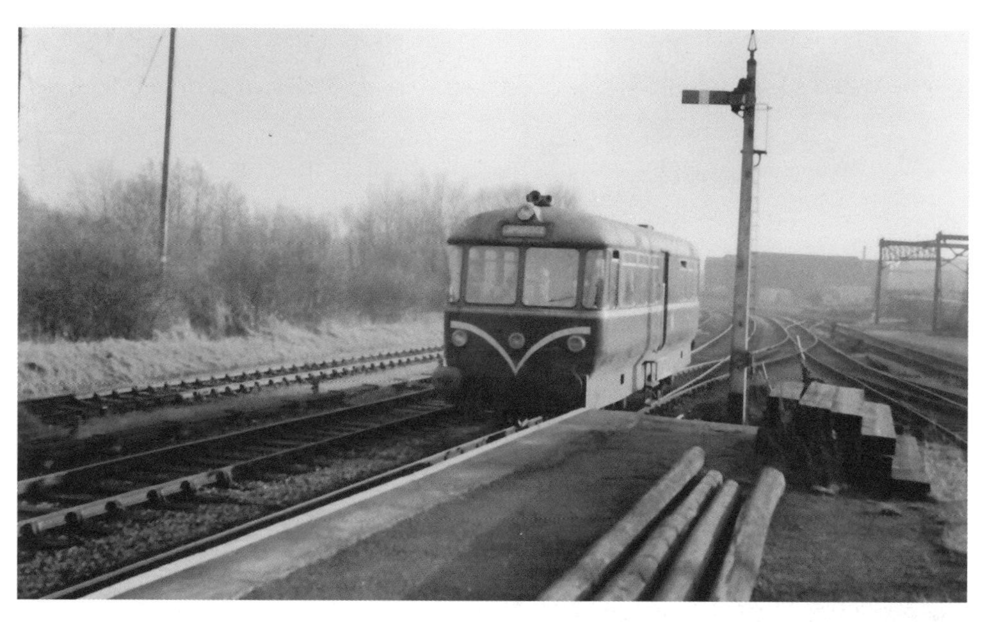

A W&M railbus arrives at the station. Although not dated, it is probably sometime in 1961 as there is ongoing S&T work, installing a new ground frame at the platform end which took over the working of this connection after the signal box closed. Unusually, for some reason the Up starting signal had been converted from a lower quadrant to an upper quadrant in the line's dying days. The arm appears to be a short version, no doubt for clearance reasons. (Dr I. C. Allen/Transport Treasury)

Yeldham

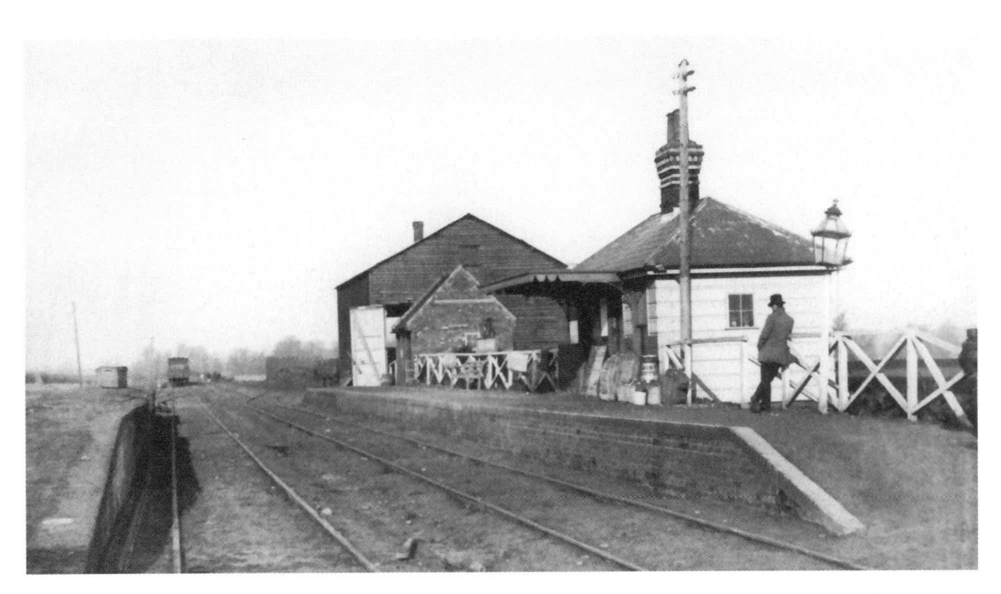

A view from around the 1880s of Yeldham, looking north from the level crossing. This view is pre-signalling. The original station building, a brick building and the goods shed can be clearly seen. Originally Yeldham was not supposed to have a level crossing over Toppesfield Road – it was to be a bridge; the Colne Valley board had chosen to ignore this fact in the act but fell foul of the Board of Trade inspector, who forced the CV&HR to get powers to change the original Act to agree to a level crossing. Whether the CVR board did or not, I don't know. (M. Brooks Collection)

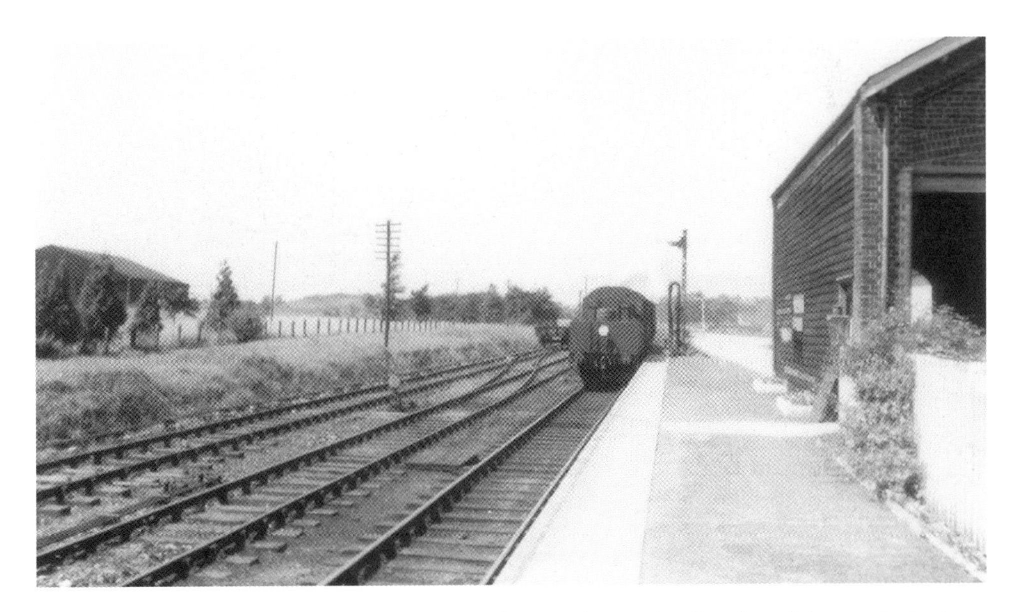

Class 2MT arriving with an Up passenger working in the 1950s; the edge of the goods shed can be seen on the right. (Stations UK)

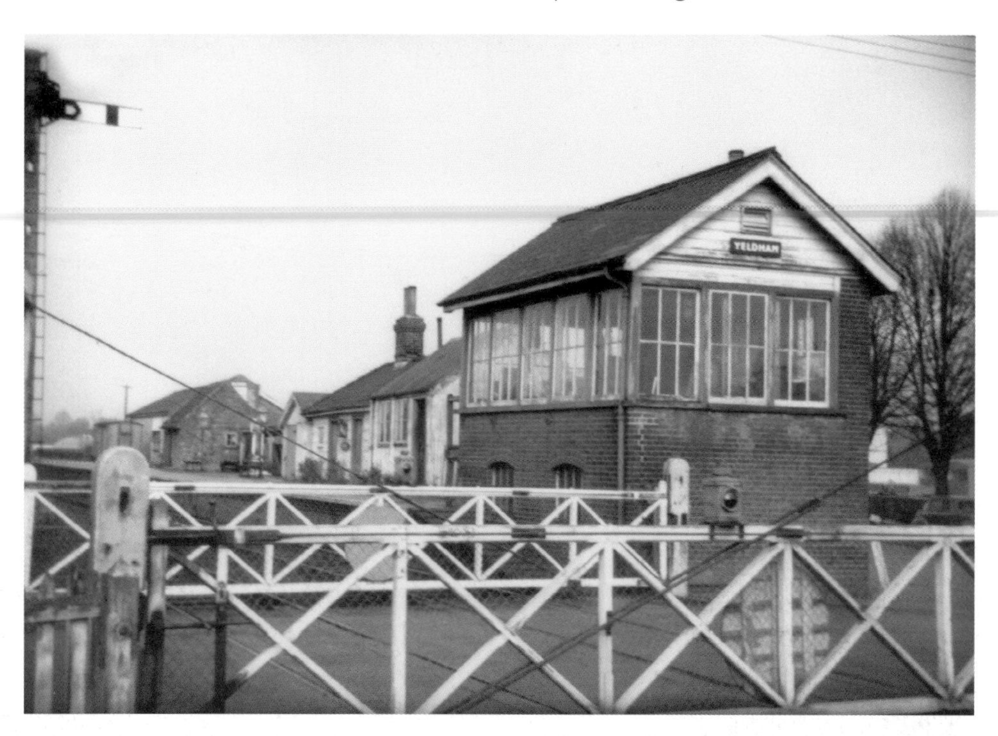

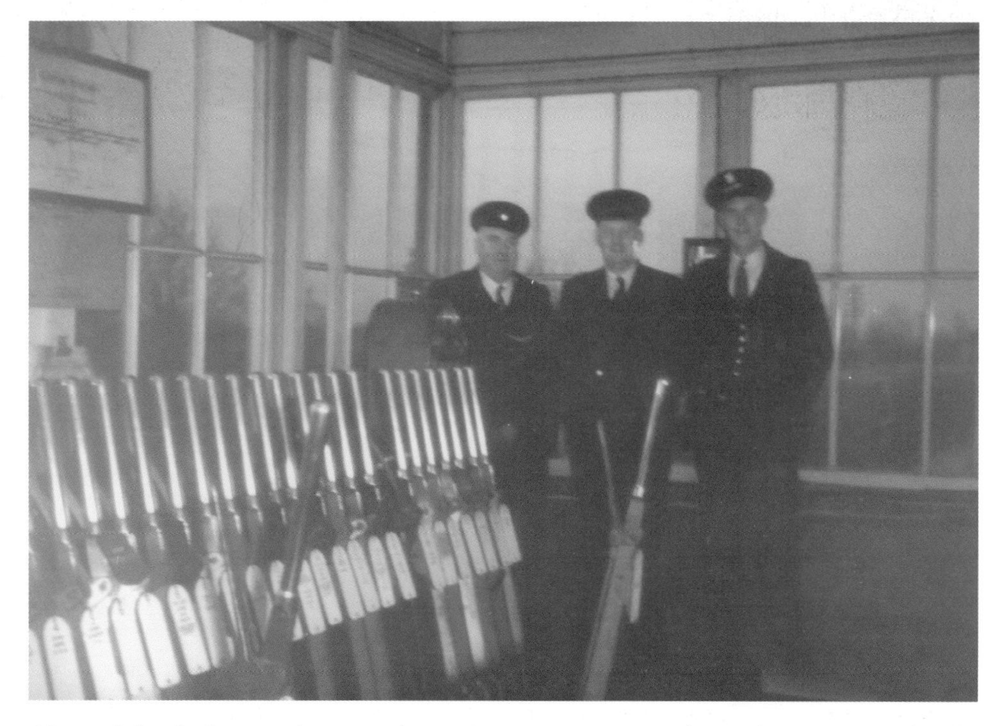

Above: A local photographer gets the stationmaster, porter and signalman to pose for the camera adjacent to the lever frame. Even in a dark black-and-white view, the shiny levers still stick out – the local staff kept everything clean and tidy. (Ron Hutley)

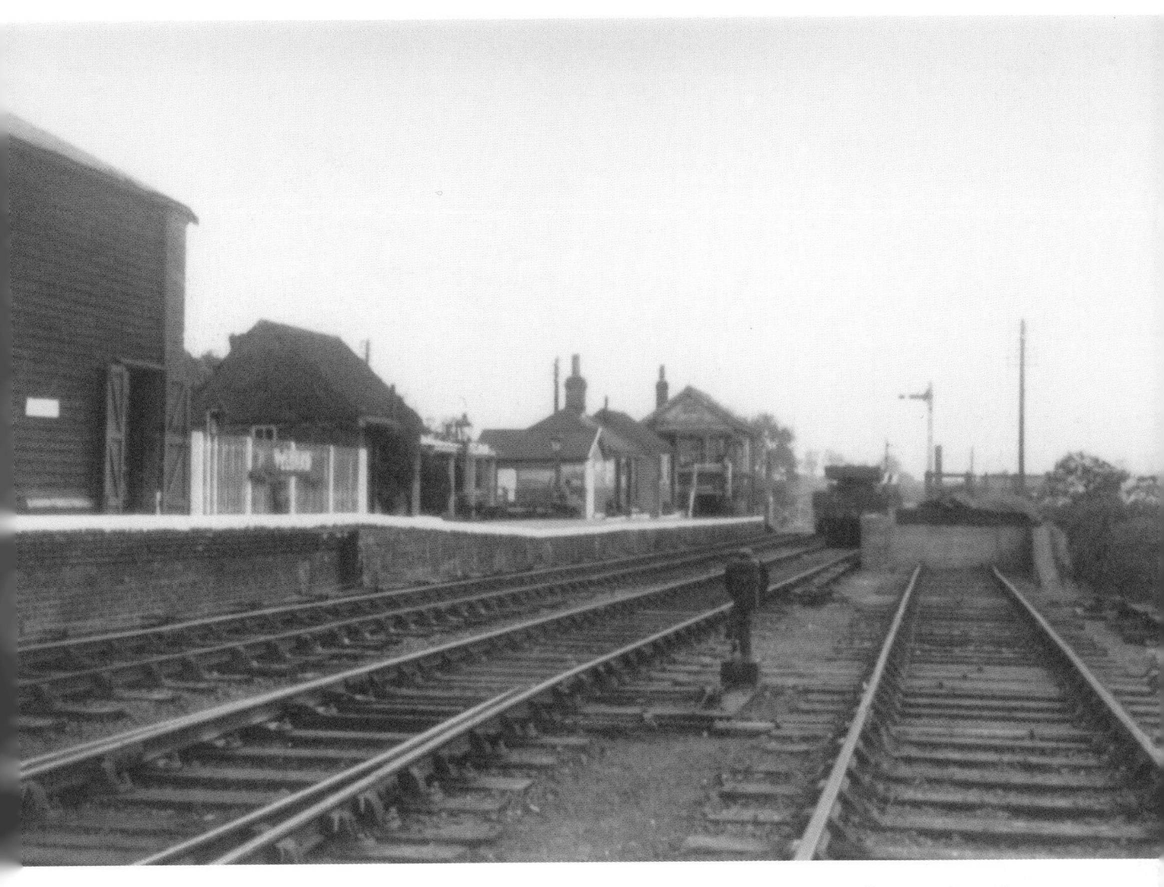

A general view of the station and loading dock as seen *c.* 1947, just prior to the British Railways takeover. This picture clearly shows the original platform and the slightly higher extension that was built at the north end; the platforms still exist some fifty years after closure, although this whole area is now covered with trees, all grown in the intervening years. (Historical Model Railway Society – ABD110)

Opposite above: The signal box and level crossing with the station in the background; when compared to the earlier view, one can see that the station had gained an additional building as well as the signal box. The signal box benefitted from a gate wheel to work the gates. The replacement concrete up starting signal can be seen on the extreme left. (Ron Hutley)

Birdbrook

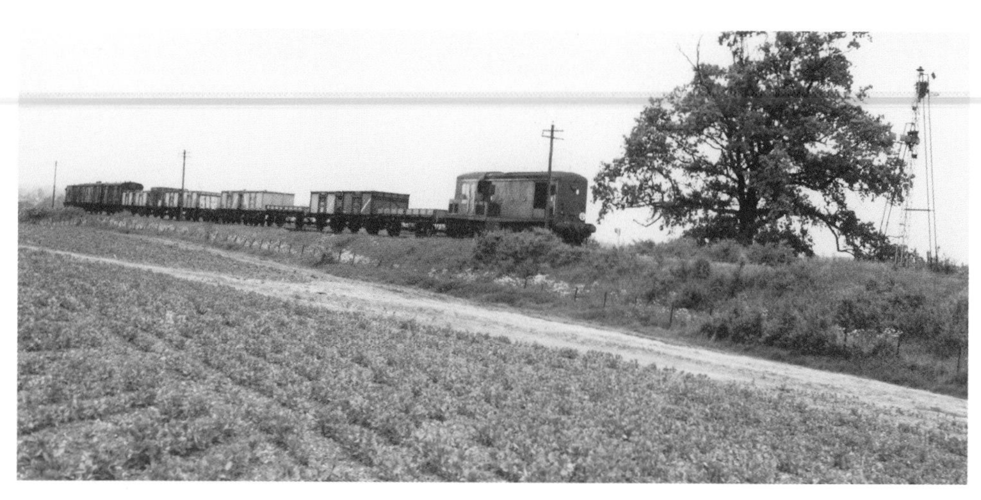

The first of two undated views of Type 1 (later Class 15) D8227 approaching Birdbrook Up home Down starting signal with a selection of goods vehicles and a brake van. The signal is of lattice post construction and had been modified twice in its life. The first was in April 1955, when the Up home arm and spectacle were joined to form a single unit. Both signals at this time were lower quadrants; sometime after that the two arms were converted from lower quadrant to upper quadrant. Even more bizarre was the renewal of the Down distant signal wooden post and lower quadrant arm with a new tubular steel post and upper quadrant arm only a few months before the line shut completely. Cynics might say that it was a typical waste of money, knowing the line was closing; for the accountants it would be another figure shown in the spend column. I wonder? (Dr I. C. Allen/Transport Treasury)

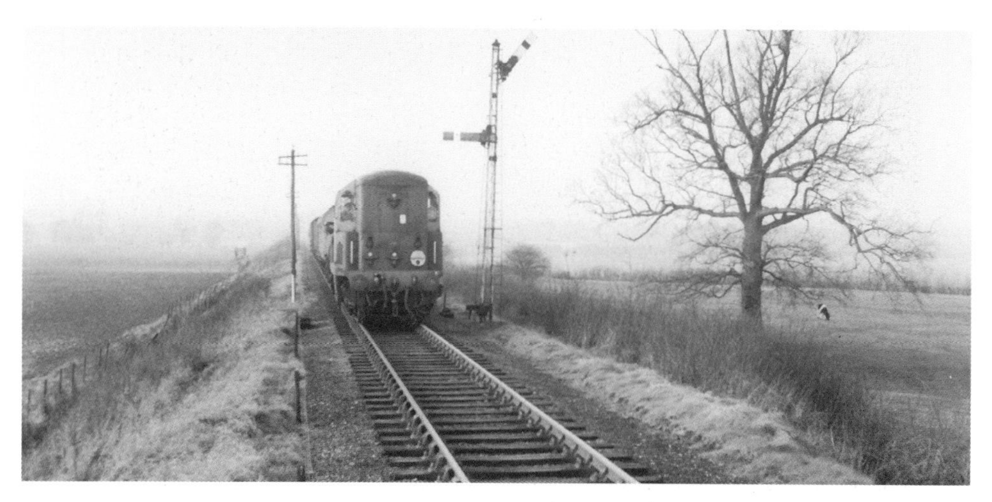

A head-on view of a diesel locomotive and freight train passing the Up home and Down starting signals previously mentioned. Whether these two views were taken on the same day I have no idea, but the absence of leaves on the tree in one view would indicate otherwise. (Dr I. C. Allen/ Transport Treasury)

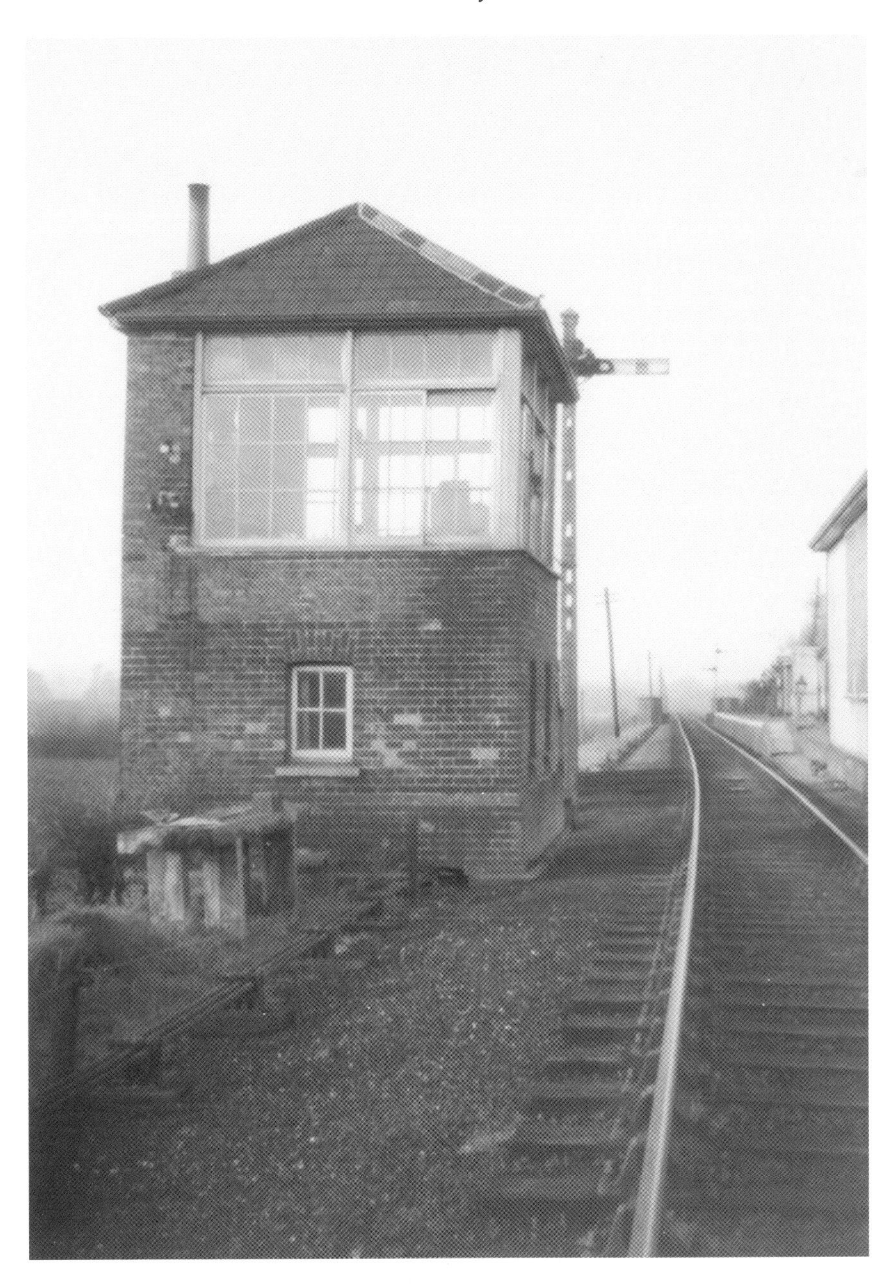

Another different Colne Valley-designed signal box. This one is nearly all brick with a small window in the lower floor and with large sixteen-pane windows on three sides giving an all-round view. The signal box was equipped with a McKenzie & Holland eleven-lever frame with ten working and one spare lever. Unusually, there were no trap points from the goods yard lines, but instead there was a worked mechanical scotch to stop any vehicle fouling the running line. (Ron Hutley)

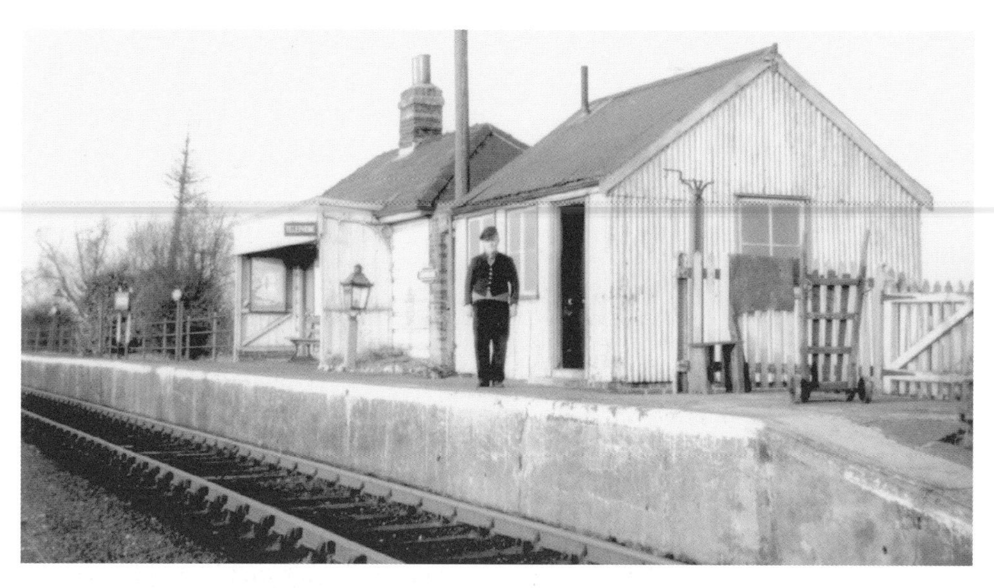

Very basic facilities were provided at the station. The original station building is shown on the left and the newer, corrugated iron-built building of 1908 vintage is on the right. In the later days only one man was employed on each shift at the station, and he would be a porter signalman who would sell tickets, look after the small goods yard and work the signal box when required. The stationmaster at Haverhill supervised the station in the later years of its existence. (Ron Hutley)

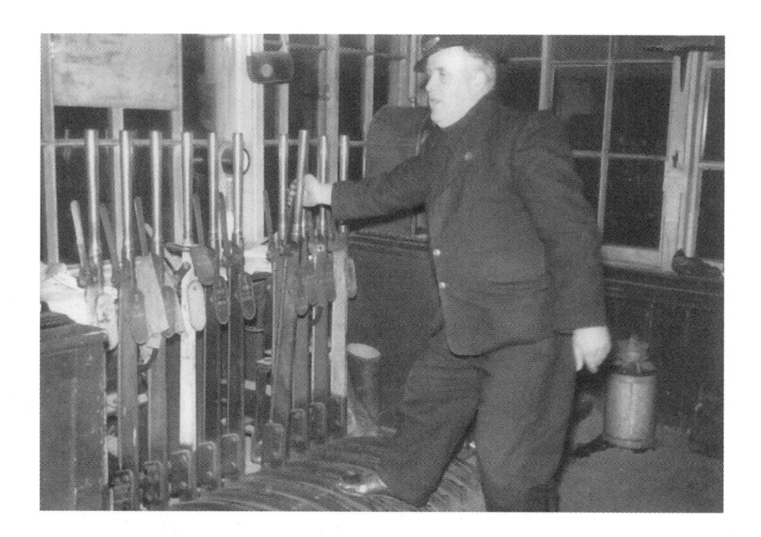

Porter signalman Charlie Chase operating the lever frame on 30 December 1961. This was the final day for the station and once the last train had passed through, the lights would be extinguished forever. A local man travelled to the station to buy the last tickets sold there that dark December night; when he died, they were passed on to the CVRPL at Castle Hedingham. (Vincent Heckford/CVRPL Collection)

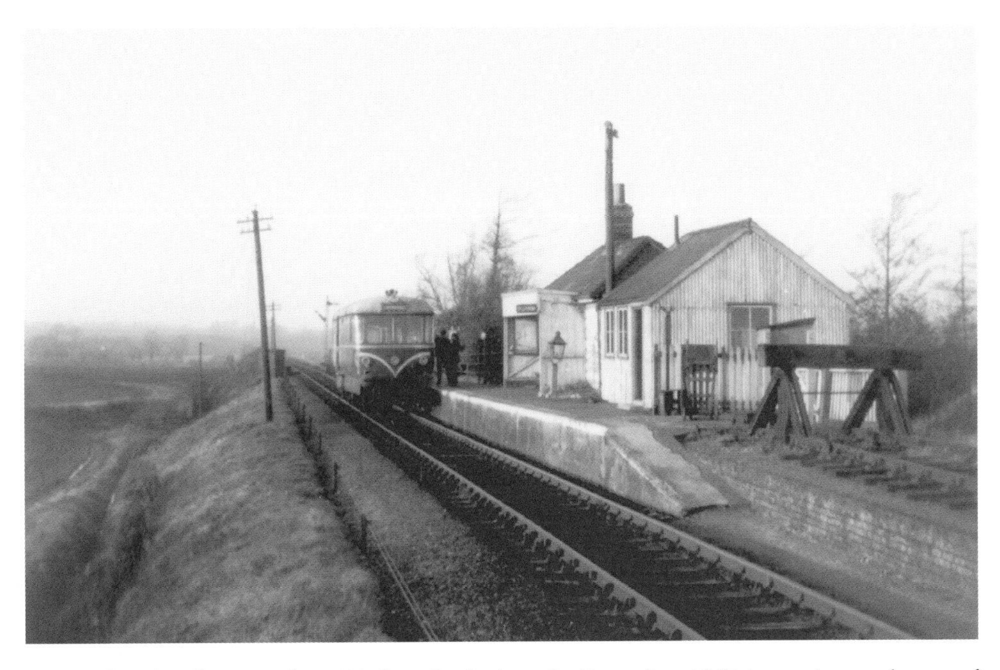

W&M diesel railbus stands at Birdbrook platform in December 1961 just prior to closure of the line; this view was taken from the signal box. (Ron Hutley)

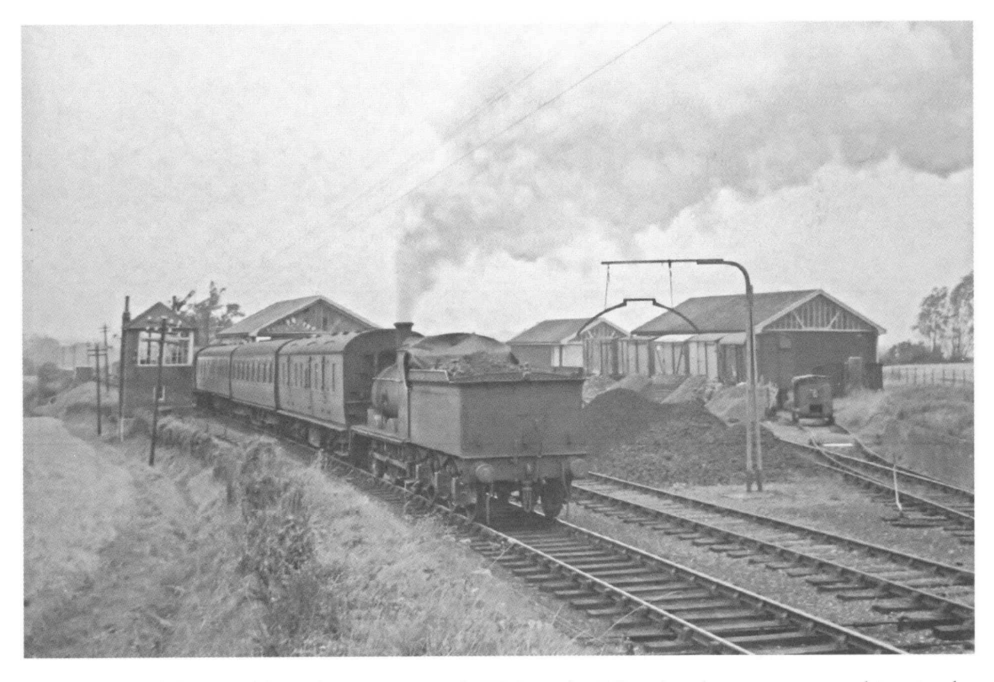

A member of the J15 class departs towards Halstead with a local passenger working in the late 1950s. The two large buildings in the goods yard were granaries. Note the permanent way inspection trolley parked in the yard. The layout at Birdbrook was very simple with a single lead off the single line which divided to serve the goods shed and goods yard. (Brian Pask)

Colne Valley Junction & Haverhill Colne Valley (South)

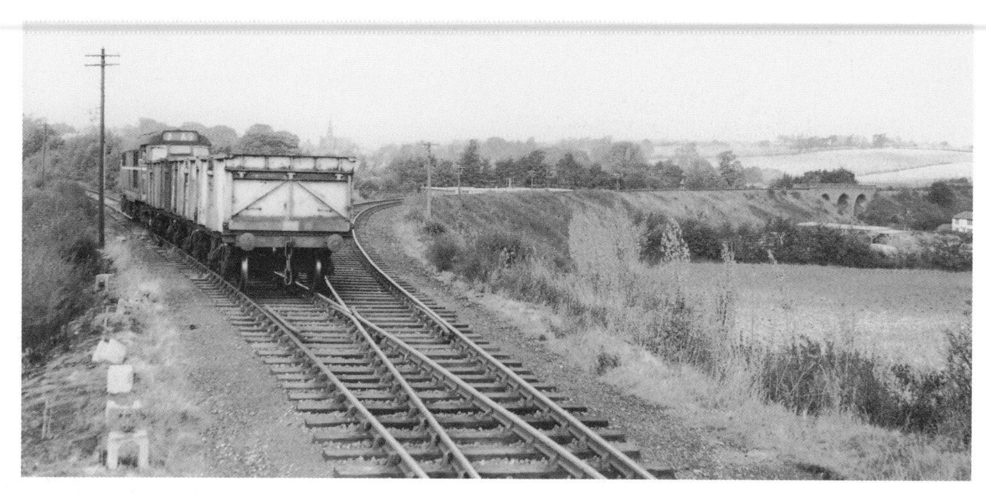

Although rated RA5, this picture shows a Class 31 propelling wagons back to the junction from Haverhill South goods yard. Once clear of the junction, the locomotive would then haul its train to the north station. In the background on the right, Hamlet Road viaduct can be seen. Although undated, this view is post-January 1962 as the ground frame-operated junction had been converted to hand operation. (Dr I. C. Allen/Transport Treasury)

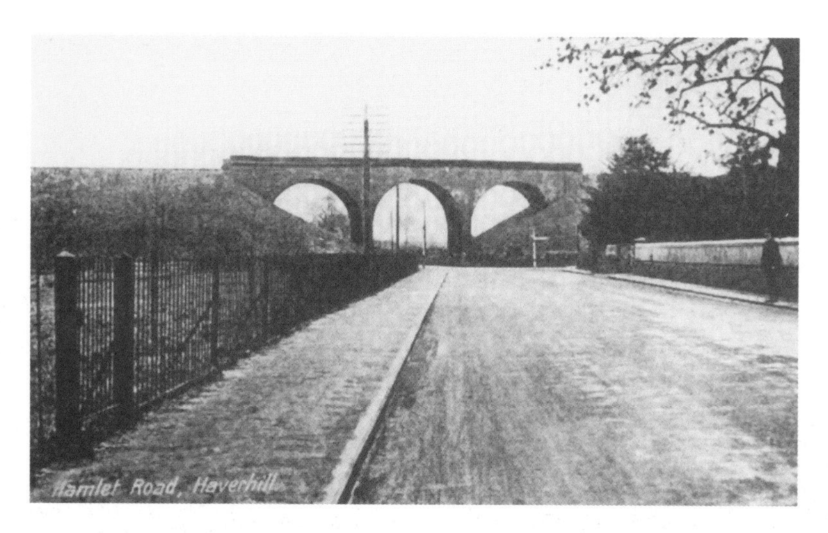

An early, uncluttered view of Hamlet Road viaduct, which was located on the connecting line between the Colne Valley line and the Stour Valley line at Haverhill. This viaduct was known locally as Sturmer Arches and is now a listed structure despite not having seen a train for fifty years. The viaduct can be walked over as it forms part of a public footpath system using former railway lines in the Haverhill area. (CVRPL Archive)

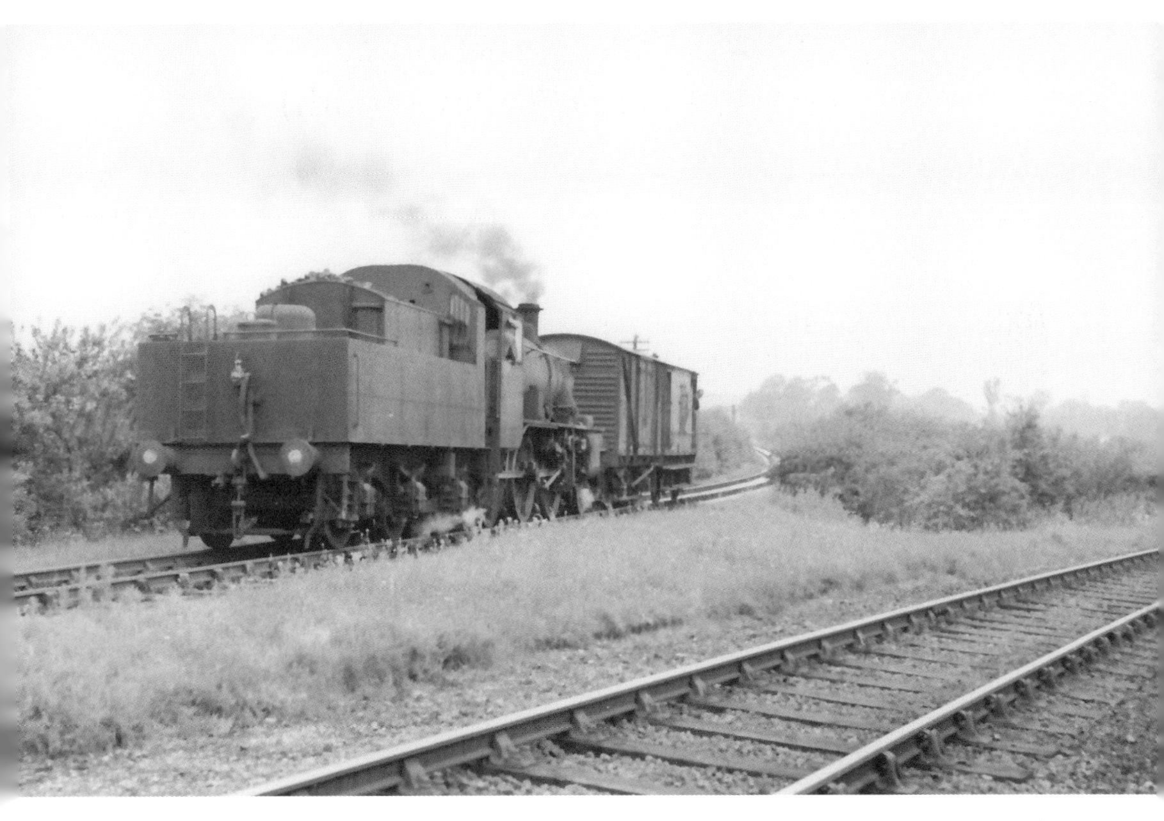

2MT class locomotive No. 46666 propels a box van and brake along the branch to the south goods depot. A local resident living adjacent to the branch told me that back in the 1950s an ageing J15 would haul a long rake of goods wagons round to Colne Valley Junction, where it would wait having a blow up, ready to push the long rake of wagons up the branch; the noise would be spectacular. (Dr I. C. Allen/Transport Treasury)

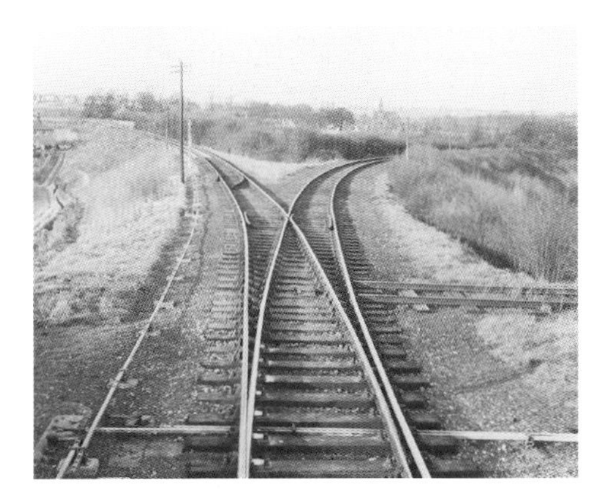

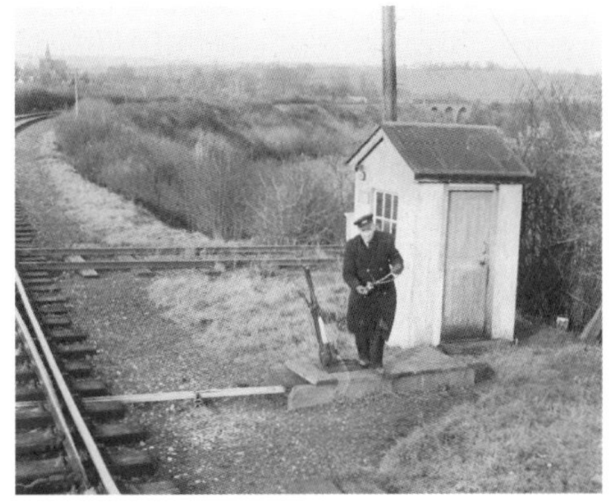

Above left and right: Two views taken from the guard's brake van showing the train waiting at the junction for the guard to change the points for the propelling move down the branch. A white marker light was provided to indicate the location of the trap points on the spur. The line to the right led to Haverhill North station. (Brian Pask)

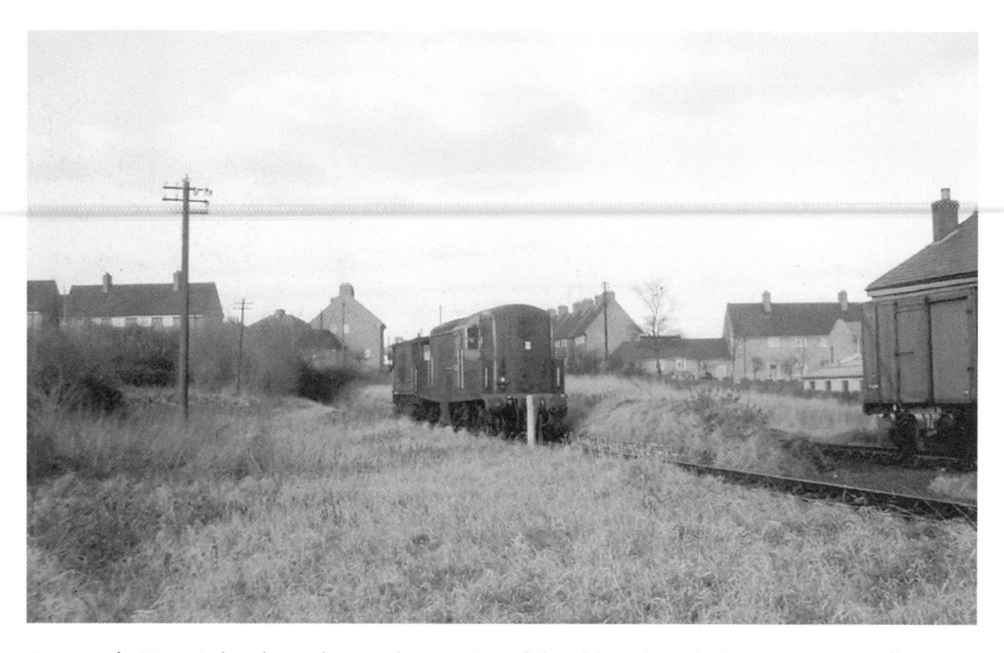

A view of a Type 1 diesel standing at the remains of the old station platform, now just a few rows of crumbling bricks and grass. This whole area has now been redeveloped into housing with some industrial use, although part of the old line is now a public footpath at the Colne Valley Junction end of the station site – with care you can walk round to the old viaduct. (Brian Pask)

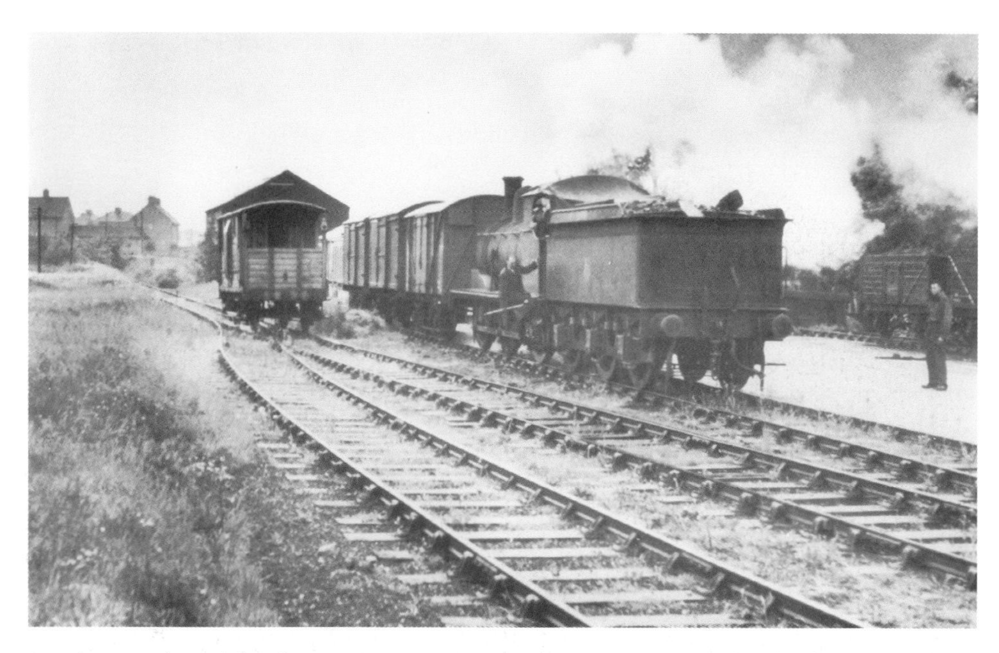

Another member of the class, No. 65573, is seen shunting vans into the goods shed sometime in the 1950s. Freight facilities were withdrawn from the south goods yard in April 1965, when many local stations lost their facilities as a consequence of BR getting out of the wagon load traffic as a direct result of the Beeching Report. (Dr I. C. Allen/Transport Treasury)

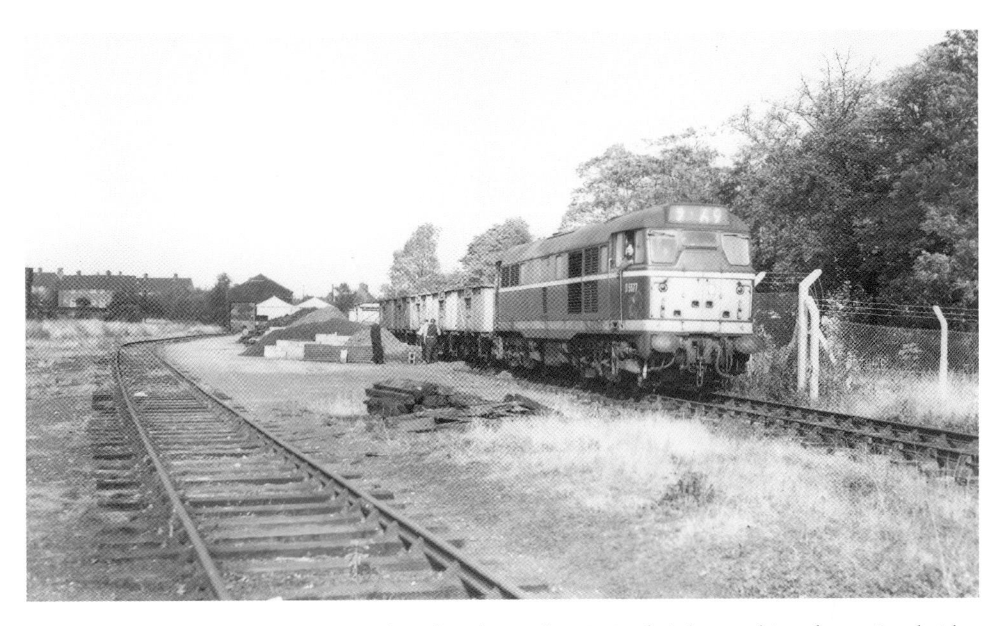

Train 7_69 was the reporting number for the early 1960s freight working from Cambridge to Sudbury; No. D5577 is seen here shunting coal wagons in one of the sidings at the goods station. Use of these heavy locomotives was surprising as the Colne Valley line was only rated as RA2. However, most of the weak bridges were on the southern end of the line – Class 31s never made it to Halstead. (Dr I. C. Allen/Transport Treasury)

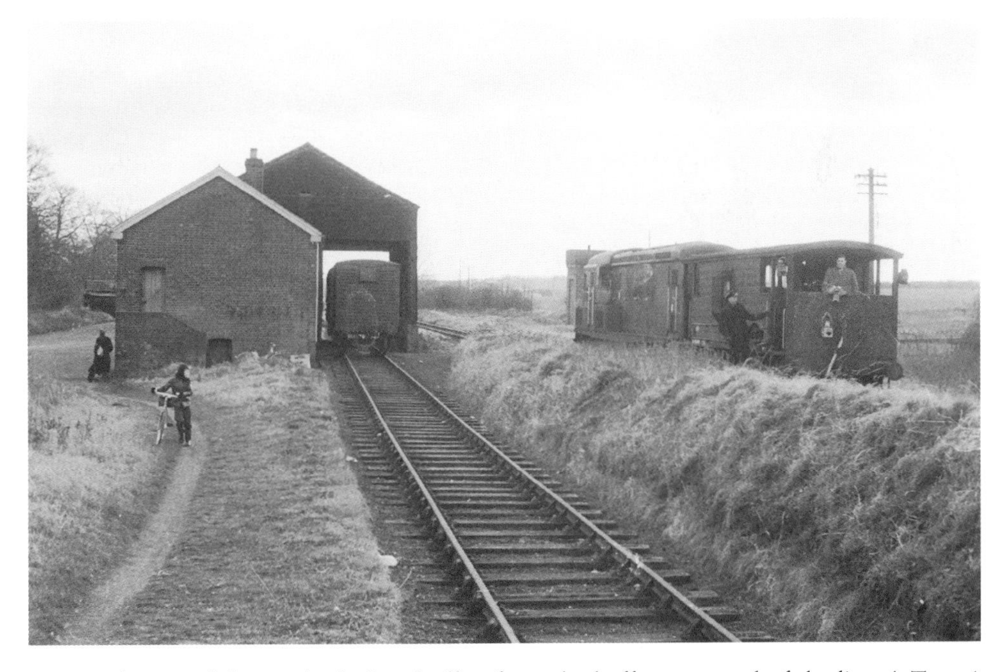

A general view of the goods shed and office from the buffer stops end of the line. A Type 1 diesel and brake van also feature; the photographer and one other person had obtained a brake van pass, which was one way of seeing this non-passenger part of the network. (Brian Pask)

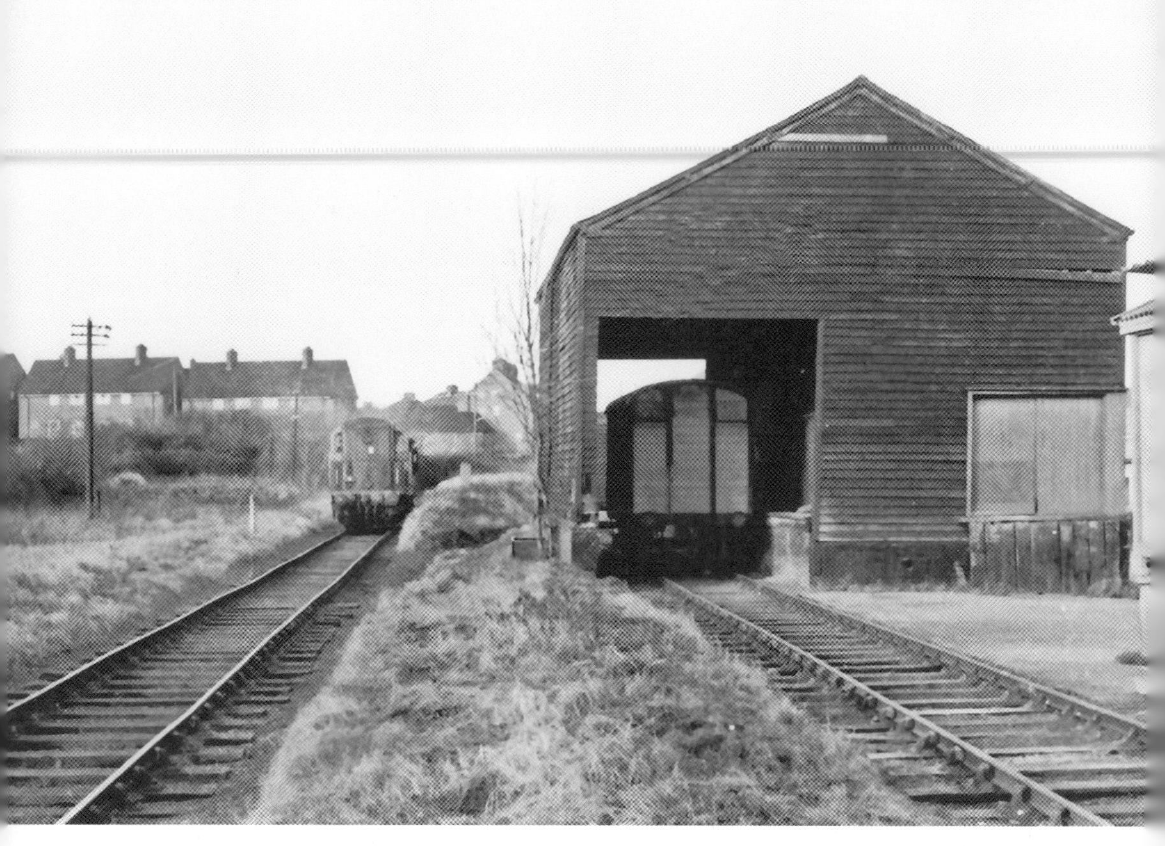

The original goods shed with a covered van neatly parked in it, ready for loading or unloading as the case may be. The locomotive is resting on the old platform line. When visiting this area a few years ago, most of the old station site had been given over to houses with some industrial development. (Brian Pask)

The Bury Branch: Long Melford to Bury St Edmunds

The line from Sudbury to Clare, with a branch to Lavenham from Long Melford and then a further extension to Bury St Edmunds, had been authorised in June 1846 as an official extension of the Colchester, Stour Valley Sudbury & Halstead Railway (CSVS&HR); this company had also obtained powers at the same time to extend from Lavenham to Bury St Edmunds and to lease the whole undertaking to the Ipswich and Bury line, which in July of that year was formally leased by the Eastern Union Railway (EUR). By 1854 the former CSVS&HR extensions had passed into the hands of the Eastern Counties Railway; alas, still no construction commenced and the powers to build were allowed to lapse.

Construction of the Bury branch had to wait until the coming of the Great Eastern Railway in 1862; powers previously obtained by the ECR were renewed, which allowed for the Stour Valley extensions and the branch from Long Melford to Bury St Edmunds.

The lines from Haverhill to Sudbury and from Long Melford to Bury opened on 9 August 1865 with intermediate stations at Lavenham, Welnetham and Bury East Gate; additionally, goods sidings were provided at Cockfield and Sicklesmere. Unfortunately, Welnetham was the location of a train derailment after only a few weeks of being opened; thankfully, nobody was seriously injured.

From the opening the Bury branch was worked by the train staff & ticket system with just two sections, Melford to Lavenham and Lavenham to Bury Junction. Two accidents occurred in 1871 and 1877 at Welnetham and Bury Junction respectively; both required a BoT investigation. Cockfield goods siding became a passenger station from November 1870; on the other hand, Sicklesmere was closed by 1875. Melford station officially became Long Melford from 1 February 1884.

The branch benefitted from resignalling from 1889, signal boxes being provided at all stations although Cockfield, Welnetham and Bury East Gate were not block posts. None of the new signalling system could do anything about the next accident to plague the line, which happened in October 1891 between Lavenham and Long Melford when a train derailed, the locomotive ending up down an embankment; although there were some injuries to passengers and staff, none were fatal. The branch benefitted from a bridge rebuilding or strengthening programme in 1894.

Bury East Gate station closed to passenger traffic on 1 May 1909; its signal box was also closed at the same time. The First World War brought increased traffic to the Bury line; electric tablet working was introduced between Long Melford and Bury St Edmunds Junction in 1916. After the First World War the GER was grouped into the London & North Eastern Railway (LNER) on 1 January 1923.

The LNER made economies with the closure of Welnetham signal box; this took place in 1926, the connections to the sidings then being worked from a ground frame. The passenger service in the 1930s reached its peak at six trains each way over the line. The wartime traffic over the Bury line was heavy and was mostly freight; by 1942, the passenger service had been reduced to five trains each way. To cope with the ever increasing freight traffic, the Bury line remained open overnight, as did the line through to Marks Tey. Traffic started to ebb away from the line after the Second World War; this accelerated further after the lifting of petrol rationing in the 1950s.

Modernisation in the form of diesel railbuses and multiple units arrived in January 1959; the passenger service that summer consisted of only three Down trains and four Up trains. The writing was on the wall for the branch passenger service, which was duly withdrawn on 10 April 1961. The last passenger train to run over the whole branch did so on 4 June 1961, when a diesel-hauled ramblers' special ran to and from London Liverpool Street to Bury St Edmunds via Sudbury and Long Melford. The section between Lavenham and Long Melford then closed completely; this portion of the line was duly dismantled in 1962.

Freight continued to be handled at the branch stations, the daily service travelling out and back from Bury St Edmunds. Following publication of the Beeching Report, the process of closing small goods yards commenced. Welnetham closed as a public delivery siding in July 1964 and Cockfield and Lavenham went in April 1965; dismantling of the track soon followed. The final freight train actually ran on 15 April 1965, hauled by diesel locomotive No. D8221.

Following demolition the land and stations were sold off for further use. Today, Welnetham station is a private house, Cockfield is disused but intact while Lavenham survived for a number of years before eventually it disappeared when the whole area was redeveloped into a large factory; this factory eventually closed and the site was cleared for future development, probably housing. Part of the old track bed near Lavenham has been turned into a country walk by the local authority, as has a short section near Long Melford.

Bury St Edmunds Branch

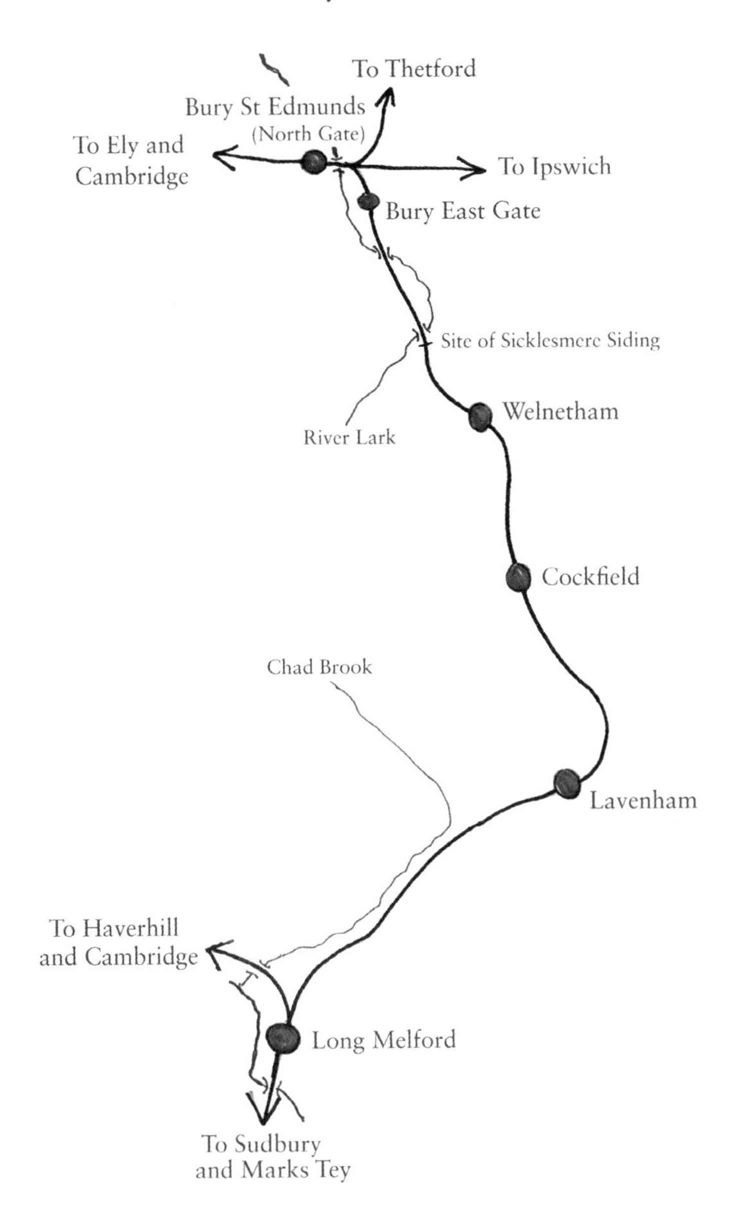

Lavenham

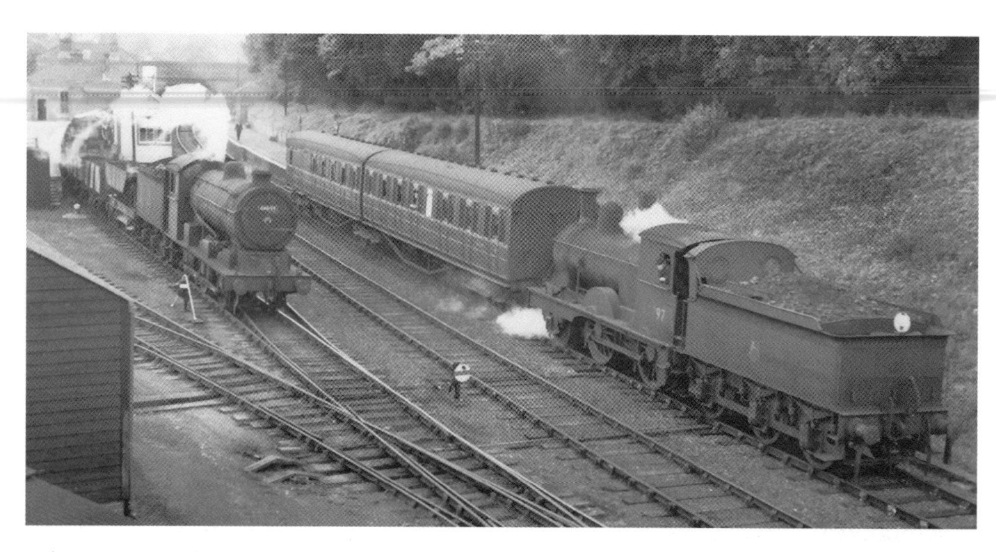

A busy scene at the station showing E4 class locomotive No. 62797 with the two-coach branch passenger train departing towards Cockfield sometime before March 1957, when this veteran engine was finally withdrawn from service. In the yard J19 class No. 64659 stands with a goods train blowing off, waiting its turn to proceed. Lavenham was the principle crossing place on the Bury branch. (Dr I. C. Allen/Transport Treasury)

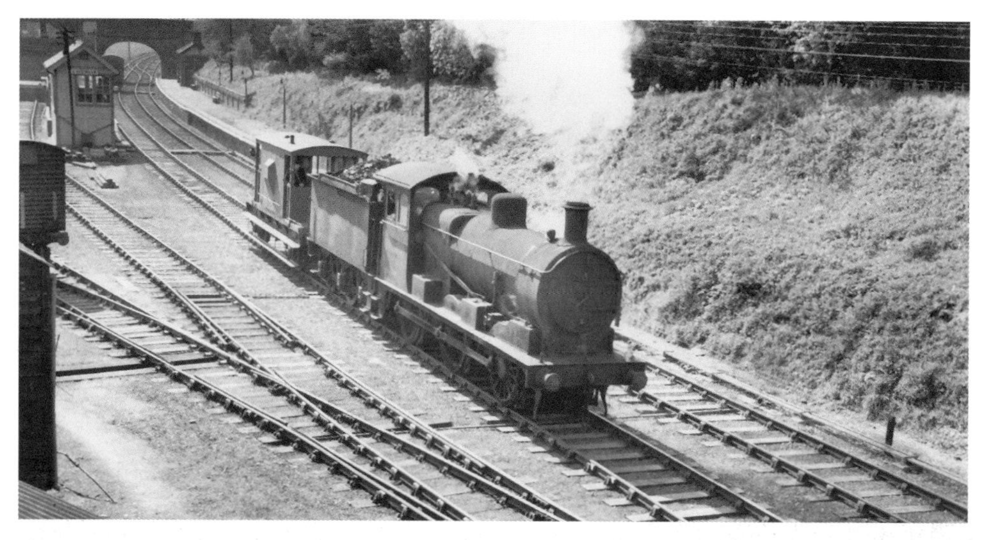

An undated and unidentified J19 and brake van shunting. By this time twelve points next to the box had been removed and a couple of recovered Dodds can be seen stacked next to the signal box. Comparing the two pictures, there seems to have been other track work, with the double slip reduced to a single lead plus new traps protecting the dock line. After the passenger train service was withdrawn in April 1961 the station continued to be served by goods trains until total closure in April 1965. (Dr I. C. Allen/Transport Treasury)

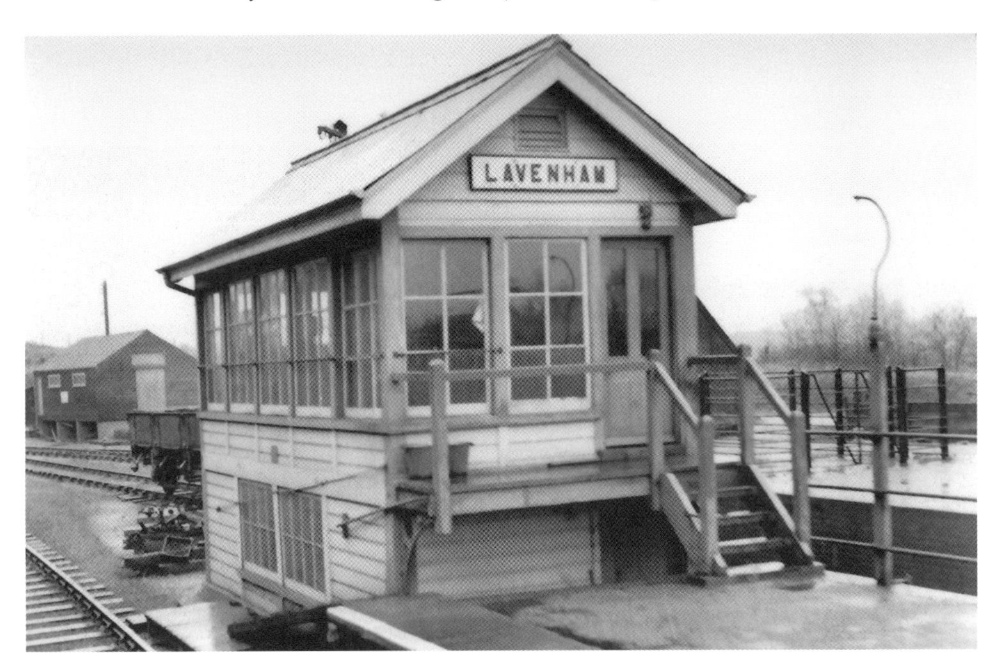

Lavenham signal box seen on 3 April 1961, which was a week before the passenger service was withdrawn. As can be seen, the previously mentioned twelve points had already been removed. The signal box was fitted with a twenty-six-lever Saxby & Farmer frame and was opened in 1892 and closed on 14 October 1962; it was all wood construction and measured 23 feet by 10 feet 4 inches. After closure the signal box was demolished. (Railway Correspondence & Travel Society Archive)

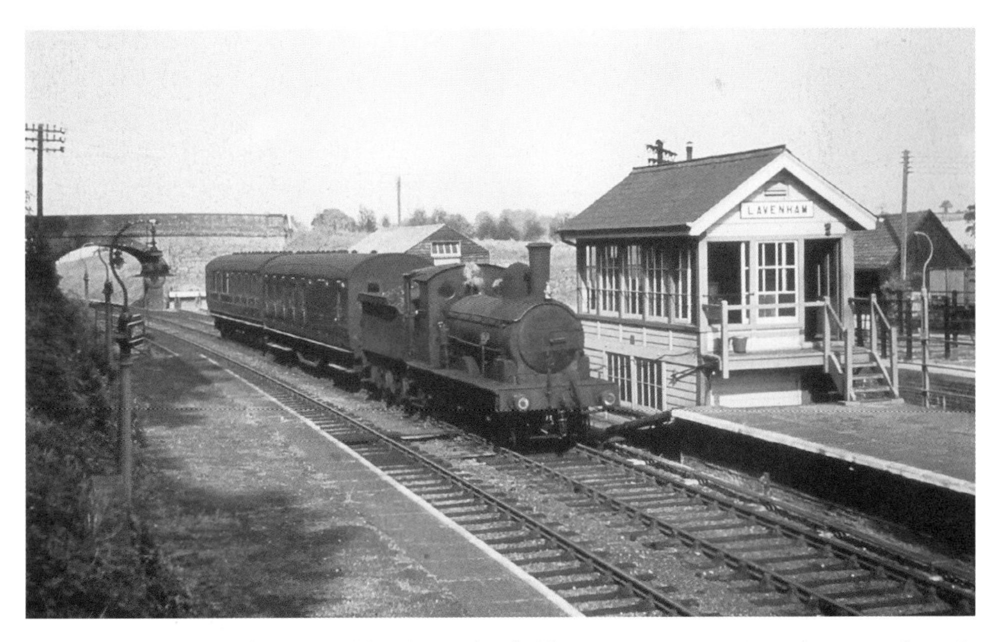

A view of a Long Melford-bound local train hauled by J15 No. 65477. Lavenham was the only crossing place for passenger trains on the branch. The branch had benefitted from an upgrade to electric tablet working from 1916. (BR/CVRPL Collection)

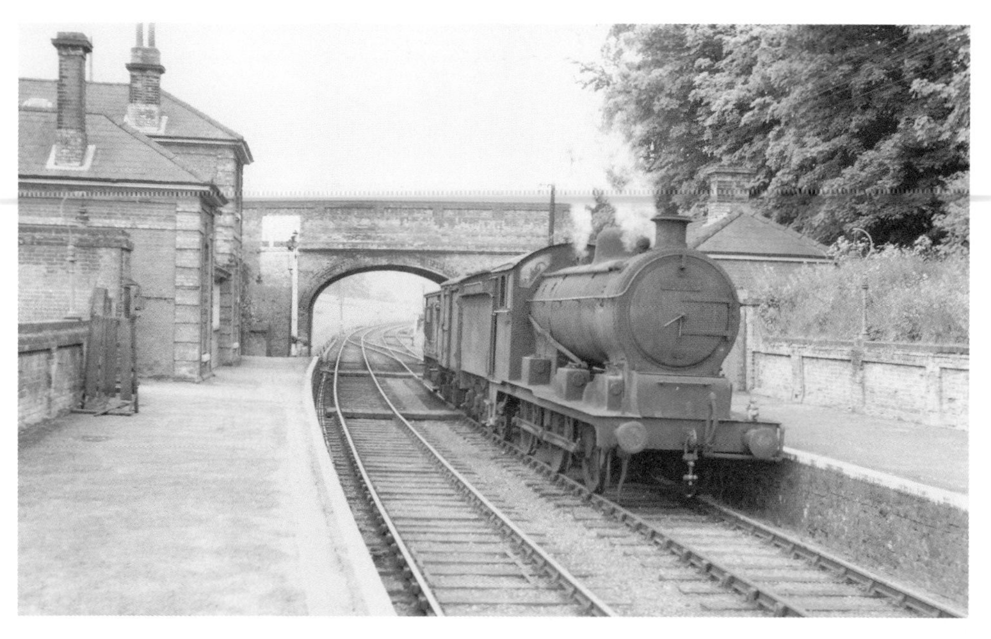

LNER J19 class locomotive No. 64656 stands in the Down platform loop with a very short train of one covered wagon and a brake van, a tiny load for such a powerful engine. The station had over bridges at both ends which survive to this day; unfortunately, the station does not. (Dr I. C. Allen/Transport Treasury)

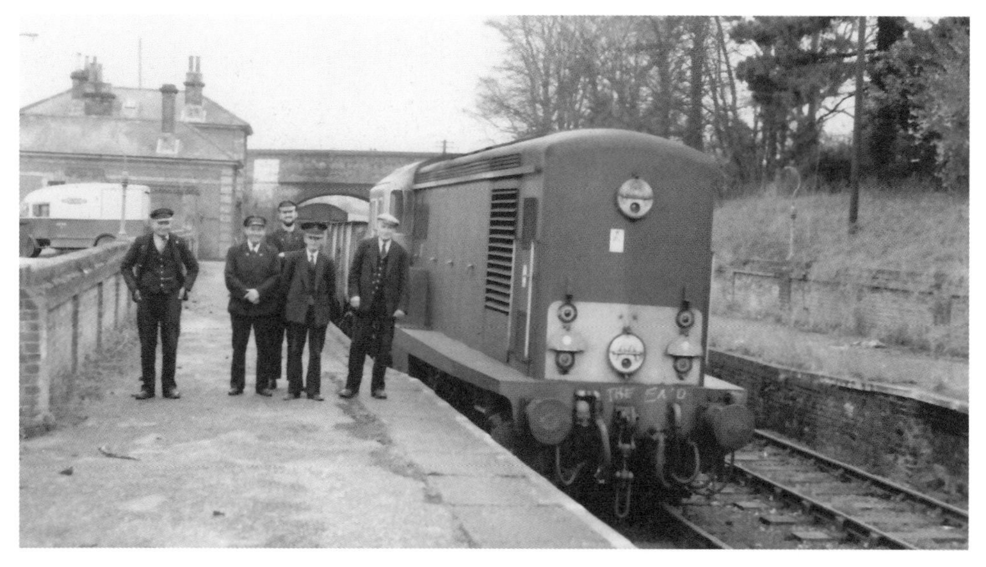

The train crew and stationmaster line up for a picture on the very last day, 15 April 1965, next to locomotive No. D8221 plus its train. Freight facilities were officially withdrawn on and from 19 April, a bad day for many stations in East Anglia. The section of track between this station and Long Melford Junction had been lifted during the summer of 1962; the remaining line to Bury remained for a short while before it too was lifted by the scrap men. Their task was completed by the summer of 1966. (Dr I. C. Allen/Transport Treasury)

Cockfield

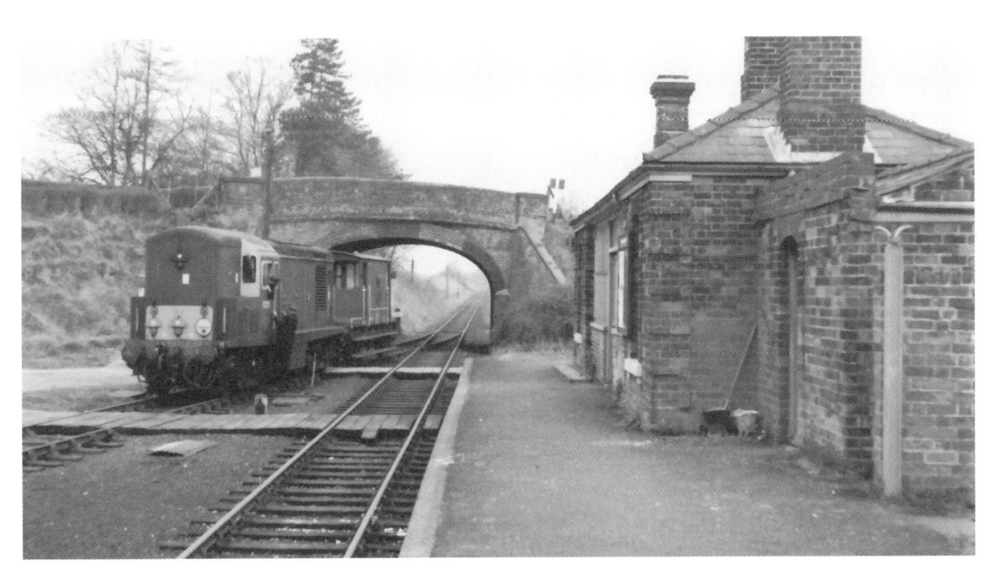

Class 15 diesel D82xx shunts a brake van in the loop siding at Cockfield between October 1962 and April 1965. The remaining freight ran to and from Bury St Edmunds daily and served the three remaining stations on the branch. (Dr I. C. Allen/Transport Treasury)

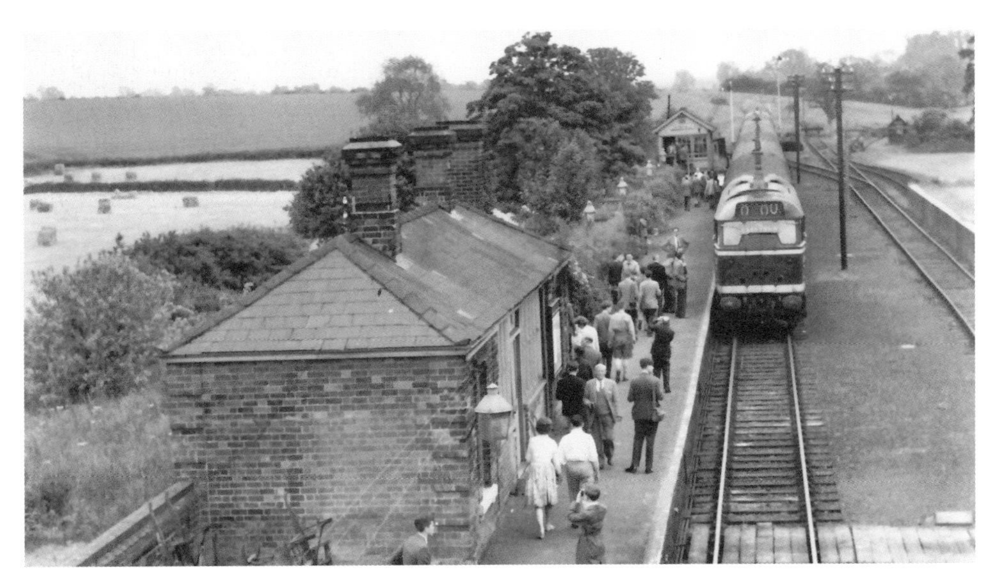

The last through passenger train to transverse the whole line was the ramblers' special which ran on 4 June 1961; it is seen here standing at the station on the outward leg. The train had originated at Liverpool Street station and had travelled by way of Marks Tey to Sudbury, Long Melford to Bury and returned back to London via the same route; it was hauled by diesel locomotive No. D5537. There are many photographs of this special at the various stations; it carried a headboard that said 'The Last Train'. (A. E. Bennett/Transport Treasury)

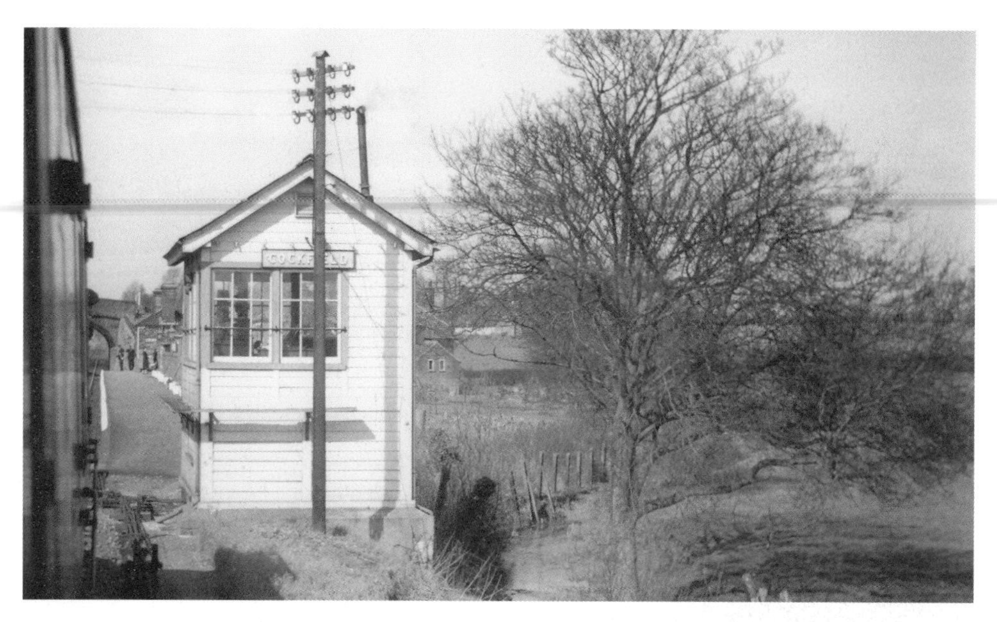

View of the signal box taken from the train on 11 November 1961; the signal box was at the Lavenham end of the station at the end of the platform ramp, a stream ran behind the structure which required substantial concrete foundations. The station was upgraded to electric tablet working in 1916 and became a tablet station, although passenger trains were not allowed to cross at this location. The signal box survived the withdrawal of the passenger service and continued to be used for the daily freight service until it closed in October 1962. (R. E. Vincent/Transport Treasury)

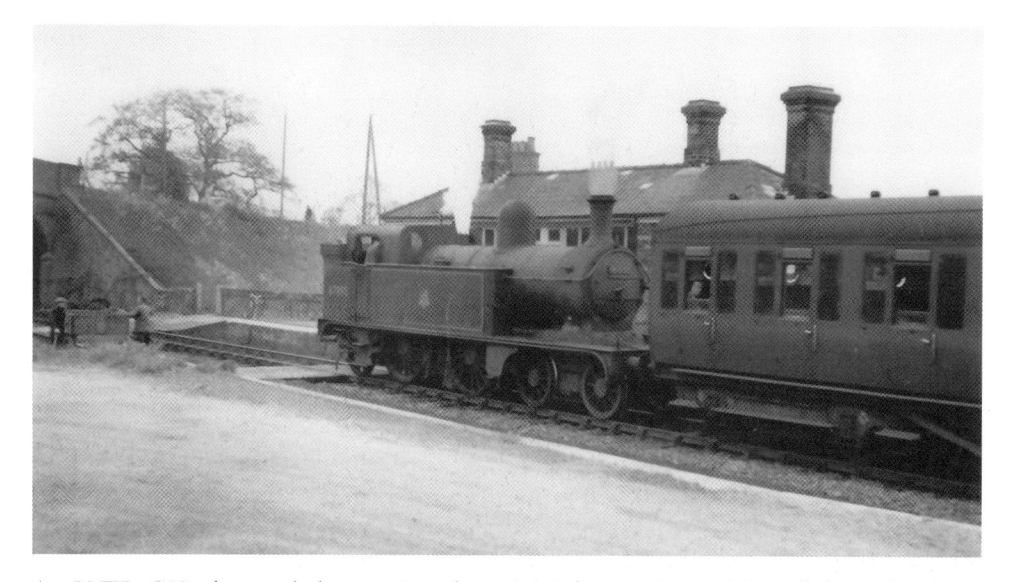

An LNER C12 class tank locomotive; these 4-4-2 locomotives originated from the Great Northern Railway and were built between 1898 and 1907. Although undated, this view shows No. 67395 on an Up passenger working, standing at the station sometime during the 1950s. These engines finished their days allocated to Bury St Edmunds shed, but could be seen on the Stour Valley and Saffron Walden branches in earlier times. (Dr I. C. Allen/Transport Treasury)

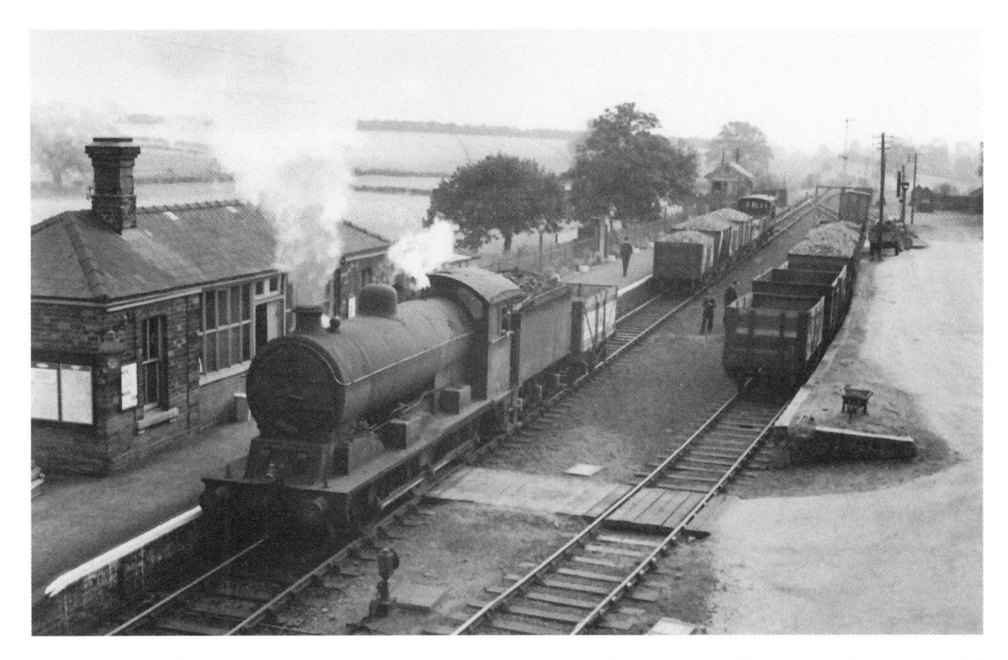

A busy scene showing J20 No. 64678 shunting wagons at the station in the 1950s; these powerful engines were often seen on freight workings over the branch. The layout at the station was very basic with a single loop siding with a head shunt and short spur. The arrival of the daily goods train would see a hive of activity at the station before things returned to normal after the train had departed. During the Second World War the line would have seen a continuous stream of trains carrying goods and wartime materials. (Dr I. C. Allen/Transport Treasury)

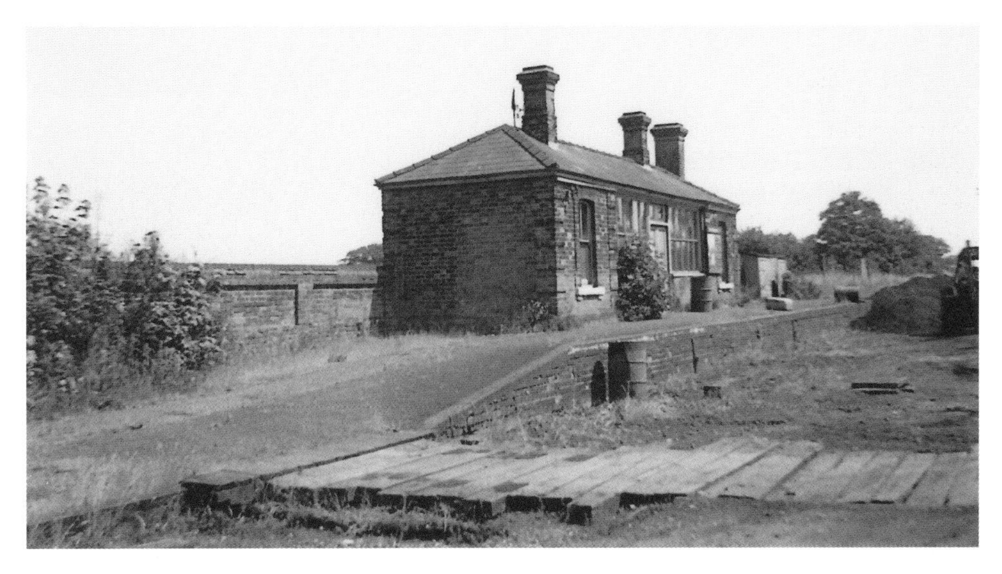

Freight facilities were withdrawn completely from the remaining Bury branch stations on and from 19 April 1965. In this view taken on 30 June 1966 the track had already been lifted, just leaving the platform and station building, which surprisingly still stand to this day, albeit in need of a bit of restoration. (Railway Correspondence & Travel Society Archive)

Welnetham

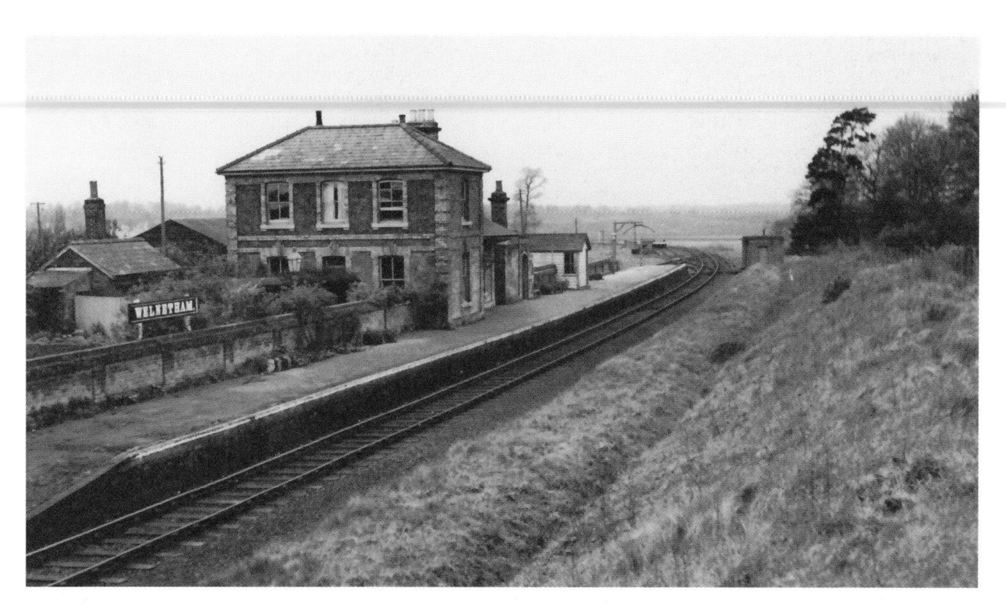

A general view of the station, taken looking in a northerly direction towards Bury St Edmunds. The station had a simple layout with two connections off the single line worked from the adjacent ground frame. There was originally a signal box containing an eighteen-lever Dutton frame at the north end of the platform which had been removed by the LNER in 1926 and replaced by a three-lever ground frame, released by the section tablet. The station closed to passengers on 10 April 1961 and remained as a public delivery siding for goods traffic until 13 July 1964, when the station closed completely. (C. Gammell/Photos from the Fifties)

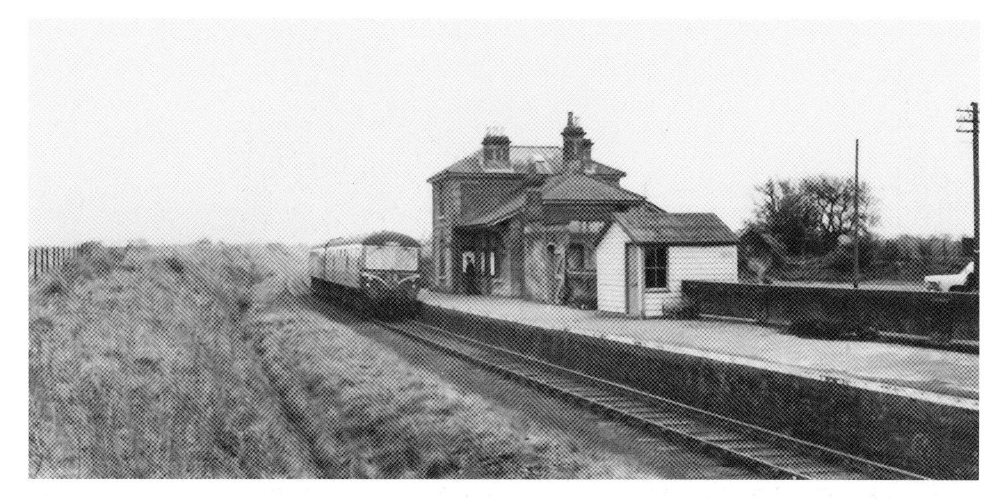

A Cravens-type diesel multiple unit, later designated Class 105, calls at the station on the last day of service with a train for Bury St Edmunds. DMUs had taken over the passenger services from 1 January 1959, which resulted in service improvements on the Stour and Colne lines but the Bury line was reduced to just three Down and four Up services in its final year. (Stations UK)

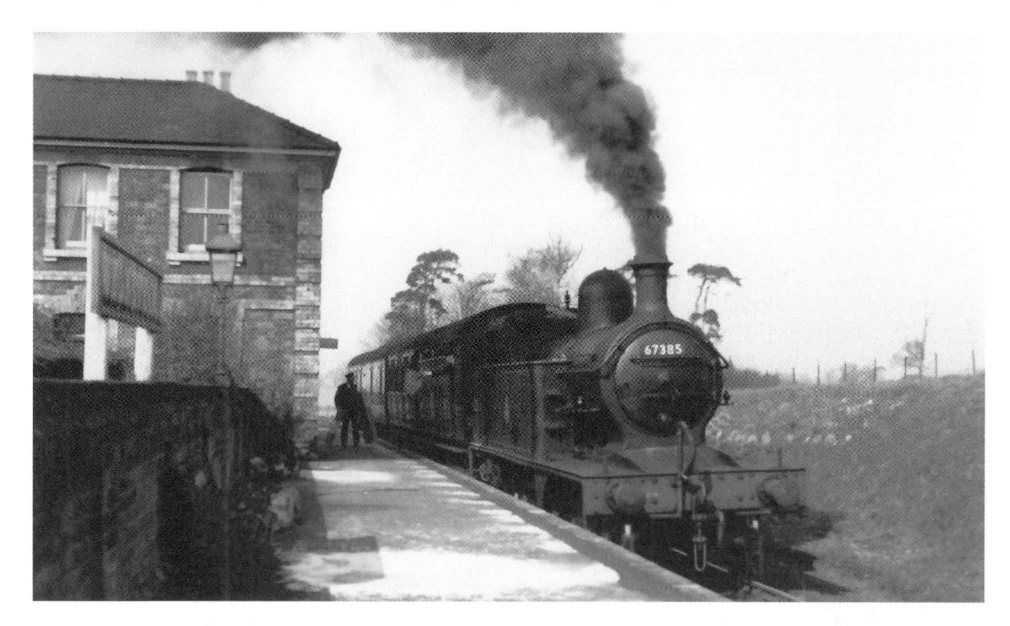

An LNER C12 class locomotive, No. 67385, calls at the station with a Long Melford-bound train. Although undated, this has to be before April 1955 when the engine was withdrawn for scrapping; the last three of these engines had finished their days based at Bury St Edmunds shed. These locomotives could be seen on many of the branch lines in East Anglia, even straying as far as Swaffham in Norfolk. (Dr I. C. Allen/Transport Treasury)

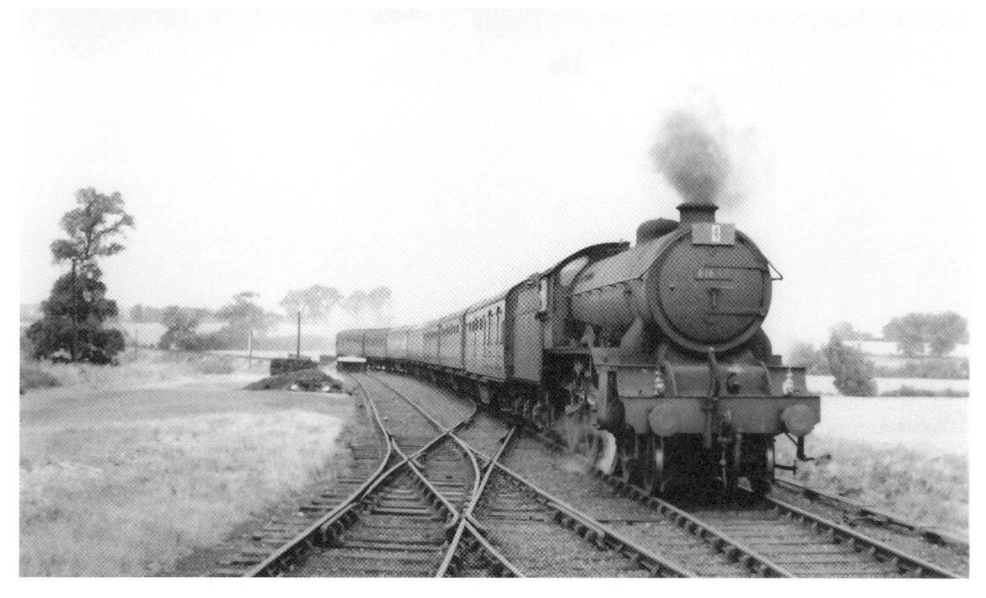

B17/6 class locomotive No. 61653 *Huddersfield Town* is seen approaching the station while working a Manchester to Clacton excursion train on a summer Saturday in the 1950s. These through expresses were for the benefit of Butlins holiday camp at Clacton; later on in the 1950s they started from Leicester and after the Bury line closed they ran via the Stour Valley line. The simple layout of the goods sidings at the station can clearly been seen. (Dr I. C. Allen/Transport Treasury)

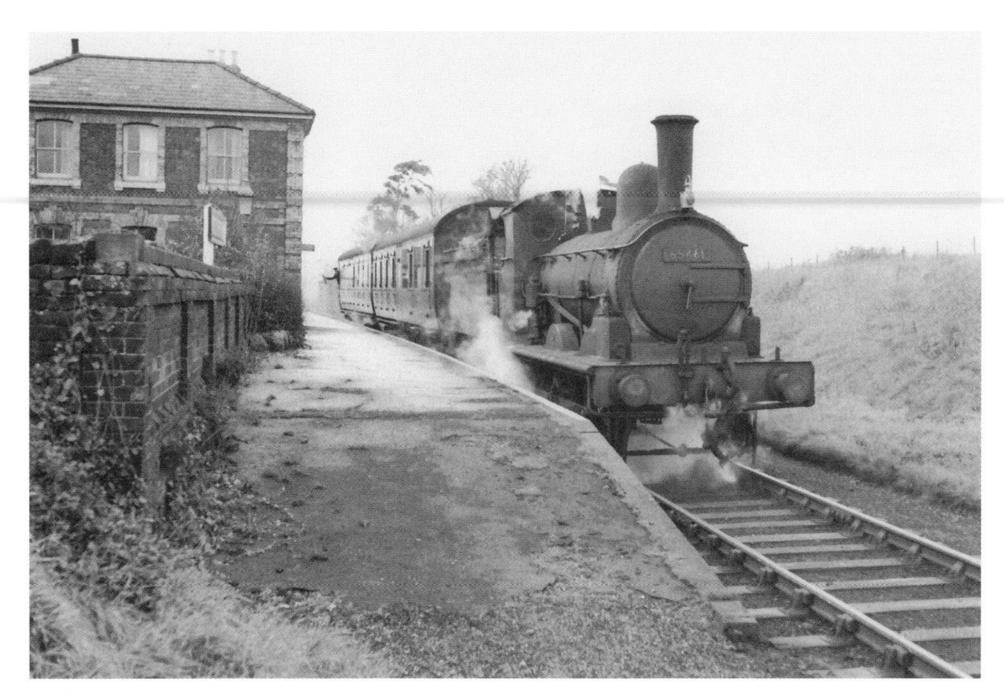

J15 class locomotive No. 65461 is seen departing from the station with a southbound local passenger service. Locomotive No. 65461 was a Cambridge-based engine, having been at that depot since June 1947, and just survived into the 1960s, being withdrawn from service on 28 April 1960. (Dr I. C. Allen/Transport Treasury)

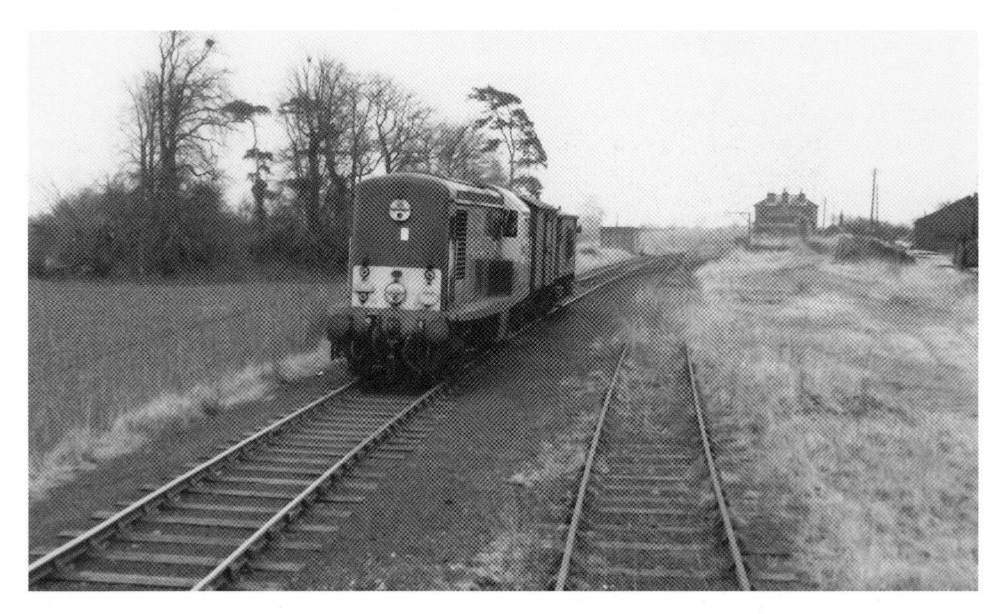

An unidentified BR Class 15 diesel locomotive of the D82xx series is seen passing Welnetham siding en route back to Bury St Edmunds with a very short freight train consisting of one covered van and brake. The station can be seen in the background; the weeds seem to be taking a hold in the station siding. (Dr I. C. Allen/Transport Treasury)

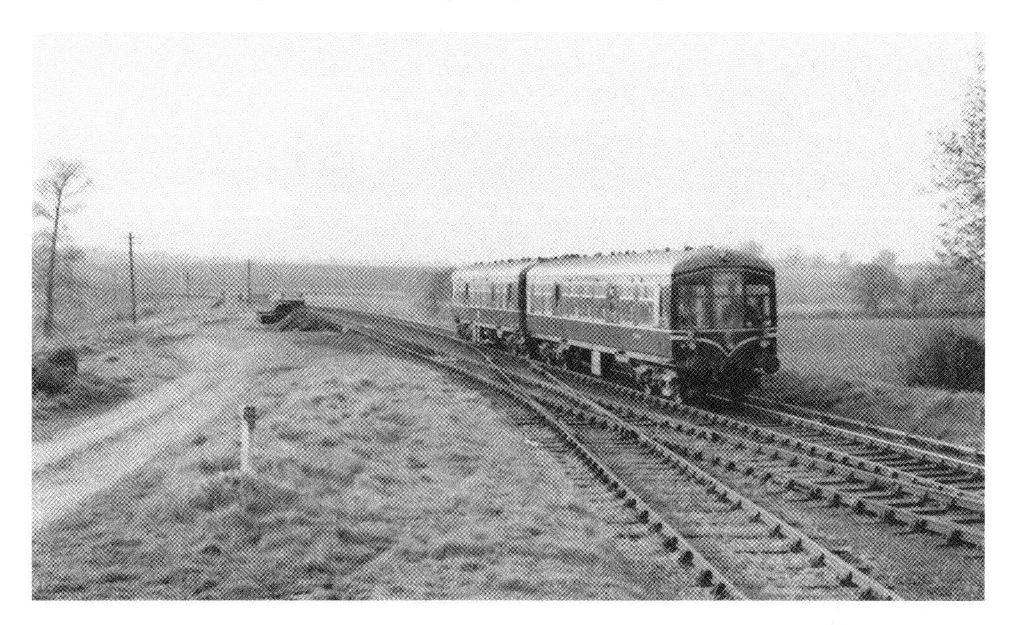

A southbound Derby lightweight DMU passes over the yard point work as it enters the station during the period between 1 January 1959 and 10 April 1961. Note the milepost on the left. The siding accommodation consisted of a long head shunt and spur running back into a dock level with the north end of the passenger platform; the two were connected by a single slip. (Dr I. C. Allen/Transport Treasury)

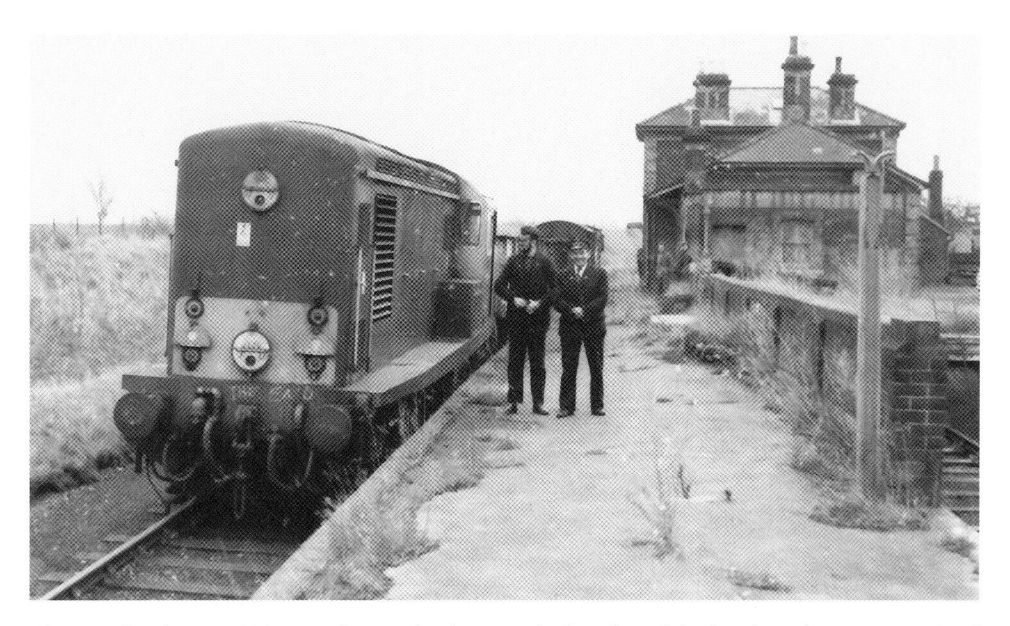

Class 15 diesel No. D8220 stands at Welnetham on the last day of the freight-only service, 15 April 1965, while the train crew pose for the photographer. Note the weeds taking hold on the platform; the station had been unstaffed since April 1961 and had closed completely in July 1964, although trains continued to pass through until April 1965. The station is now a private dwelling; the original buildings still stand albeit extended to suit their new use. (Dr I. C. Allen/Transport Treasury)

Bury St Edmunds Eastgate

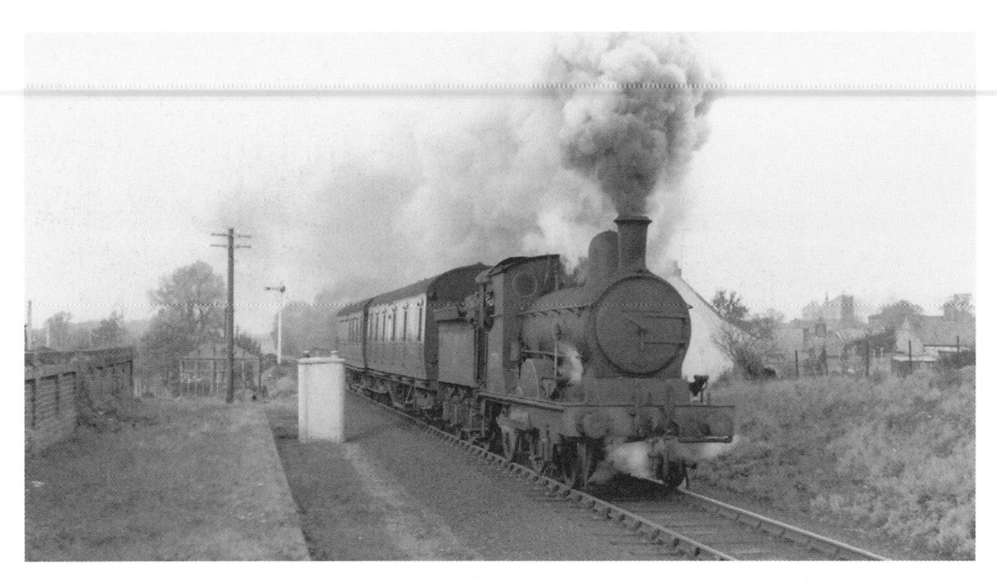

Veteran LNER E4 class No. 72785 is seen at the remains of the station with a branch Up passenger service. Although undated, this was probably during the 1950s; this locomotive was the last of the class to be withdrawn from service and was selected for preservation as part of the national collection and is currently at Bressingham Gardens Steam Museum near Diss. (Dr I. C. Allen/Transport Treasury)

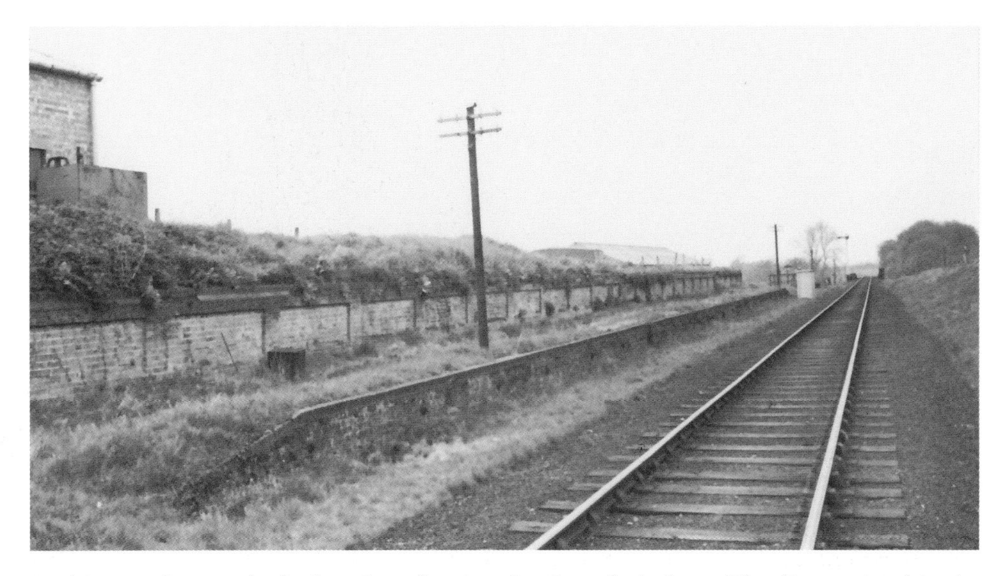

Looking north towards the junction, showing the disused platform. The distant signal in the background is Bury St Edmunds Down branch fixed distant, the junction with the main line being about ½ mile further on. The station had originally closed back in 1909; this part of the old line is now buried under the A14 trunk road. (Stations UK)

Bury St Edmunds

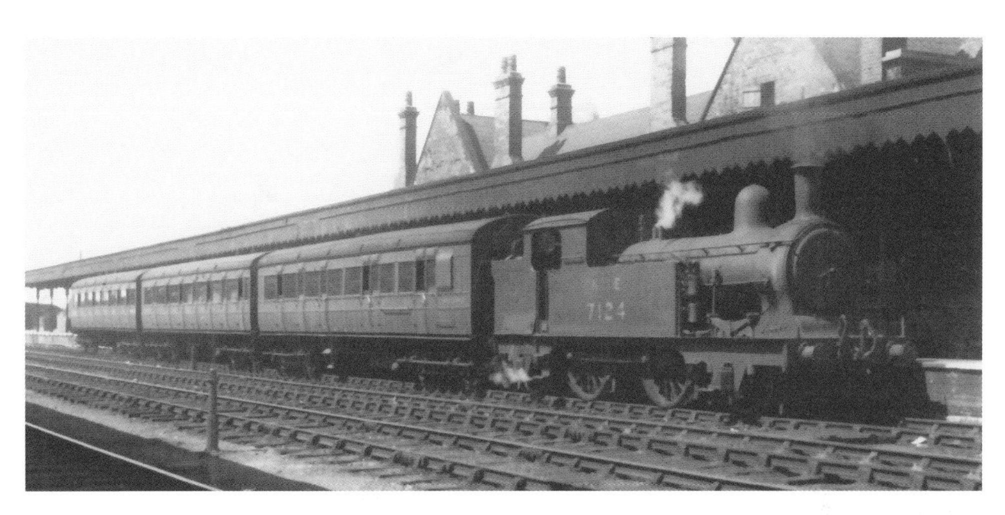

Five and a half months after the formation of British Railways, F4 class 7124, still in its LNER livery, is seen standing at the Down platform with a local passenger train on 18 May 1948. At this time the station had a Down through line and an Up carriage road avoiding both platform lines. (Stephenson Locomotive Society 28868)

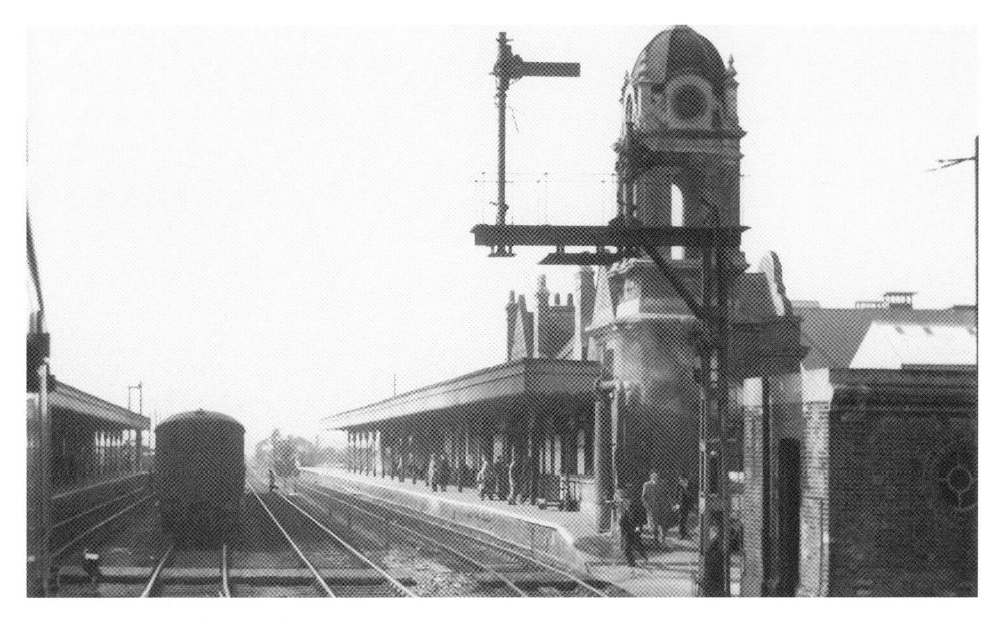

A general view of the station taken from an arriving branch train which was completing its journey from Marks Tey via Sudbury and Long Melford in1952. The lines shown are, from left to right: the Up platform, Up through siding, Down through and Down platform. The bracket signal shown is the down through starter controlled from Bury St Edmunds Junction signal box, with the platform signal controlled by the yard signal box and slotted by the junction signal box. (R. E. Vincent/Transport Treasury)

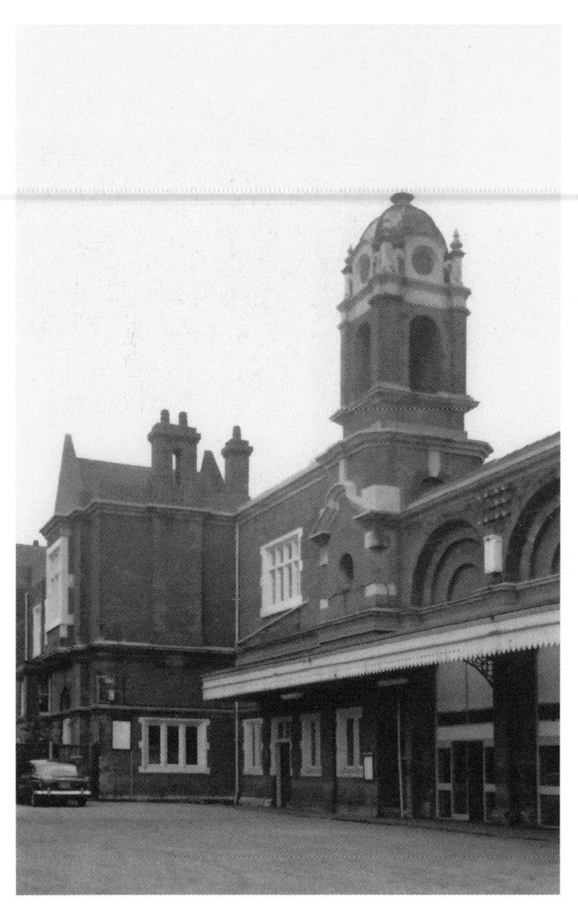

Left: A view taken in the station forecourt of the Up side main buildings with the magnificent towers. This view was taken on 16 August 1968. Even in its reduced layout the station continues to give good service, with a regular passenger service between Ipswich and Cambridge and also a service running from Ipswich to Ely and Peterborough. Freight trains also use this route between Ipswich and Felixstowe and the north via Ely and Peterborough as an alternative to running via London. (Railway Correspondence & Travel Society Archive)

Below: 2MT class No. 46465 arriving at the platform on a local passenger working. Five of these versatile machines had been allocated to Cambridge and Colchester sheds and could be seen working on various main and branch lines in the area. In the background on the right can be seen the engine shed and depot. The large station layout was originally controlled by two signal boxes; the yard signal box is still giving good service. (L. R. Freeman/ Transport Treasury)

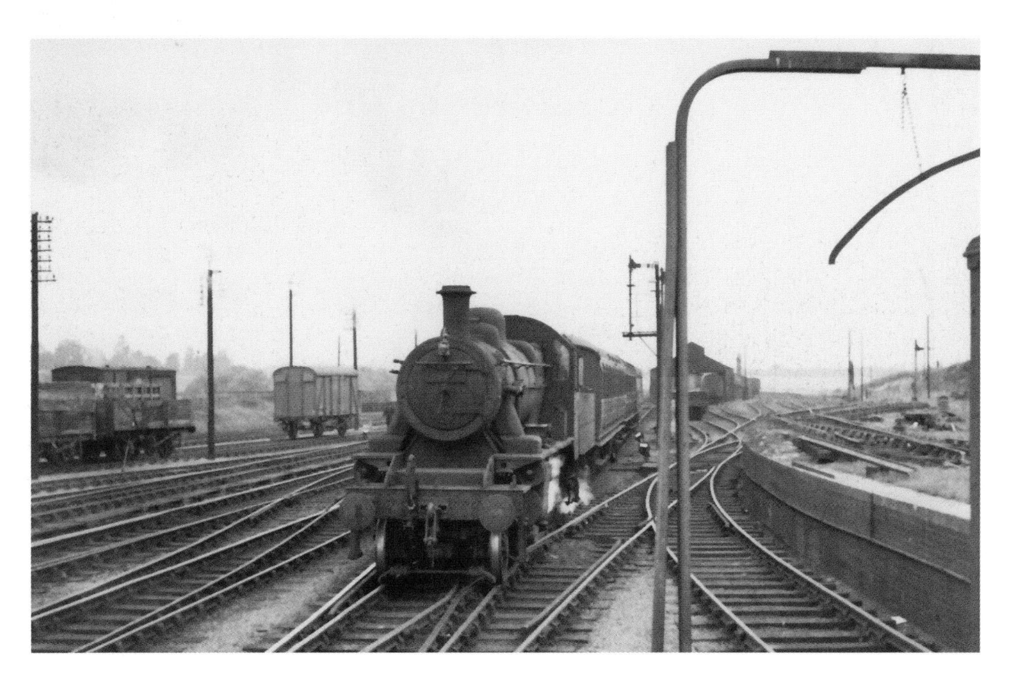

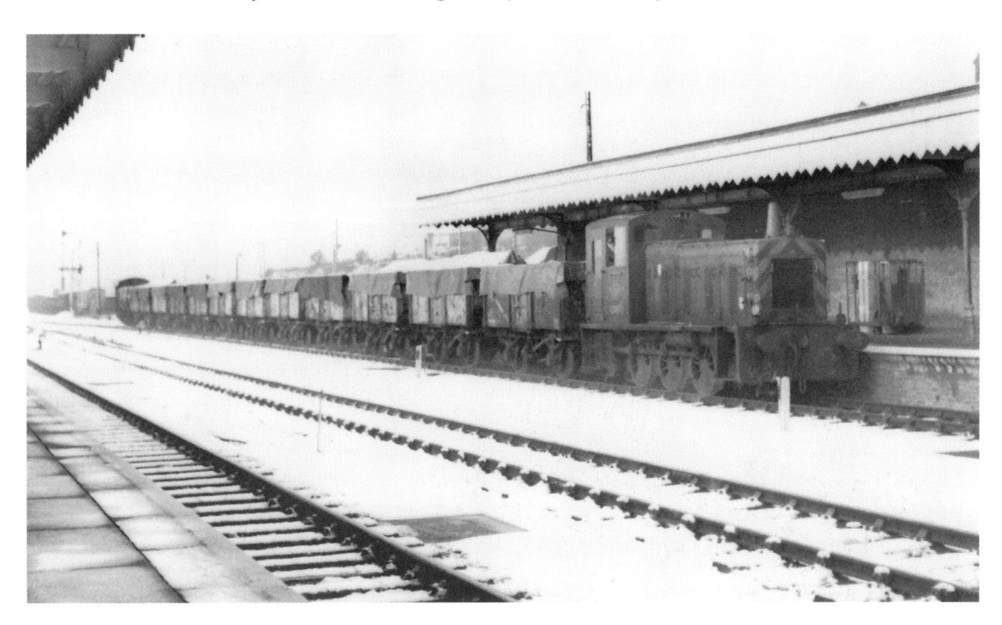

A small 0-6-0 diesel shunter, now designated BR Class 03, with a rake of tarpaulin-covered trucks moving through the Down eastbound platform. The Down through line had been abolished in March 1965, and by the time of this view on 7 January 1967 the track had been lifted and the Up through line had been shortened to a siding with a buffer stop erected at the Ipswich end of the station. (Railway Correspondence & Travel Society Archive)

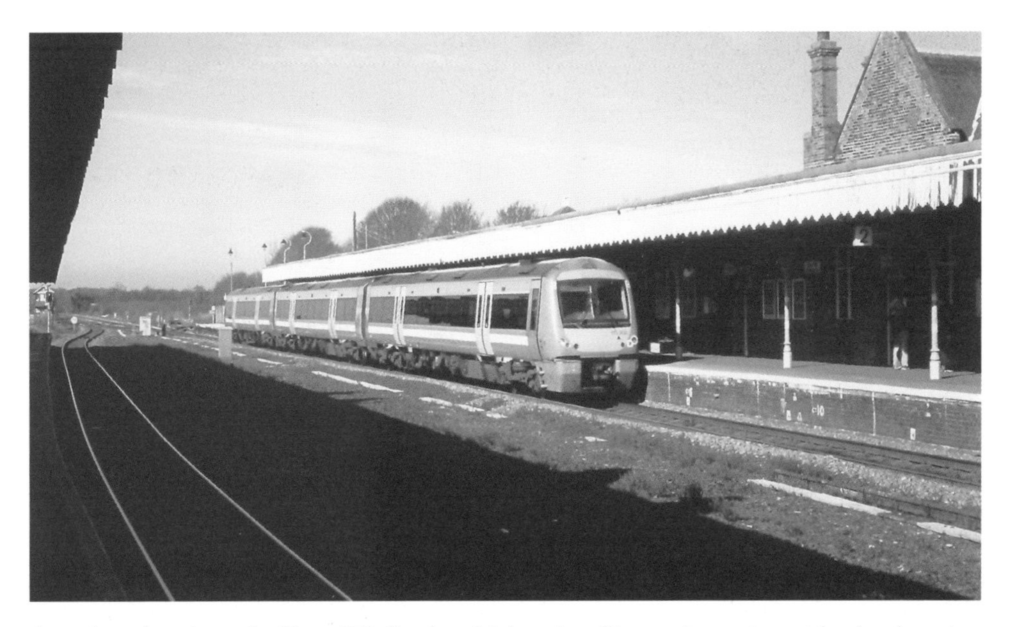

A modern-day view of a Class 170 diesel multiple unit calling at the station with a local service. All the centre roads have long been lifted, just leaving the two platform lines; all the remaining sidings are now at the Cambridge end of the station, the remaining layout being controlled from Bury St Edmunds Yard signal box, which controls trains going west towards Chippenham Junction, and to the east it fringes with Colchester power signalling centre. (Ray Bishop)

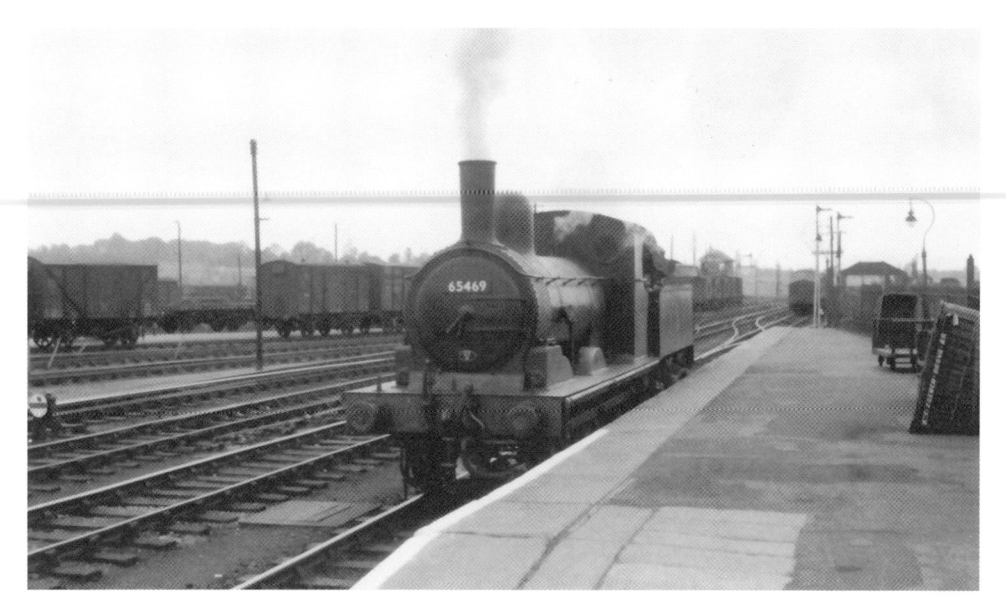

J15 class No. 65469 standing at the Down eastbound platform at the station, waiting for its next working, as seen on 11 June 1960. At this time East Anglia was being slowly dieselised, with DMUs, railbuses and diesel locomotive-hauled trains on the longer journeys. By 1962 the region was to be completely steam free. (R. C. Riley/Transport Treasury)

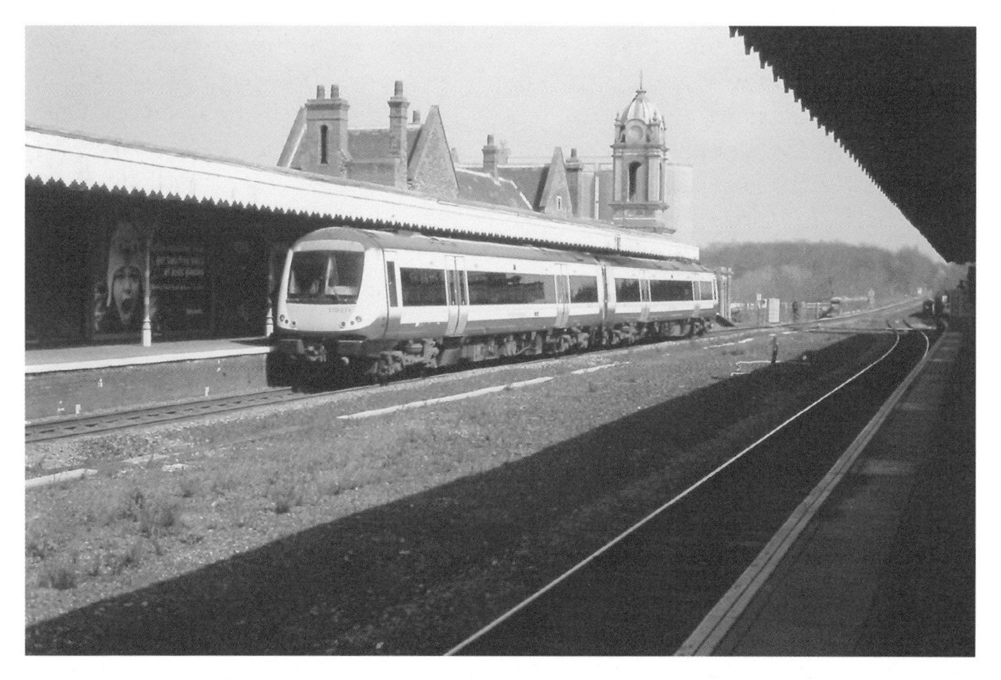

A two-car version of a Class 170 DMU departs eastbound on a local working towards Ipswich. The station retains all its fine features, including the magnificent towers on both platforms. Like many stations now, the passenger usage has grown from 210,000 annually ten years ago to some 500,000+ in 2014, justifying an increasing service. (Ray Bishop)

The Saffron Walden Branch: Audley End to Bartlow

When the Northern & Eastern Railway was sanctioned on 4 July 1836 to build the main line from London to Cambridge, it became clear that Saffron Walden was to be bypassed by the new railway; the nearest station was to be Wenden, later renamed to Audley End, which was 2 miles from the town.

It was to be the Eastern Counties Railway which finally built the main line from Newport to Brandon via Cambridge and Ely. A request to build a branch to Saffron Walden was dismissed by the ECR, which led local people to form the Saffron Walden Railway; powers were obtained in July 1861. Raising the necessary finance proved difficult, but with assistance from the new Great Eastern Railway the line was completed and duly opened on 23 November 1865.

Prior to the opening, the Saffron Walden Railway Company had obtained additional powers in June 1863 to extend their line to Bartlow on the Stour Valley line. Construction was slow but eventually the line opened on 22 October 1866; the branch had its own platform at Bartlow and was connected to the Great Eastern station by a short pathway, the actual railway forming a junction slightly to the west of Bartlow station.

The Saffron Walden Railway struggled as an independent concern until it was declared bankrupt in 1869 and an official receiver was appointed. The railway remained in his hands until the whole concern was bought outright by the Great Eastern Railway (GER) on 1 January 1877. Saffron Walden received new sidings and a new signal box and signalling by 1891. The residents of Ashdon petitioned the GER to provide a halt on the line near to their village; this took place when a plain earth and clinker platform with a wooden sleeper face was provided on 14 August 1911, although no buildings were provided until an old coach body was used as accommodation from 1916.

After the First World War the railways were grouped into four large companies and the old GER became part of the LNER on and from 1 January 1923. Two major rail strikes at the beginning of the LNER regime forced more passengers and freight off the branch, some never returning. The remaining years of the 1920s and 30s remained fairly quiet, although there was a slight increase in passenger usage with the coming of paid holidays. The train service at this time reached eighteen trips to the main line, with only seven starting at or going to Bartlow.

In the autumn of 1939, a petroleum depot opened near Saffron Walden. Many special trains were run to the new depot, usually routed by Shelford and Bartlow; this facility closed in 1949. Heavy wartime use of all of the railways took its toll as maintenance was minimal; diversions regularly took place over the branch. The LNER ceased to exist, with the nationalisation of the railways taking place from 1 January 1948.

In July 1951, push-and-pull working was introduced over the branch using ex NER G5 0-4-4 tank locomotives plus two adapted ex GER coaches; these in turn were replaced by N7 class locomotives and Gresley-designed push-and-pull sets; some of these workings were extended to Haverhill in 1958, with reversal taking place at Bartlow.

On 25 March 1957, a new halt built by Acrow Engineering was opened by the company for use by their employees in getting to and from work; it was named Acrow Halt and was built out of reinforced concrete. The British Railways modernisation plan of 1955 had proposed the replacement of steam traction with diesel or electric, and in line with this policy diesel railbuses took over the branch workings from 7 July 1958. These vehicles proved unpopular with local passengers but sufficed for the majority of trains, a couple of trips still being run to and from Haverhill.

The Beeching Report, which was published on 27 March 1963, spelt the end for the line. The formal hearing into the future of the railway took place on 13 December 1963, only to be adjourned until the end of the month. The Transport Users' Consultant Committee (TUCC) recommended closure and a date of 2 March 1964 was published by British Rail. This had to be postponed until 7 September 1964 as due process had not been completed by the earlier date.

The last passenger trains ran on Sunday 6 September; railbus No. E79963 was the rostered motive power for duty on this day. Freight was still being handled at Saffron Walden, albeit only for a few more months. Acrow and Ashdon halts both closed on 7 September. A Class 03 shunter was kept at Saffron Walden to haul the remaining freight trips to Audley End. A few weeks later British Railways announced the closure of Saffron Walden to goods traffic; this duly took place on and from 28 December 1964, the last actual freight train having trundled back to Audley End on 24 December.

By late March 1965, the junction between the main line and branch at Audley End had been removed; this also included the Up dock line behind the Up platform. Some of the redundant signals were recovered by December 1965, including some of the branch platform track. The remaining lines remained silent until the summer of 1968 when they were torn up, starting at Audley End and moving onto Saffron Walden and ending at Bartlow; the demolition trains arrived on the branch from the Bartlow end. All of the former railway lines at Audley End were eventually turned over to car parking. Most of the former railway has now disappeared, with many of the cuttings and embankments being filled in or flattened. The station site at Saffron Walden was used as a garage complex until being redeveloped as housing many years later; the station buildings were refurbished as part of the new housing. Acrow Halt remains crumbling away among tree and bush growth, Ashdon Halt still stands together with its rotting coach body, and the shell of Bartlow Junction signal box stood for many years until the rotting roof timbers collapsed in on themselves.

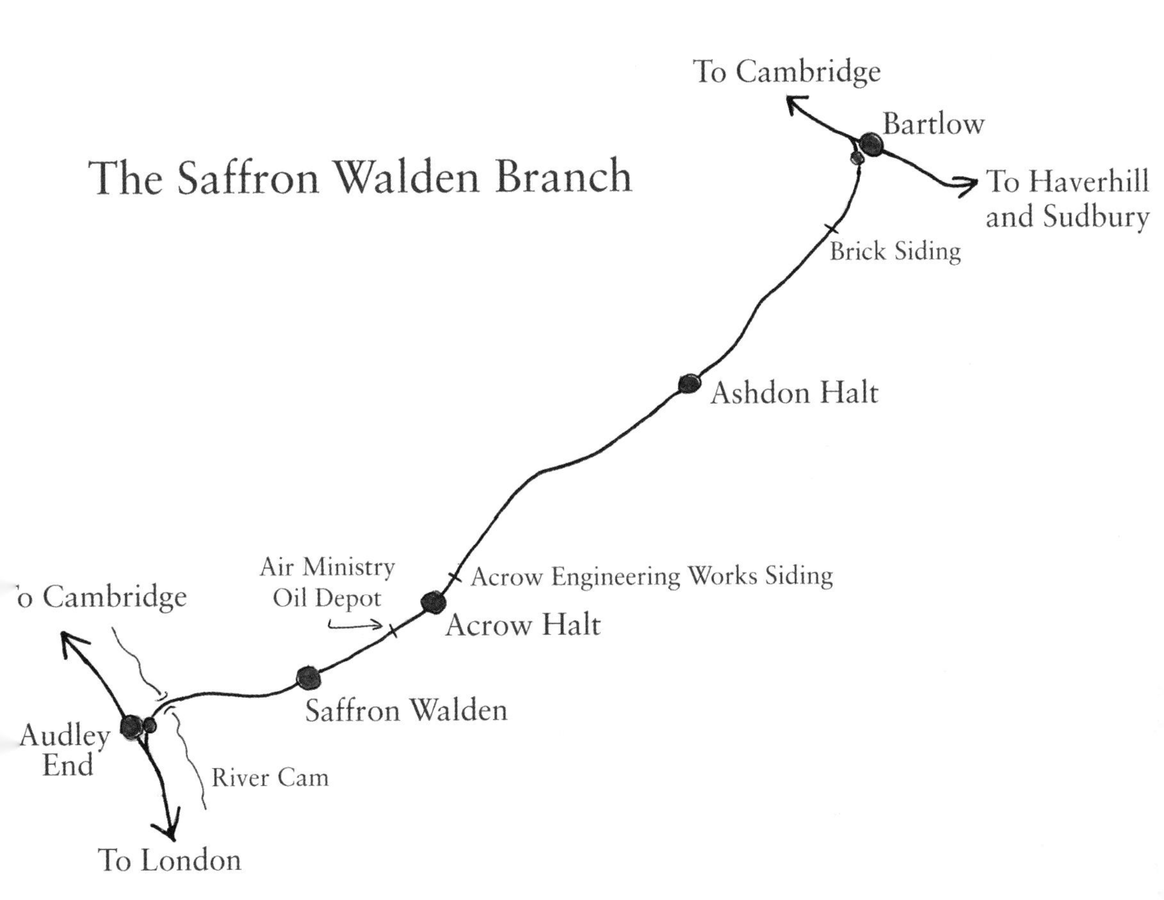
The Saffron Walden Branch
To Cambridge
Bartlow
To Haverhill
and Sudbury
Brick Siding
Ashdon Halt
Air Ministry
Oil Depot
Acrow Engineering Works Siding
Acrow Halt
o Cambridge
Saffron Walden
Audley
End
River Cam
To London

Bartlow Branch Platform

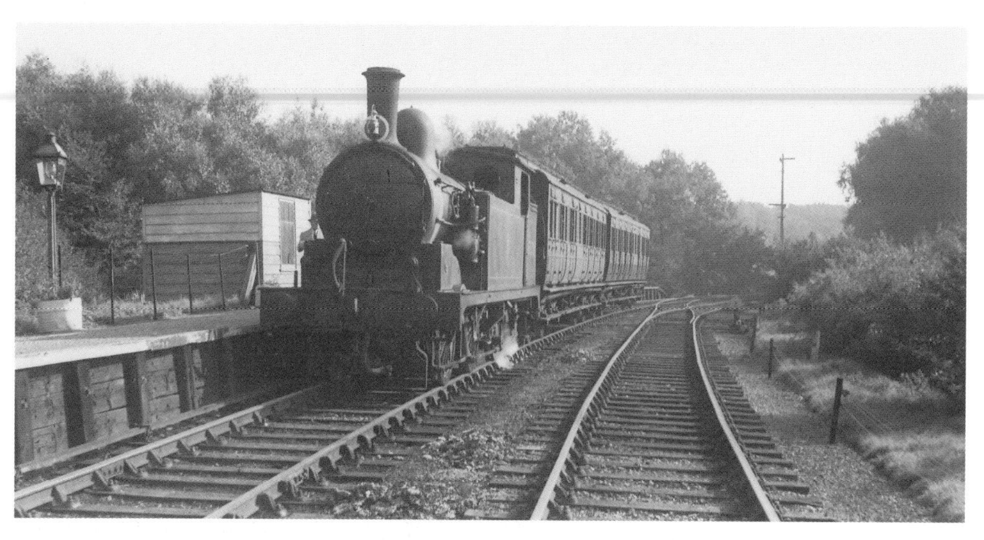

G5 class locomotive No. 67322 is seen at the branch platform with a push-and-pull working, getting ready for the return journey to Saffron Walden. The G5s had been transferred to the branch to work the service, having previously been used on the Palace Gates branch. The three locomotives continued to work the branch until replaced by the N7s in October 1956. (Dr. I. C. Allen/Transport Treasury)

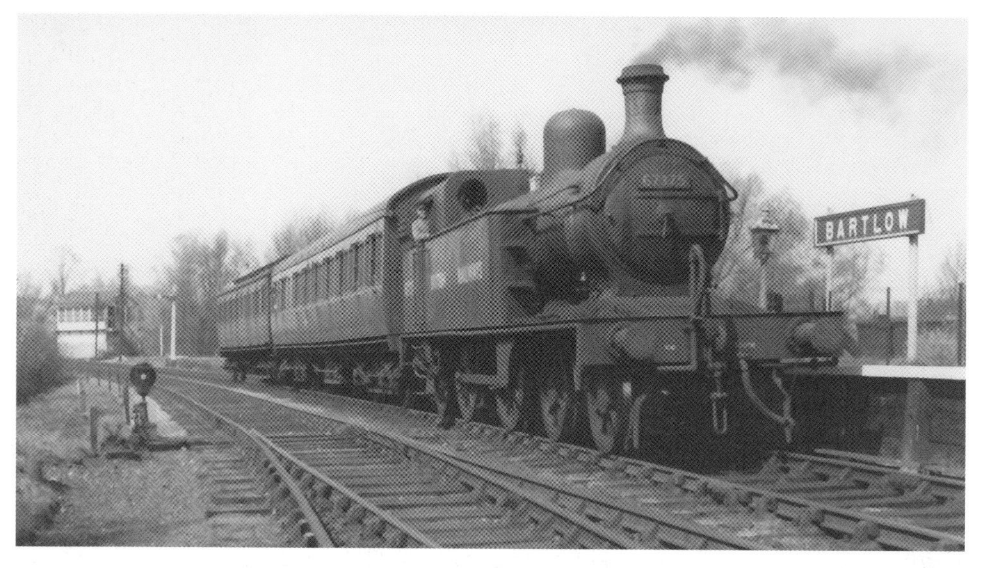

LNER C12 class stands with two coaches at the branch platform awaiting departure. The C12s first appeared on the branch in 1938 when the G4s were withdrawn or moved on before scrapping; two of the class were sub-shedded at Saffron Walden. The junction signal box can be seen in the background; the line in the foreground was the run-round loop. (Stephenson Locomotive Society – 28654)

Right: The very tall branch Down home and branch Up starting signals survived right up to the line's closure; the down home was worked by lever thirty-eight and up starter by lever four in Bartlow Junction signal box. The branch platform and simple wooden waiting shelter can be seen in the distance. (Paul Smith)

Below: Bartlow Junction signal box, installed in 1891 when new signalling was introduced on the Stour Valley line. Originally, there were two signal boxes at Bartlow until the LNER rationalised signalling and the junction box took control of the whole layout. The junction was originally equipped with a thirty-eight-lever Saxby & Farmer lever frame with twenty working and eighteen spare levers; in 1925 this changed to a thirty-nine-lever frame with thirty-seven working and two spare levers. In 1939 the branch double junction was reduced to a single lead and the signal box was altered to thirty-three working and six spare levers. The signal box closed on 17 April 1966. (N. L. Cadge)

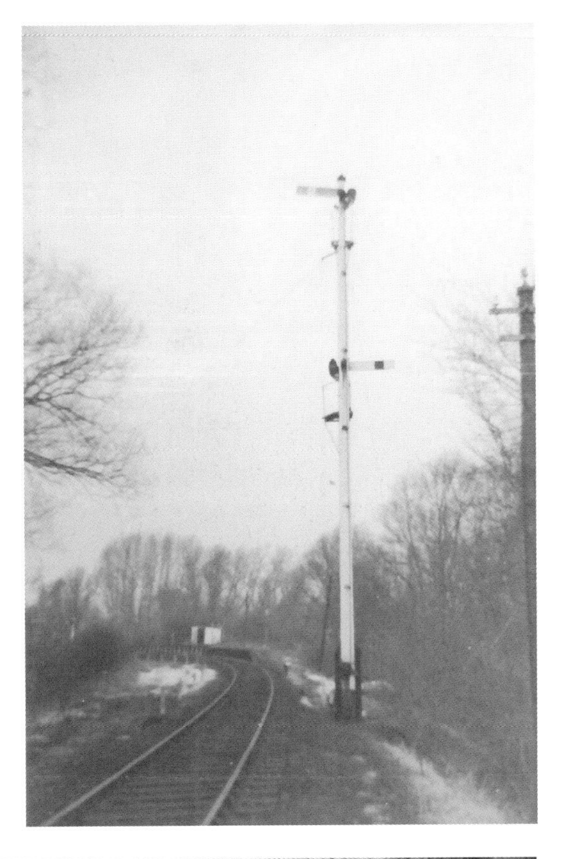

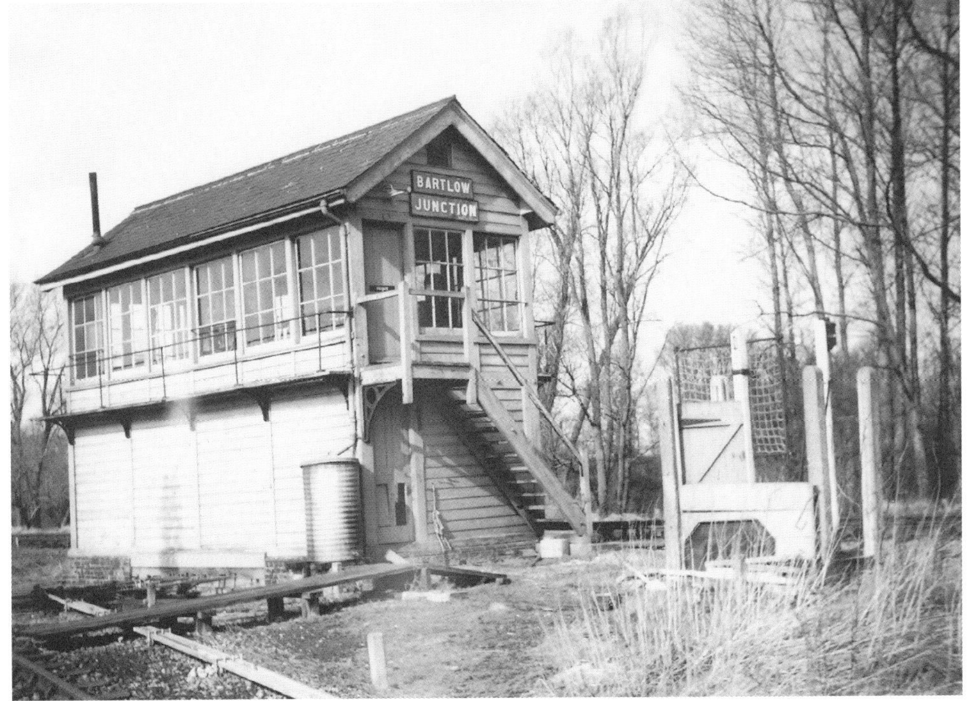

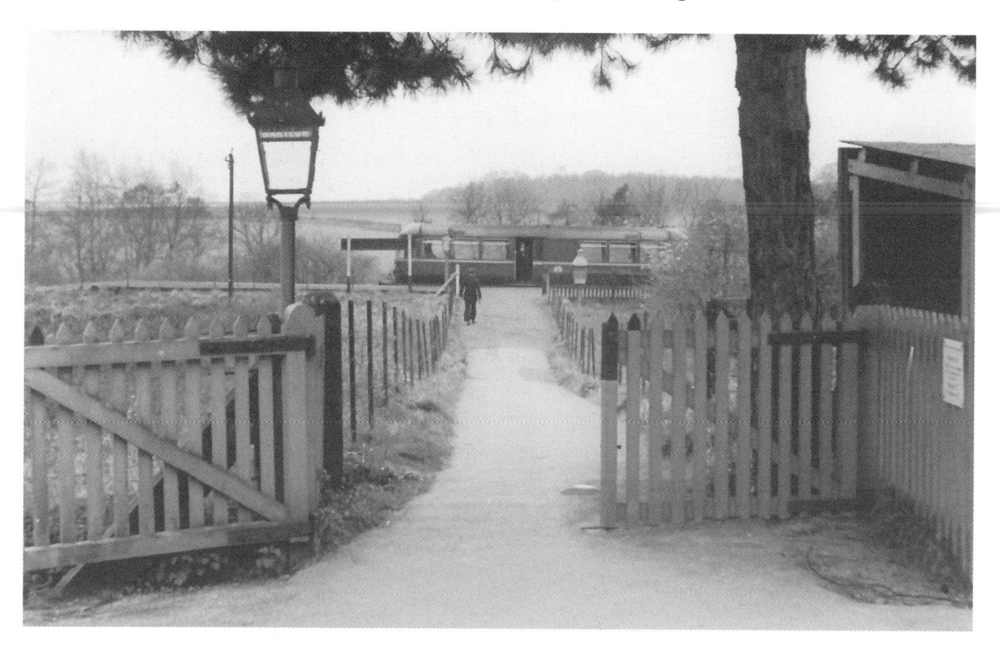

The connecting footpath between the main station and branch platform with a railbus standing waiting to depart. The diesel railbuses were introduced to the branch in July 1958; at first they were unreliable but when most of the gremlins had been sorted out, they were in charge of the branch workings until the end of the passenger service in 1964. (D. Lawrence/Photos from the Fifties)

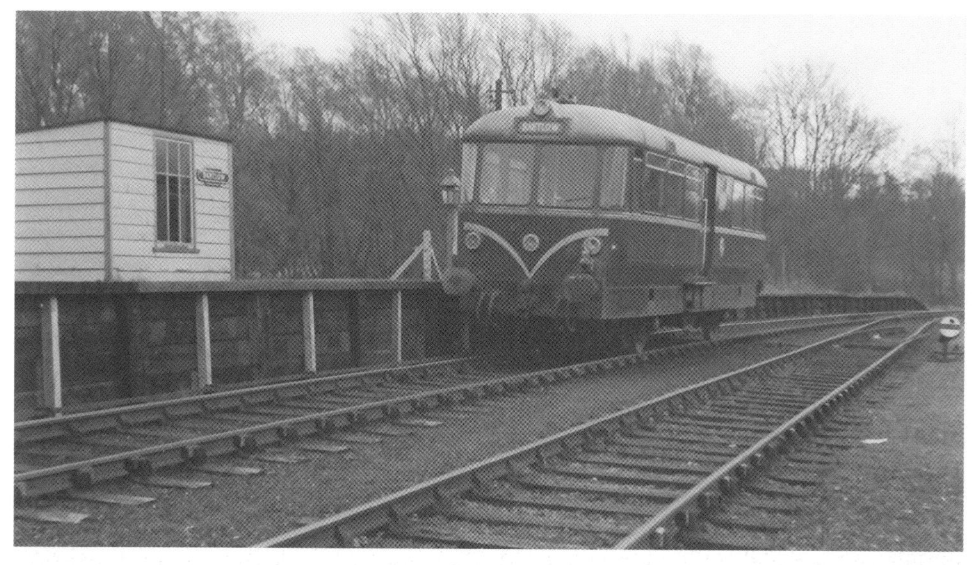

A track-level view of a Waggon und Maschinenbau diesel railbus built in Germany, one of five different types of similar vehicles built for British Railways to be assessed on lightly used branch lines. Five of this design saw service on various branch lines in East Anglia. They could seat fifty-six passengers and had two power-operated doors. Most of the workings shuttled between Saffron Walden and Audley End, with seven workings being extended to Bartlow and three of these continuing on to Haverhill after reversal at Bartlow Junction. (D. Lawrence/Photos from the Fifties)

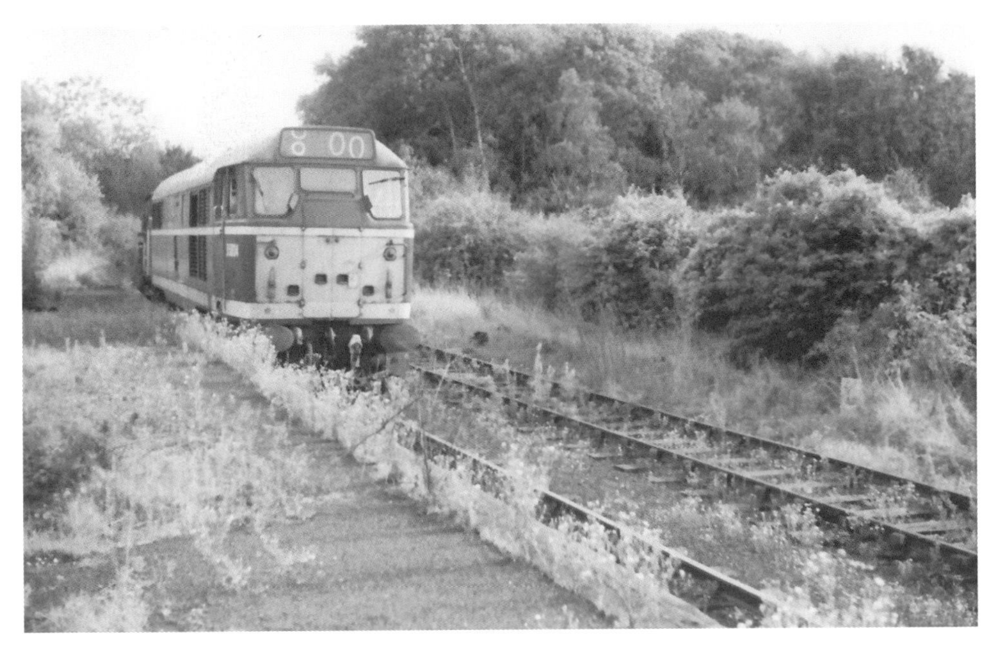

A sad scene from the summer of 1968 as a Brush-type diesel, later designated Class 31, passes through the branch platform with a loaded demolition train en route back to Chesterton Junction Permanent Way Depot. The weeds are already taking hold on the platform and track. All rail activity had ceased on the branch in December 1964, and in March 1967 on the neighbouring Stour Valley line, until the demolition trains arrived in the summer of 1968. (Brian Barham)

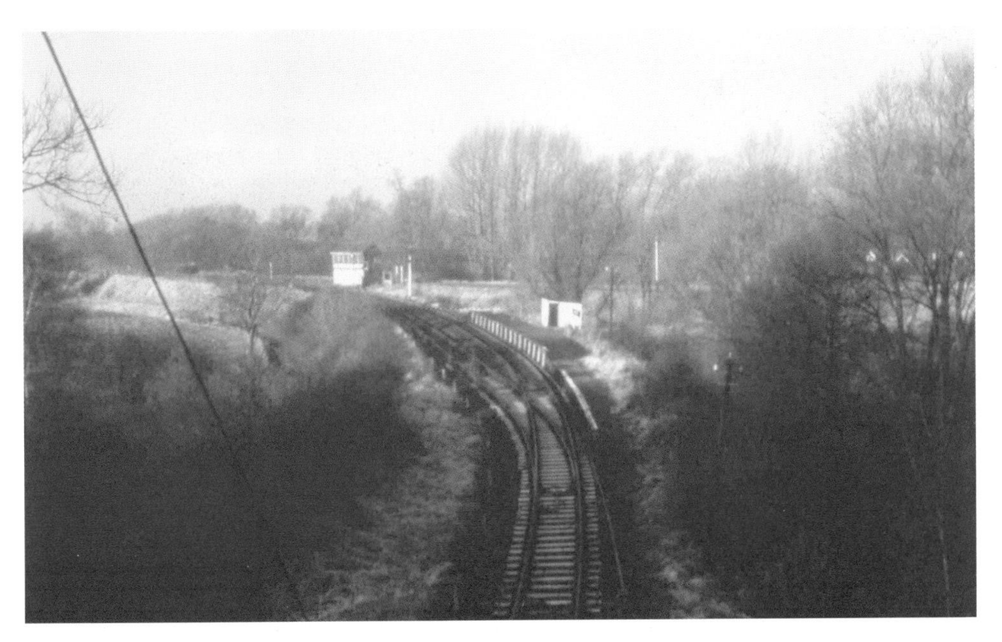

An elevated view taken from the Down home signal post, looking at the branch platform and signal box. This view was taken some fifteen months after the branch passenger service was withdrawn on 26 December 1965; the low winter sun and frost can be clearly seen. (D. J. Plyer)

Ashdon Halt

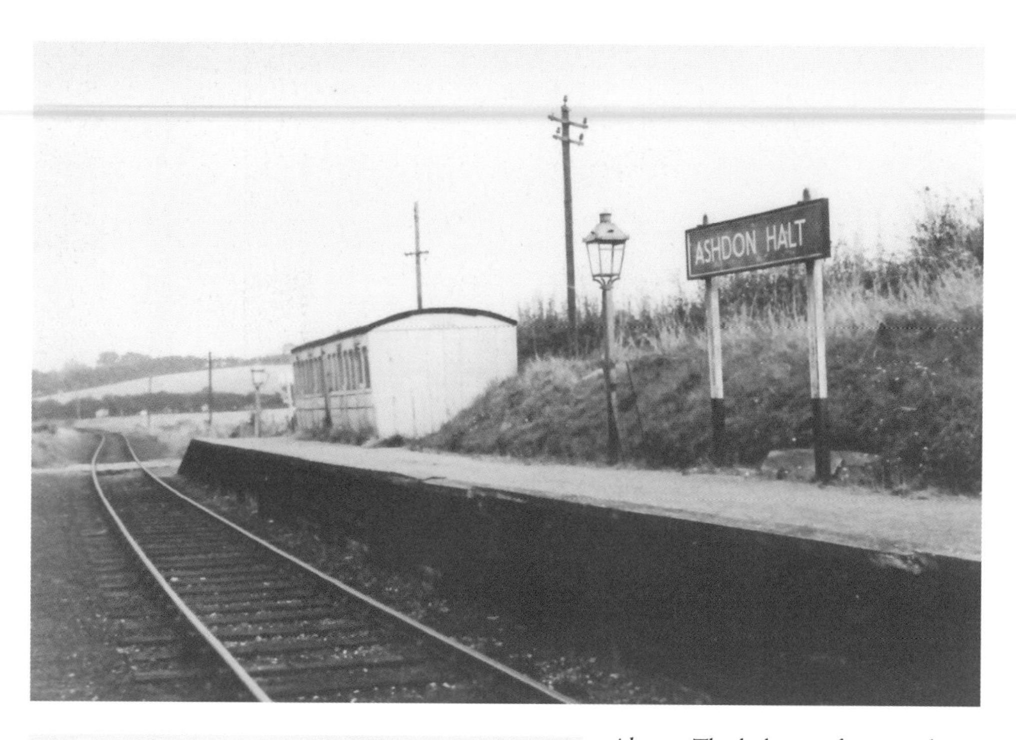

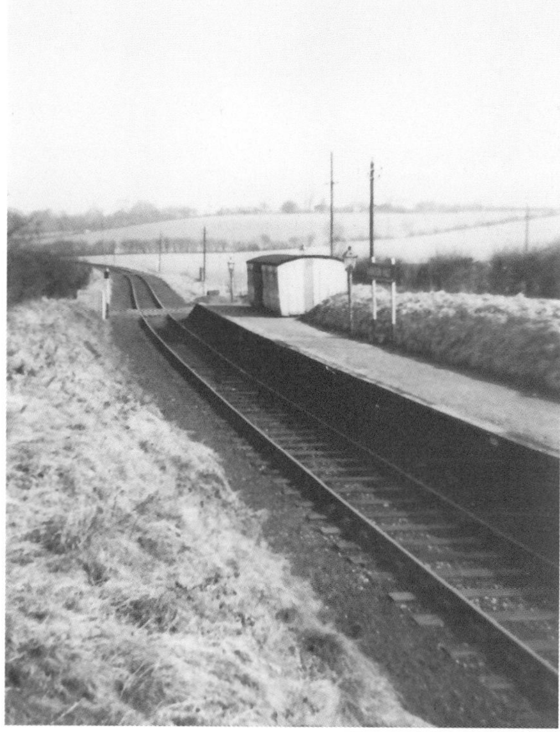

Above: The halt seen from track level, looking towards Bartlow, on 5 September 1964, a couple of days before the withdrawal of the passenger service. The halt had been built for the low cost of £73 and opened without any accommodation on Monday 14 August 1911. The old GER carriage body was provided in 1916, having had all its internal compartments removed and replaced by seats around the edge of the coach. (D. J. Plyer)

Left: Another view of the platform, this time taken from the Down side embankment. The platform was 210 feet in length, adequate for up to three coaches in the days of locomotive-hauled stock; most trains in later years were only two coaches long plus engine and the railbuses were only just over 45 feet. (Paul Smith)

Acrow Halt

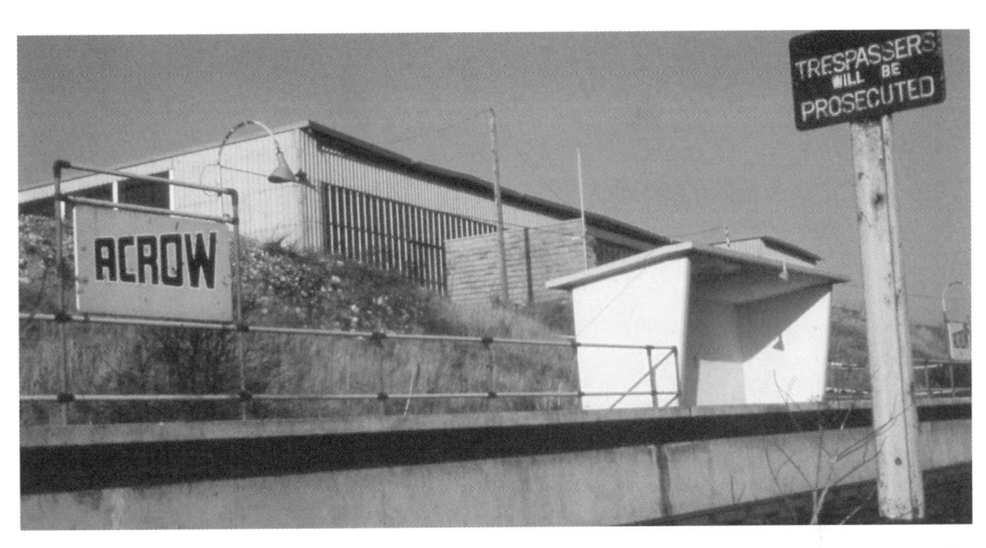

A view of the halt, purpose built to serve the engineering firm of the same name adjacent to the railway. This was taken on 26 December 1965, and the line had been completely closed for over a year before. The halt had opened on 25 March 1957 for the benefit of workers at the nearby Acrow Engineering Ltd. (D. J. Plyer)

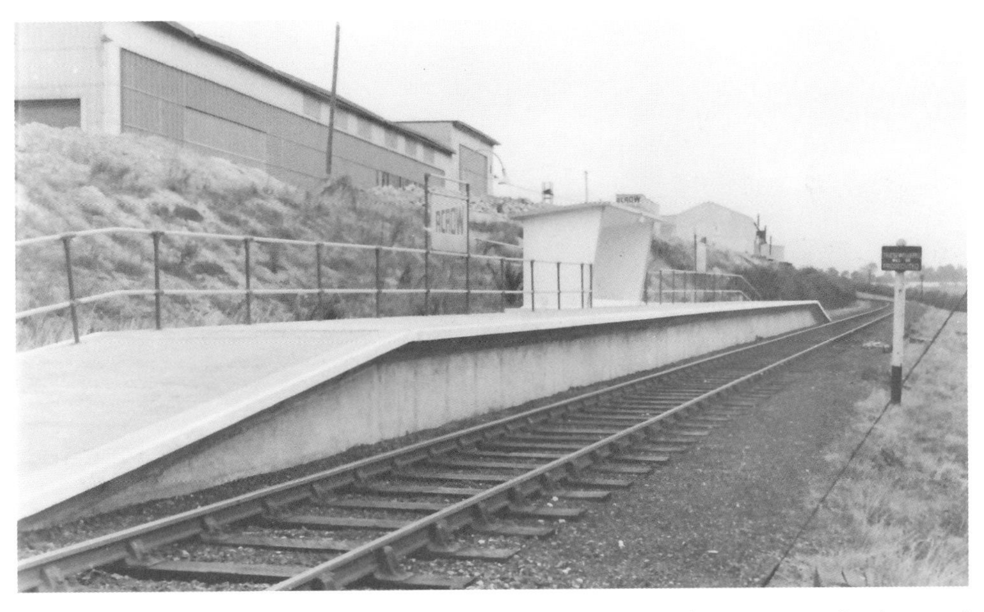

A track-level view of the halt, looking towards Bartlow; the platform was 230 feet long and had been constructed by the engineering firm using concrete and metal shuttering. Surprisingly, the halt still stands, slowly crumbling away, hidden among the trees and bushes. The halt was 2 miles and 73 chains from Audley End and 3 chains on the Bartlow side of Ashdon Road under bridge. (Lens of Sutton Association)

Saffron Walden

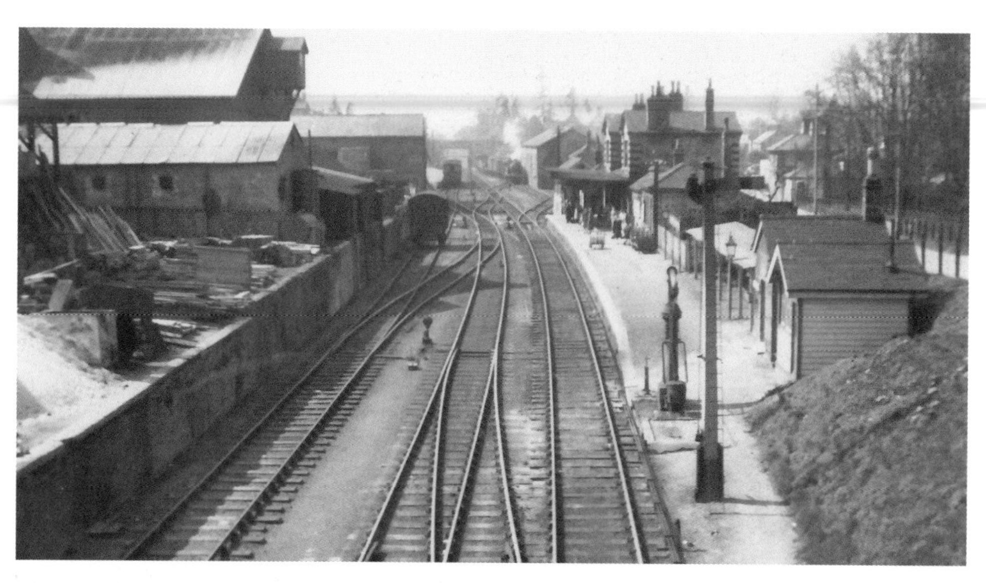

The view from South Road over bridge, looking west at the station. The tracks in view are the main single line serving the platform; then next to that the run-round road, off which ran a further siding that ran past the locomotive depot; the tracks next to the wall served the railway foundry at the eastern end and the loading dock at the western end. (Lens of Sutton Association)

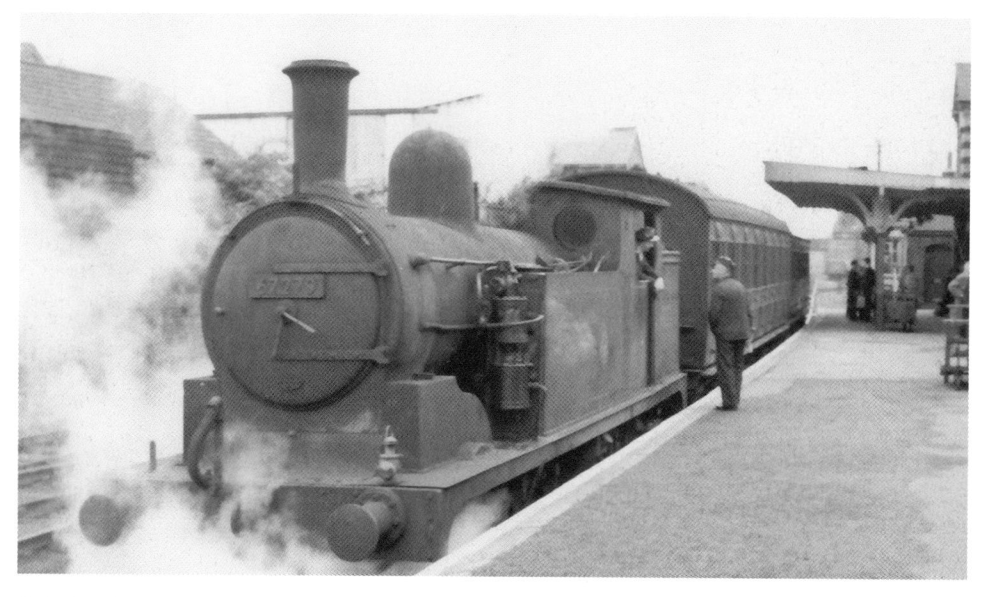

G5 class locomotive No. 67279 stands at the platform with a push-and-pull working on 21 July 1956, just a couple of months before the class was replaced with N7 tanks; No. 67279 was withdrawn from Cambridge shed in November 1956 for scrapping. They had entered service with the North Eastern Railway between 1894 and 1901. (L. R. Freeman/Transport Treasury)

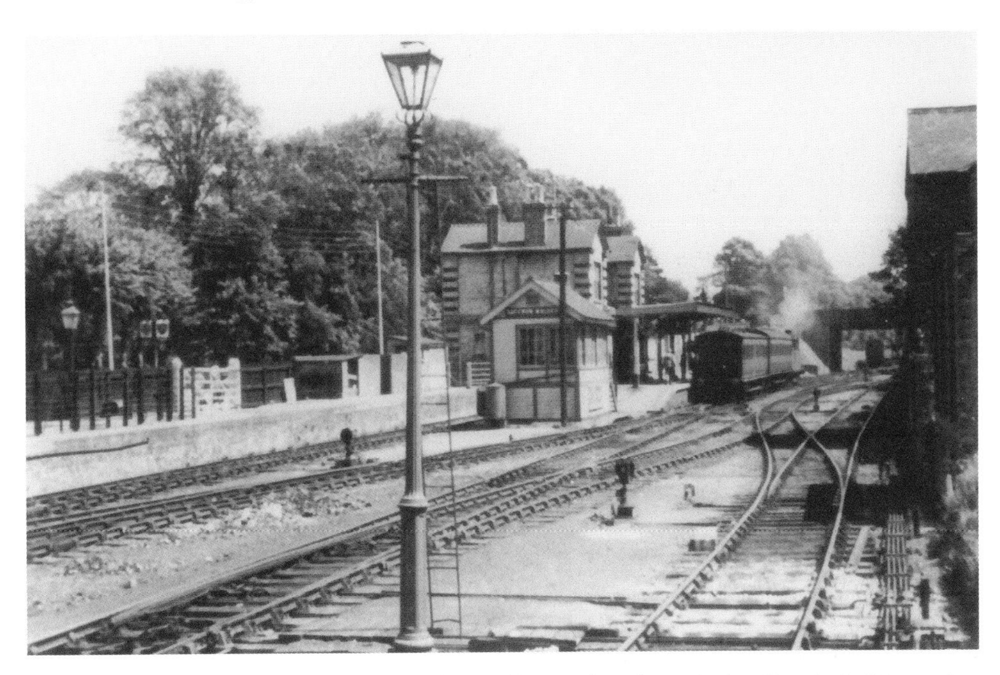

A general view, looking at the station and signal box, taken from the loading dock. The station buildings can clearly be seen and there is a train in the platform. Out of view to the left there were four sidings and a large goods shed. (Rail Archive Stephenson)

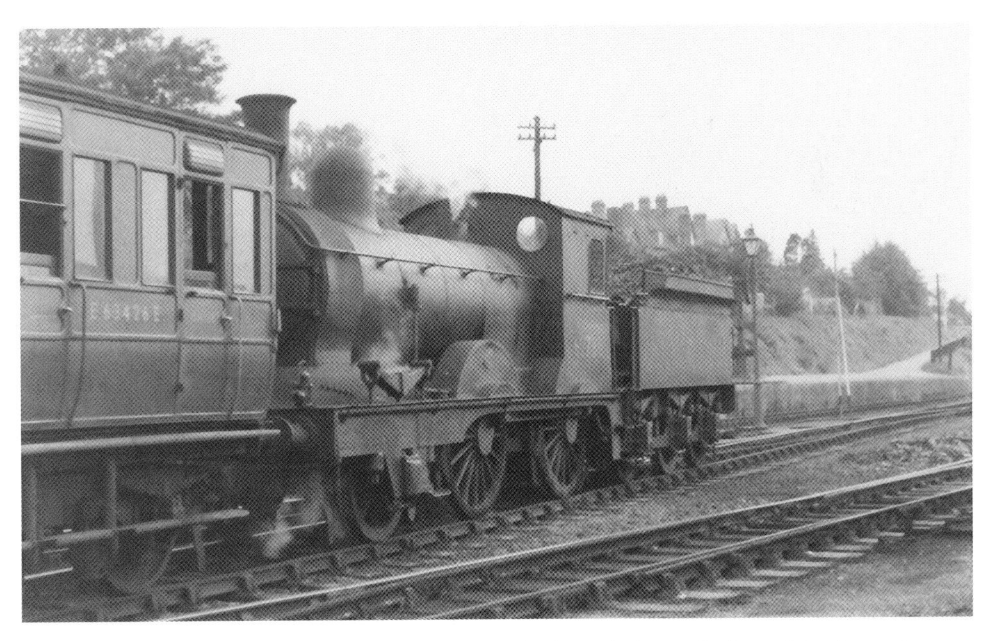

The LNER E4 class, known as Intermediates, worked regularly on the branch in the early years of the twentieth century. Many years later, they occasionally worked on the branch when one of the G5s or C12s was not available. In this view, No. 62788 is seen on a passenger working on 8 September 1956. (R. C. Riley/Transport Treasury)

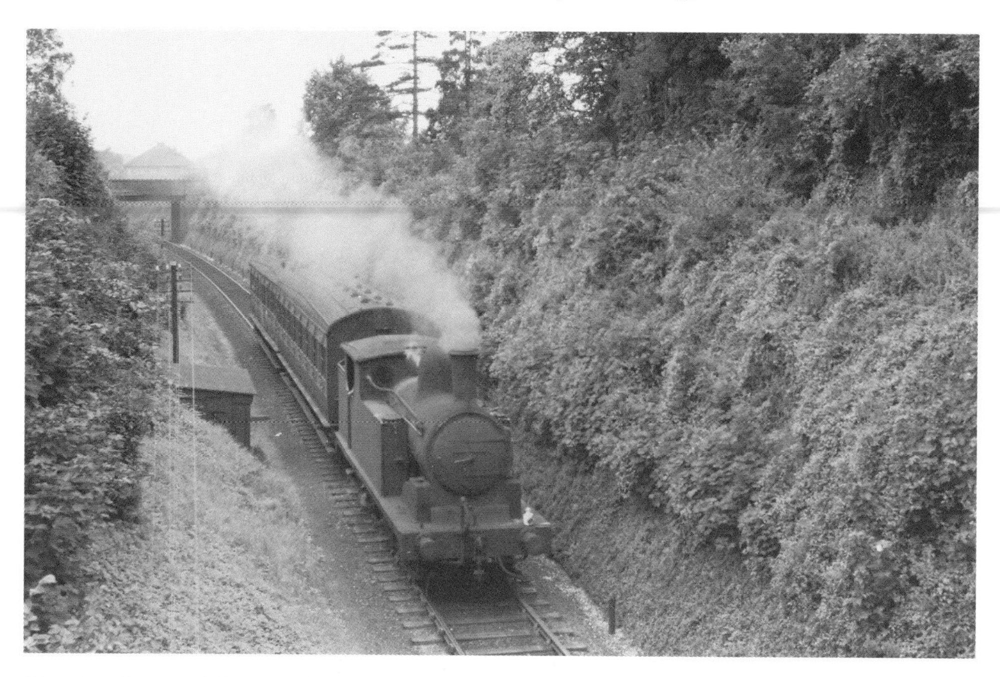

The view from Debden Road over bridge as a G5 push-and-pull working enters the station with a Bartlow-bound passenger train. The wooden permanent way hut on the left of the picture survived the closure of the line; one local resident told me a story that the cutting was filled in with chalk, including on top of the hut, and many years later the wooden roof of the hut collapsed and a square hole appeared in the garden of a house built on the former railway land! (R. E. Vincent/Transport Treasury)

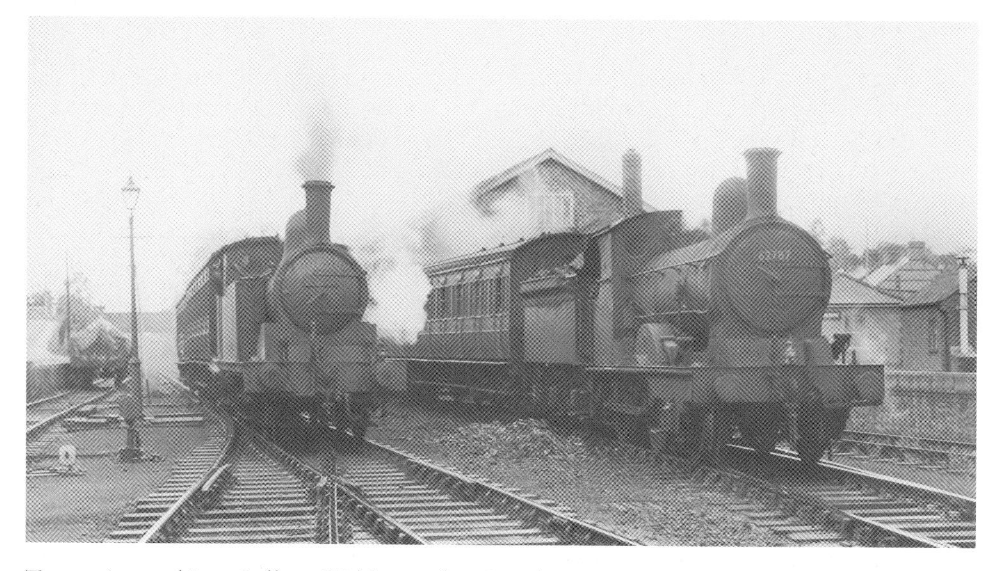

Two-train working, Saffron Walden style! G5 class No. 67322 is seen passing E4 class No. 62787 standing in the siding adjacent to the running line. The goods shed can be seen behind the locomotive; the loading dock, with a solitary sheeted wagon, can be seen in the loading dock road. (R. C. Riley/Transport Treasury)

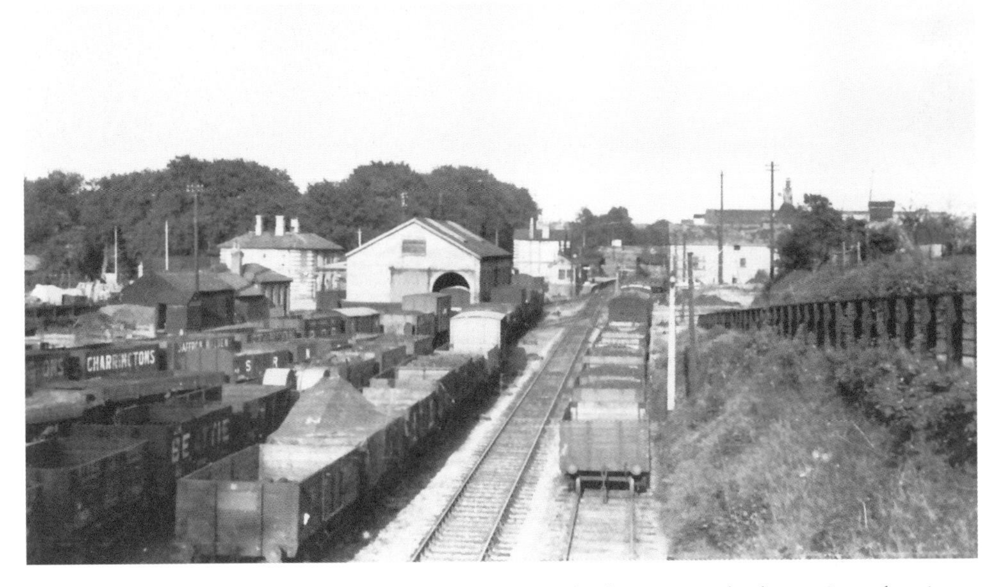

A view from circa 1936, from Debden Road bridge looking towards the station, showing a very busy goods yard. There seems to be a varied selection of open wagons large and small plus closed vans. The large goods shed and station buildings can be clearly seen; the signal on the right is the up starter worked by number four lever in the signal box. (Stations UK)

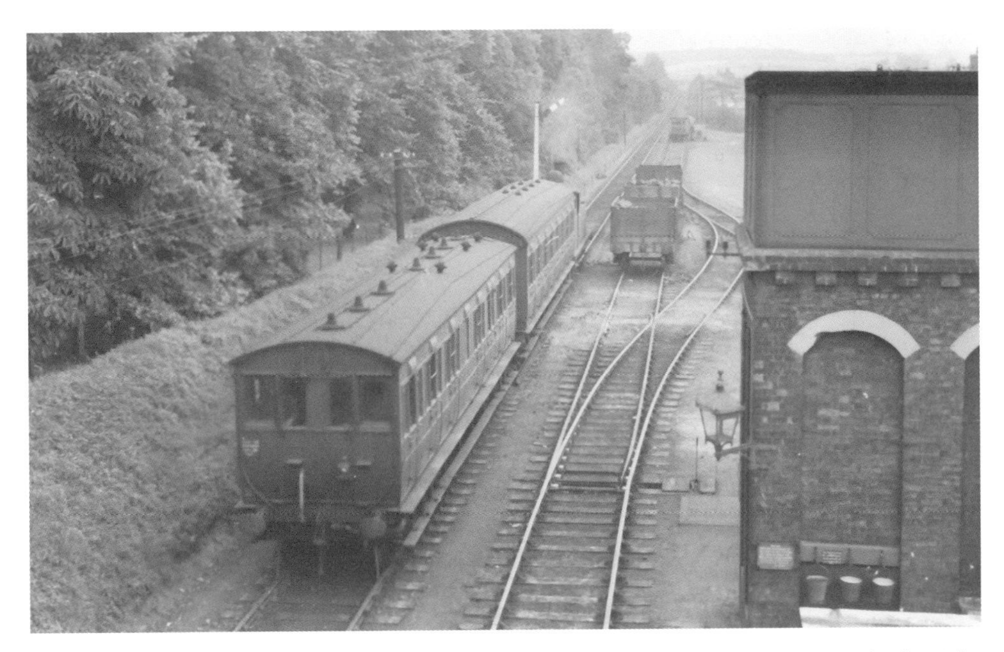

A push-and-pull working arriving into the station as seen from South Road over bridge. The locomotive depot is located on the right. The G5 locomotive is propelling the coaches; the driver has basic controls in the front coach. This method of working saved time at the end of each journey as no running round of the locomotive was required; it was used from 1951 until the line was dieselised. (R. E. Vincent/Transport Treasury)

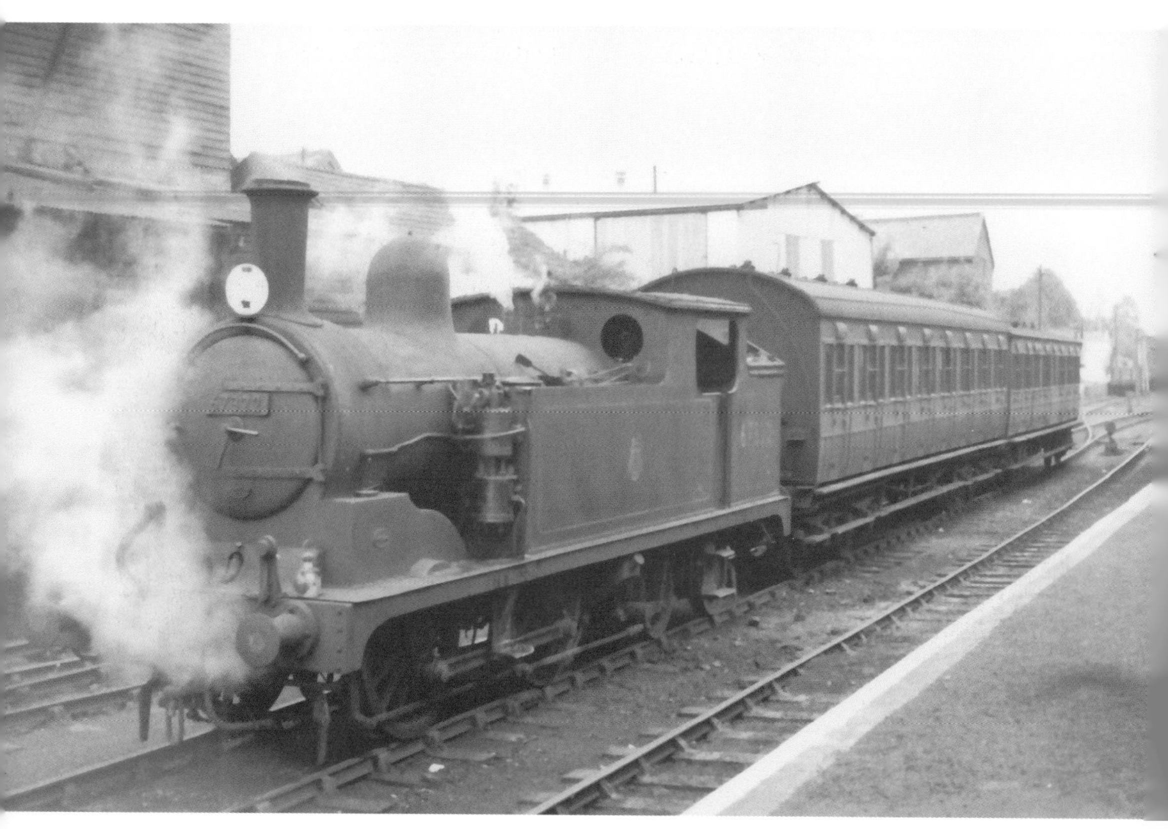

Another view of a G5 class locomotive with two coaches. This engine is No. 67322 and is seen on 21 July 1956; the train is standing in the run-round road. Two engines and two sets of coaches were required to run the service, the trains passing at Saffron Walden. In the early 1950s there were sixteen passenger workings to Audley End and back; only five trains ran on towards Bartlow and back from that station. (L. R. Freeman/Transport Treasury)

Audley End – Branch Platform

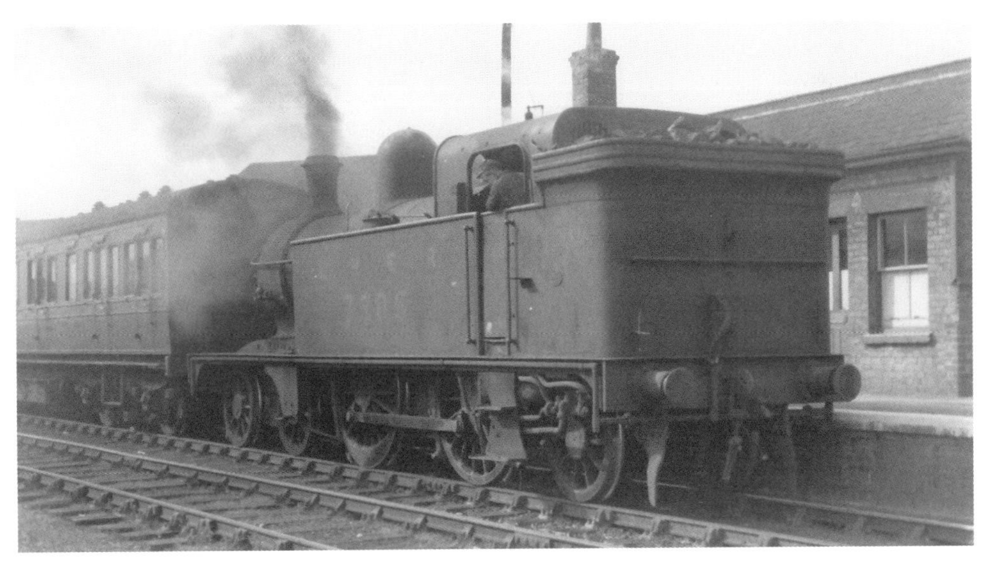

LNER C12 class locomotive No. 7385, still in its LNER livery, on 24 September 1950, awaiting departure to Saffron Walden and Bartlow. The C12 class had arrived on the branch in about 1938 to work the local services; they in turn were ousted by the G5 tank engine when push-and-pull working was introduced in 1951. (R. E. Vincent/Transport Treasury)

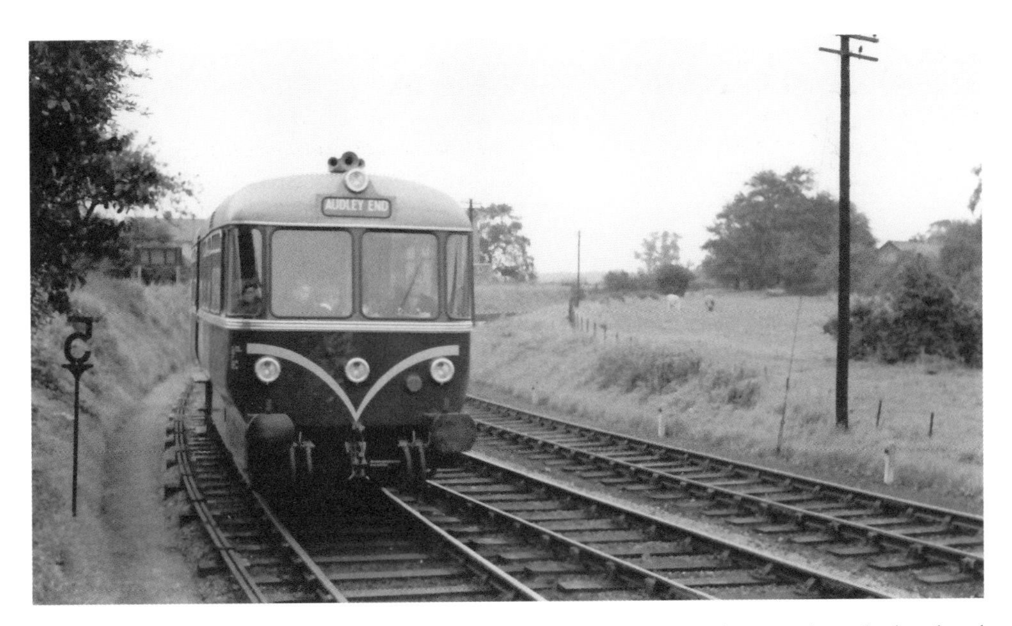

A diesel railbus approaching the branch platform on 23 August 1958. These machines had replaced the steam-operated service in July 1957; they had limited capacity and were not universally liked by the passengers, but they were cheap to run and certainly helped to reduce costs although this did not save the branch passenger service. (Hugh Davies/Photos from the Fifties)

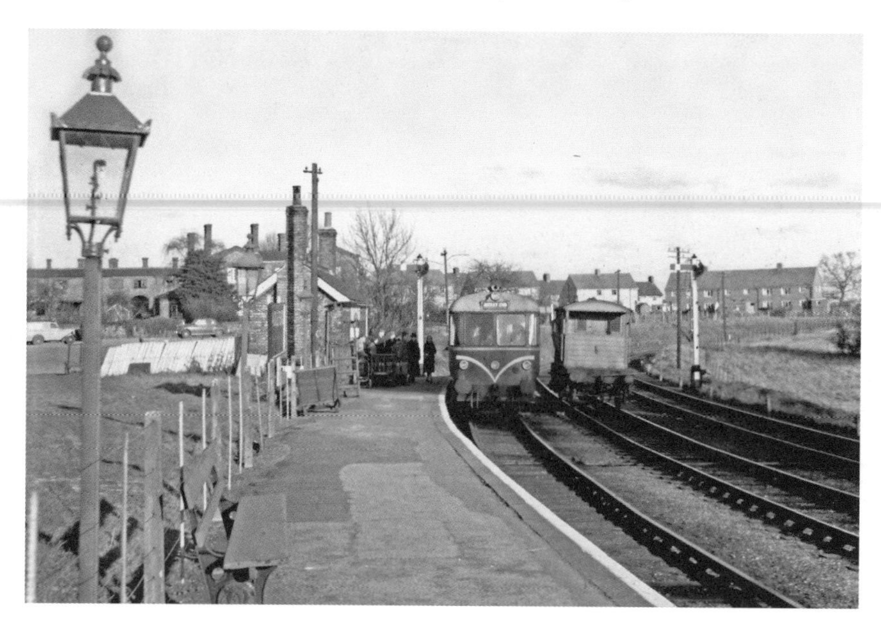

On a nice, bright December day in 1961, we have a picture of the railbus sitting in the branch platform waiting for its next trip down the line. Of the five different types of railbuses ordered by British Railways in 1957, the Waggon & Maschinenbau examples proved to be long-lived once all their teething troubles were sorted, including some being re-engined. Four of the five examples survived into the preservation era; two can be seen on the Keighley & Worth Railway and two at the North Norfolk Railway. (Brian Pask)

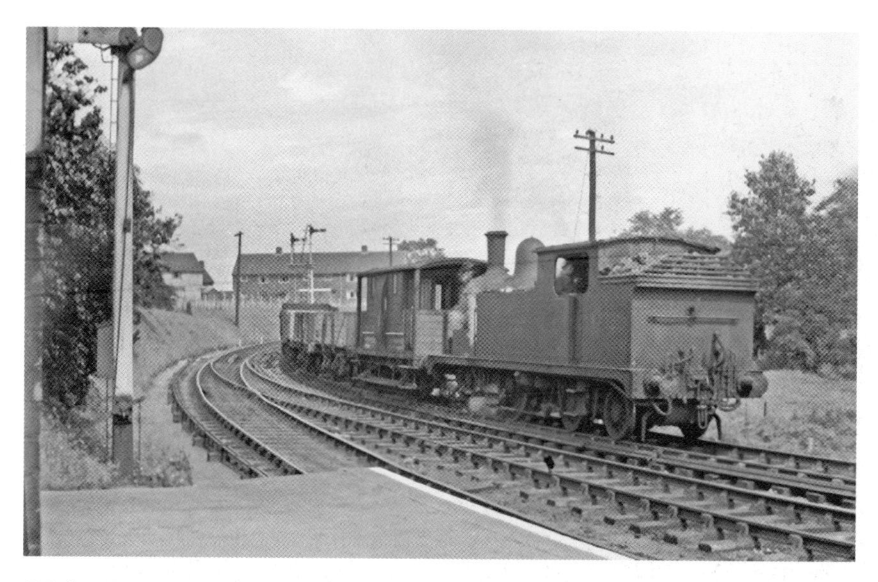

G5 class No. 67322 shunting freight vehicles in the branch siding line on 8 August 1956. The days of these old engines were numbered; this example was withdrawn for scrapping in November 1956. N7 class locomotives replaced the G5s before they too were displaced by the diesel railbuses. (Brian Pask)

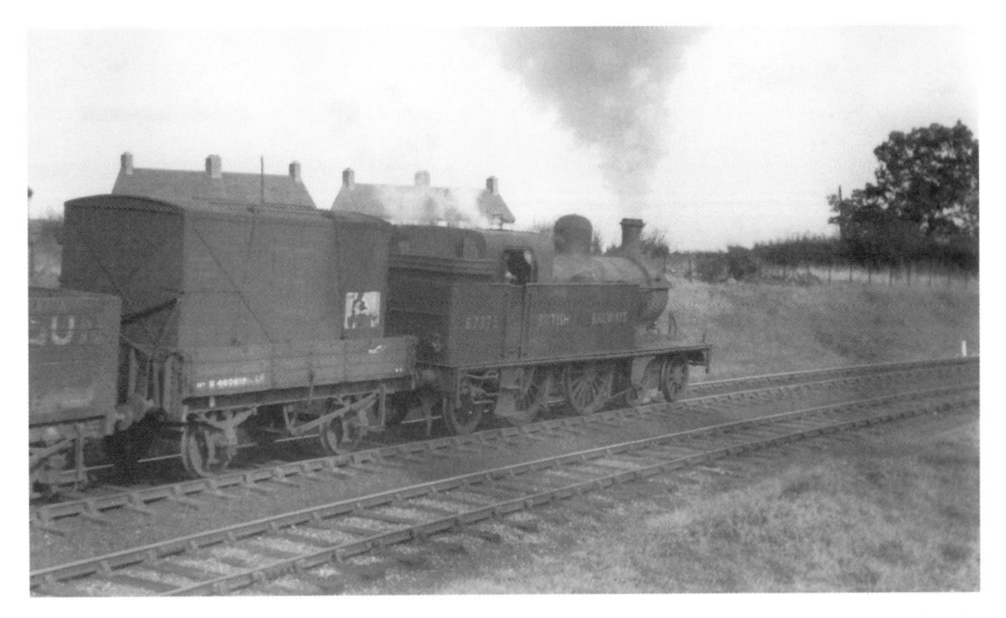

LNER C12 class locomotive No. 67375 departs from Audley End with a branch freight working. This is one of four examples that could be seen working on the branch; they were allocated to Cambridge shed, with two being out based at Saffron Walden. After push-and-pull working was introduced in 1951, the C12s could be seen working on the Bury branch as well as on the Stour Valley line. This engine finished its days at March Depot, being withdrawn in April 1955. (R. E. Vincent/Transport Treasury)

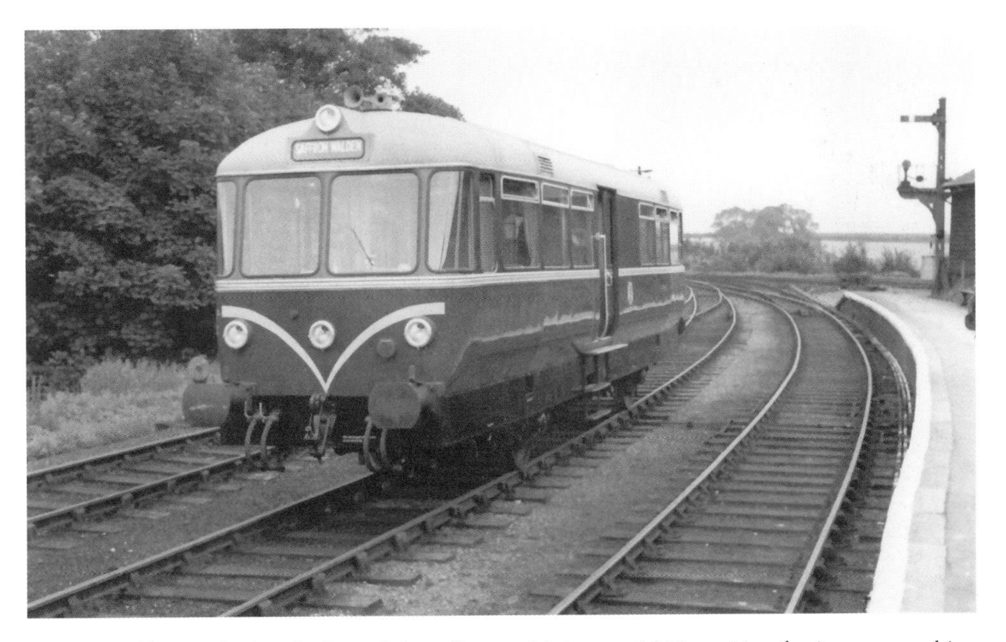

A diesel railbus parked in the branch loop line on 23 August 1958, waiting for its next working to Saffron Walden, Bartlow or even Haverhill. Except at peak times, the vehicles were adequate for all the later branch loadings. (H. Davies/Photos from the Fifties)

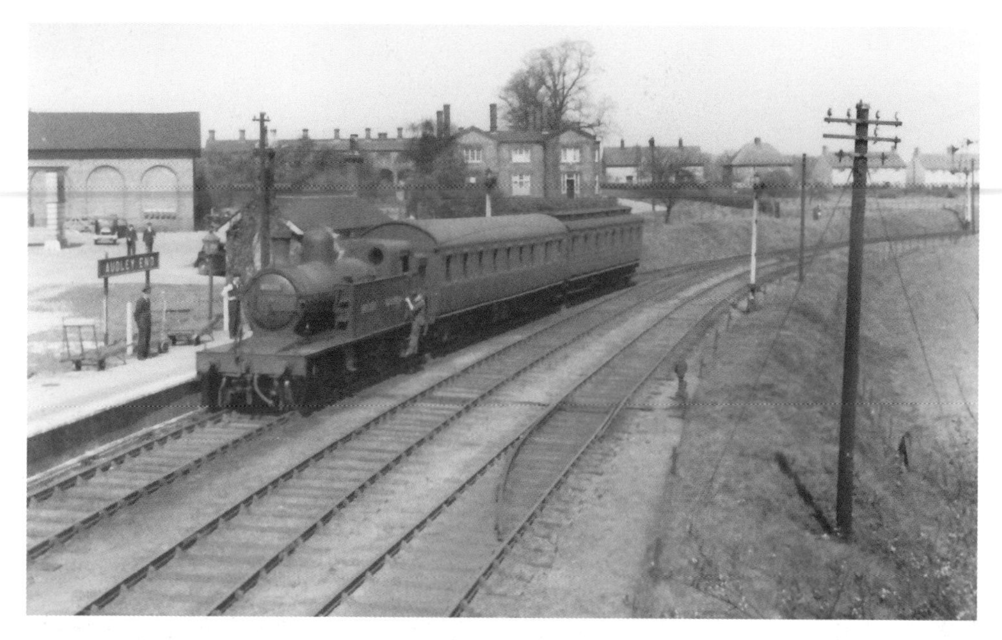

An elevated view of C12 class locomotive No. 67375 arriving at the branch platform with a two-coach passenger train on 16 April 1947. The whole area seen in this view, including the track area, is now part of a huge car park as Audley End is now the railhead for commuters to London and Cambridge; a Haverhill, Bartlow and Saffron Walden to Audley End shuttle would be a godsend now. (Stephenson Locomotive Society)

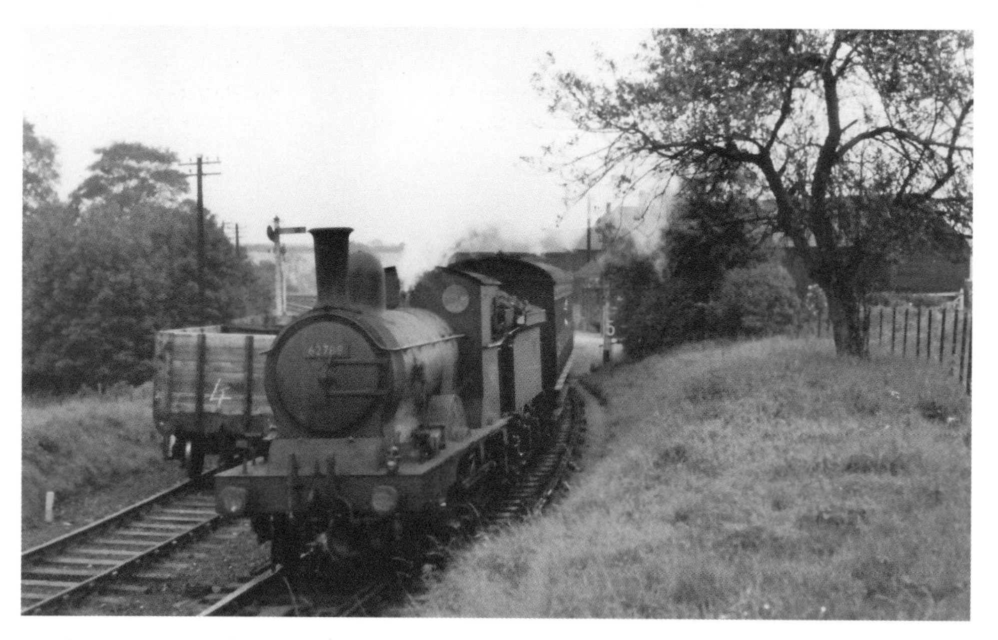

E4 class No. 62788, hauling a passenger train, departs from Audley End on 8 September 1956; this veteran locomotive would soldier on for another eighteen months before being withdrawn from traffic. A wagon can be seen standing on the branch siding. (R. C. Riley/Transport Treasury)

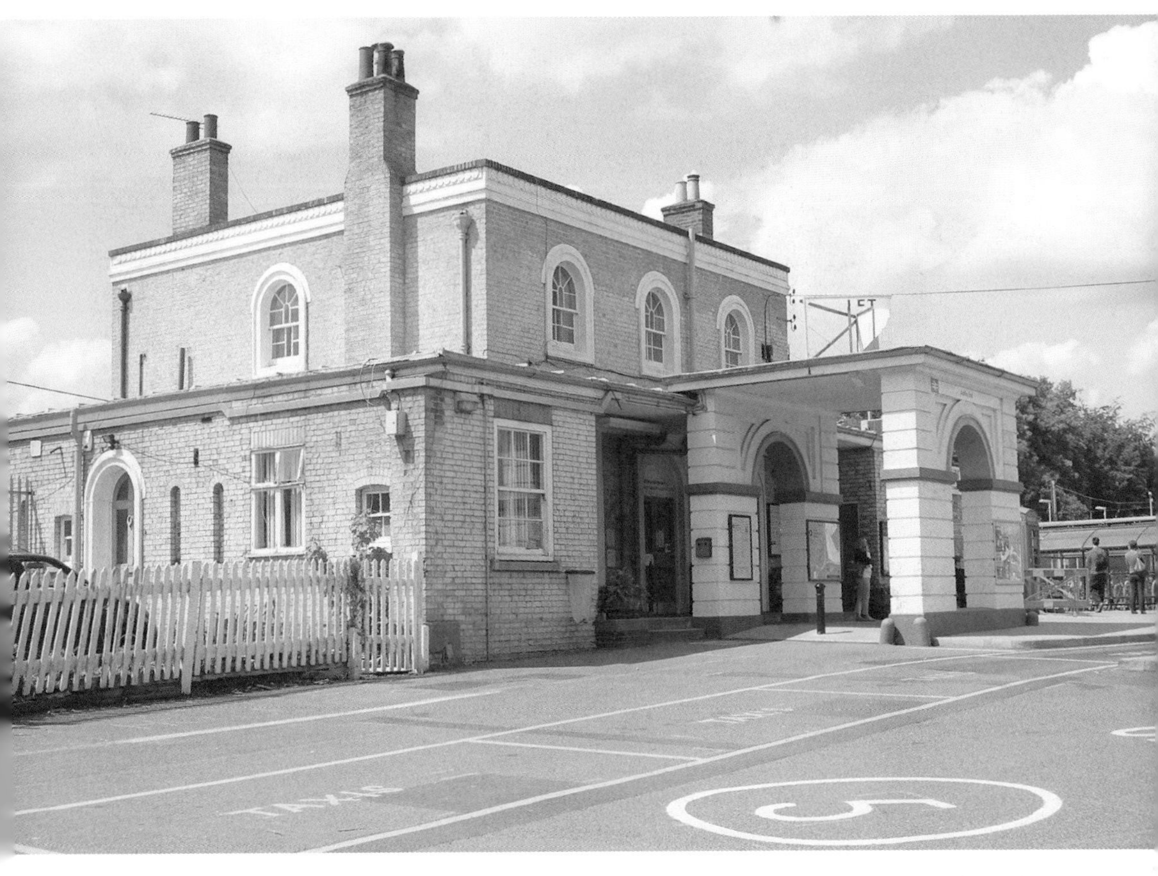

The magnificent Audley End station building, seen from the station forecourt. Dating from the opening of the railway, it has had very few changes over the years; the station now acts as a railhead for the surrounding towns and villages and is heavily used by commuters travelling to and from London. (Ray Bishop)

Acknowledgements and Further Reading

Special thanks to Ray Bishop for the modern day photographs and to Brian Barham, Brian Pask, Dickie Pearce, Lens of Suttons Association and Paul Lemon for help with the archive views. Thanks also to all the other photographers and organisations that have provided views from their collections.

For those interested, further information about the lines included in this volume can be found in the following publications:

Brodribb, John, *Branches & Byways East Anglia* (OPC, 2000).
Lawrence, E.W., *Stour Valley Album* (EARM Publications, 2011).
Paye, Peter, *The Saffron Walden Branch* (OPC, 1981).
Wallis, Andy T., *Colne Valley & Halstead Railway Through Time* (Amberley, 2011).
Wallis, Andy T., *Stour Valley Railway Through Time* (Amberley, 2011).
Wallis, Andy T., *Stour Valley Railway Part 2 Through Time* (Amberley, 2011).
Walsh, B. D. J., *The Stour Valley Railway* (EARM Publications, 2008).
Whitehead, R. A. and F. D. Simpson, *The Colne Valley and Halstead Railway* (The Oakwood Press, 1988).

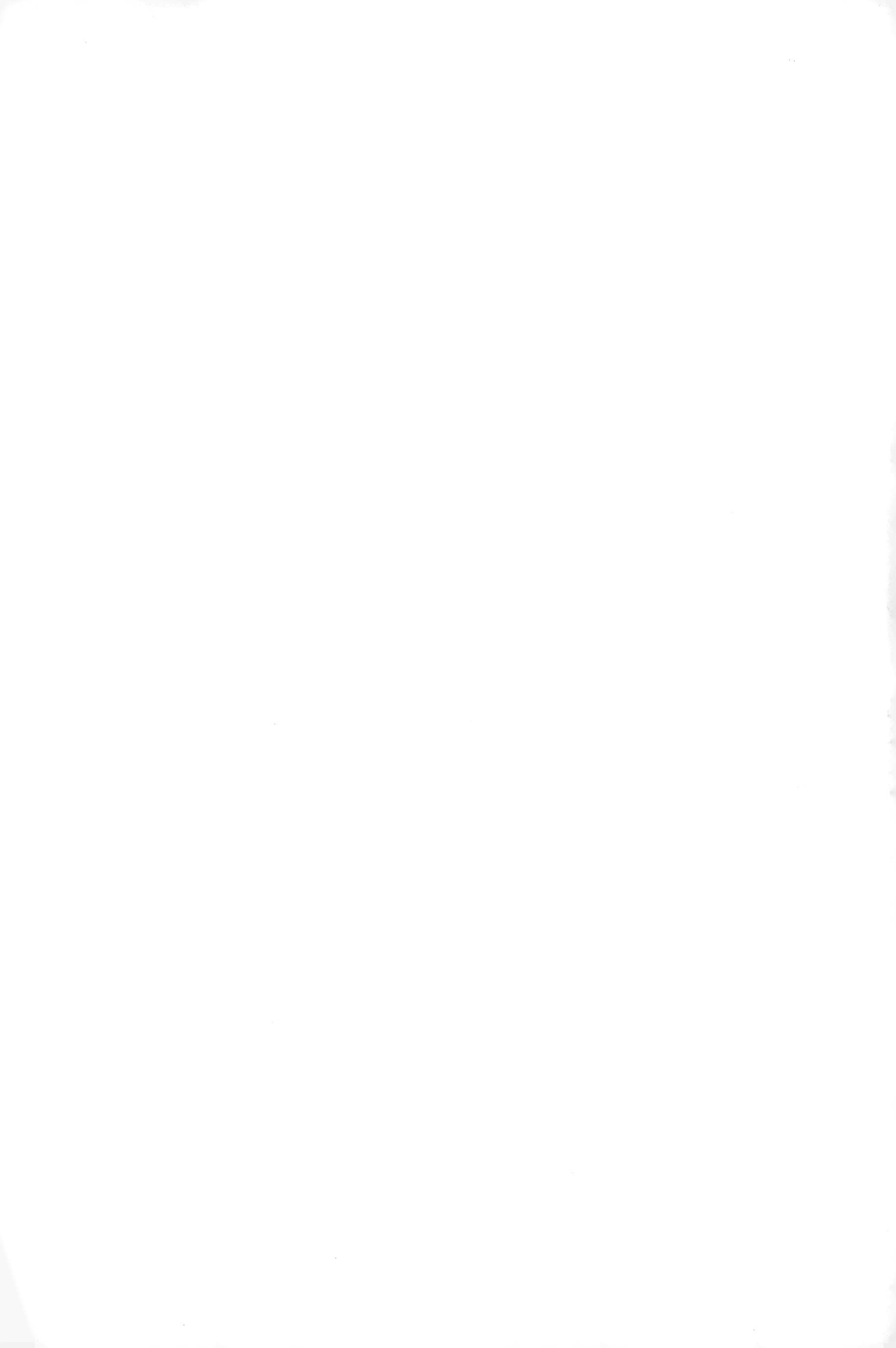